Dance
From Magic to Art

Dance
From Magic to Art

> Magic is present but never known;
> it is the source behind the
> source and the effect in front
> of the effect.
> *Parker Tyler,* artist

LOIS ELLFELDT
University of Southern California

Wm. C. Brown Company Publishers
Dubuque, Iowa

PHYSICAL EDUCATION

Consulting Editor

Aileene Lockhart
Texas Woman's University

HEALTH

Consulting Editor

Robert Kaplan
The Ohio State University

PARKS AND RECREATION

Consulting Editor

David Gray
California State University, Long Beach

Copyright © 1976 by Wm. C. Brown Company Publishers

Library of Congress Catalog Card Number: 75-11280

ISBN 0-697-07129-4

All rights reserved. No part of this publication may be reproduced, stored in a retrieval system, or transmitted, in any form or by any means, electronic, mechanical, photocopying, recording, or otherwise, without the prior written permission of the publisher.

Printed in the United States of America

Contents

	Preface	ix
1.	The Open Door	1
2.	What Is Dance?	7
	THE DILEMMA OF DEFINITION	10
	ORIGINS OF DANCE	12
	EARLY MAN AND HIS MAGIC	20
	Elements of Magic	22
	Masks	26
	Mythology	27
	Ceremony	28
3.	The Unknown Past	33
	WHAT IS PRIMITIVE?	34
	DANCE AMONG THE PRIMITIVES	36
	Characteristics of Primitive Dance	40
	Categories of Primitive Dance	45
	DANCE IN EARLY CIVILIZATIONS	53
4.	The Known Past	61
	THE FIRST GREAT CITIES	64
	Mythology	71
	MESOPOTAMIA	73
	EGYPT	75
	INDIA	76
	Ceremonies	79
	NEAR EAST	80
	EGYPT	80
	INDIA	82
5.	Link to the Past	83
	RECURRING PRIMITIVE DANCES	84
	Hunters	84
	Planters	93

	ETHNIC DANCE	98
	FOLK DANCE	103
	SOCIAL DANCE	104
6.	What We Have Today	107
	A MULTITUDE OF FORMS	109
	Acrobatic Dance	109
	Aerobic Dance	109
	Ballet, Classical, or Traditional	110
	Ballet, Contemporary, or Modern	111
	Character Dance	111
	Children's Dance	112
	Dance Drama	113
	Dance Therapy	113
	Dramatic Dance	114
	Educational Dance	115
	Esthetic, Natural, Creative, and Interpretative Dance	116
	Ethnic Dance	117
	Folk Dance	119
	Jazz Dance	121
	Modern Dance, Classical	121
	Modern Dance, Contemporary	122
	Modern Jazz	123
	Musical Comedy	123
	Pantomime	124
	Preclassic Dance	124
	Religious Dance	127
	Social or Ballroom Dance	127
	Spectacular Dance	129
	Tap Dance	129
	Hindsight	130
7.	Art Is Art Is Art	131
	THE ESTHETIC DILEMMA	132
	Esthetics and Movement	136
	WHAT IS ART?	140
	Origins of Art	143
	What They Say	144
	REPRISE	158

8.	The Artist and His Tools	163
	THE ARTIST	164
	CREATIVITY	167
	Characteristics of Creative People	169
	FORM AND CONTENT	172
	ONE STYLE OR ANOTHER	175
9.	Dance as a Performing Art	181
	THE NATURE OF PERFORMING ART	184
	DANCE: A PERFORMING ART	185
	The Dance Artist: Choreographer	188
	The Dance Artist: Performer	189
	The Dance	189
	WHAT THEY SAY DANCE IS	193
	WHAT THEY SAY ABOUT DANCE	194
	WHAT THEY SAY ABOUT DANCERS	199
	WHAT THEY SAY ABOUT TECHNIQUE	201
	WHAT THEY SAY ABOUT CHOREOGRAPHY	204
	WHEN DANCERS SPEAK	206
10.	Selected Readings	213
	Notes	229
	Index	235

Preface

A dancer is a kind of magician who sets out to perform a number of different acts of magic. He may use his powers to overcome an enemy, encourage the growth of crops, or mark the coming of age of a young man. He may dance to celebrate his national origins, perpetuate the tales of ethnic heroes, entertain his fellows, or just to enjoy himself. It is when he uses his magic to project dynamic images to an audience that the result is called "dance art."

This book cuts across the broad use of the word "dance," identifying its rise from ceremonies of magic, through its other manifestations, to dance as a performing art. And since the crux of differentiation among these dance forms lies within the realm of art, the phenomena of art will be discussed in some detail. This book is an attempt to differentiate dance as a performing art from dance for survival, for the preservation of ethnic mythology, for celebration of national culture, for socialization, for therapy, and for entertainment. One of the problems encountered was the limiting of the range and selection of relevant materials. There is so much that has had obvious effect—and "just one more myth" was hard to resist. Very specific time and place limits were set, and these were the hardest of all to cope with. There are no Greece, Rome, Dance of Death, and other fascinating historical events; no in depth examination of rituals, myths, ceremonies of dances; no cross references to then and now. Every effort was made to keep the overall view within the set boundaries of contemporary and early primitive, plus the early city-states (and then only from Mesopotamia, Egypt, and India). Presented are the basic principles of magic, a glimpse of the origins, some selected myths, ceremonies, dances and points of view on esthetics, art and finally, dance as a performing art.

This book is relevant for dance theory classes where students are concerned with the overall picture of changing emphases and forms of dance. It was written for those involved in history, philosophy, esthetics, or critical views of dance. It should be helpful to one who has puzzled about the differences between all of the confusing forms of dance, or has been unable to answer the question: "But what is it about, this kind of dance that causes you to call it an art?"

The most important purpose of this book is to stimulate the reader to venture into the almost endless materials available to him in the fields of esthetics, art, creativity, great artists and dancers, historical development of forms, mythology, magic, and many related areas, each of which open exciting avenues of thought and bases for the development of a point of view.

Only by encouraging such thinking and the resulting discussion about ideas that emerge—by personal involvement and real concern—will anyone broaden his perspective and go beyond the superficial absorption of different technical styles.

LOIS ELLFELDT

1
The Open Door

... young people everywhere must learn the forgotten art of seeing life with their own eyes.
Oskar Kokoschka, *painter*

*I*t is often said that dancers know little of their history, are uninterested in the theoretical, unconcerned with principles of esthetics, and intolerant of criticism. "Dancers should dance, not talk about it. The dancer's job is to discipline his action so that he can do what he chooses through space and in time. How can reading or thinking about it help you with this?" With such overpowering needs for strengthening muscles and gaining control of the body there is little time or energy for anything else, especially when a greater premium is placed upon this than on contemplating reasons for dancing.

What class is most popular with dancers? Is it choreography, notation, history, esthetics, criticism, or technique? Almost always it is the technique class, where the instructor tells, shows, and even imposes a formulated action, often a highly personalized series of gymnastic challenges, to a group of dancers eager "to get more technique." Obviously technique is important. Indeed it would be impossible to deny it as a basic requisite for all dancers; but knowing other things about dance can also be useful to performer, creator, director, teacher, and critic.

Why should a dancer concern himself with the confusing and controversial issues of form, style, creativity, content, expression, choreography, criticism, or art? Will this make him a better dancer? Will it help him to become a more sensitive performer? Will it enable him to be a more perceptive and creative person? Will it encourage him to try choreography? Answers to such questions vary according to convictions held about the relative values of technical virtuosity and the more nebulous aspects of art, esthetics, and creativity, both in process and product.

He who seeks *only* proof of his ability to perform movement well will have little regard for ideas, purposes, comparisons, or serious thinking about dance. But those who see dance as more than a personal satisfaction—a kind of dance therapy—will be fascinated with learning more about dance, what it has been, why, by whom, and where it was done. It will be interesting to know the views and experiences of dancers who performed in the past. Certainly anyone concerned with dance as a performing art will add to his understanding by learning more about esthetics in general and art in particular.

Most dancers collect dance pictures, programs, criticisms, magazine articles, brochures, and even some books—the latter to be read *someday*. But most of the events of the dance world are for immediate experiencing, especially for doing: seeing a concert, observing other dancers, sharing an audition, and then back to the studio to move again. But what of the reasons for dance? What happens when a choreographer designs a dance? What makes one dance better than another? Is there more to dance than the performer's technique? What are the roots of current happenings in dance? What do you know of the performers, dances, choreographers, critics, criticisms, and teachers of the past? What happens during the process called "creativity"? What is the place of dance in social development? How does it fit in the family of art? Are there common elements in all of the performing arts? What is good art? What is good dance? How do critics operate? What is the difference between dance as a performing art and a well-performed free exercise event in gymnastics? What do such confusing matters have to do with someone who just wants to dance?

Sometimes we talk about "Dance as an Art," or, more profoundly, "the Art of Dance." We infer that this phenomenon is clearly identifiable, with easily recognized form and content, but this is not true. Perhaps we are referring to a particular kind of dance, or we may just be parroting some well-worn phrase without really knowing what we mean by it. What *do* we mean by the *art* of dance? Are we ever confused by the vacillating use of the term "art" to describe such a range as the paintings of Botticelli to the spatterings of a happy chimpanzee, or from skillful rope jumping to winning at chess? We hear, "Her custards are works of art," or, "The art of teaching, like the art of making a beautiful hat, is a rare talent." What *is* art? And who is the artist?

While it may seem academic to define terms, the only alternative is confusion. It is important that anyone concerned with dance as a performing art, either as choreographer, performer, critic, viewer, or teacher, should understand something of the nature of dance as an art. It doesn't help to insist that, "*all* dance is art" or to be satisfied that only "*my* kind of dance is art."

What usually happens is that one will announce: "This dance is art, and that dance is not." What is it about a dance that causes you to say "art," and of another, "not art"? What are some of the criteria of dance as art—or, for that matter, for the phenomena called art? These are questions that most people would rather not investigate. Instead they maintain and perpetuate the popular stereotypes, immediate likes and dislikes, and the slow accretion of prejudices accumulated through the years. What appeals to any of us? Don't we value what is familiar, tested, practiced, accepted by the majority, cherished by our contemporaries, praised by the critics, and sponsored by audiences? Are these the standards of art?

Underlying such confusion is the slippery nature of our views of "the esthetic," "the artistic," as well as "dance." Growing out of personal experience and idiosyncrasy, one's values and point of view about art and esthetics have little logical basis and are used loosely to cover or hide what we really mean. How does one go about establishing a point of view about esthetics or art? There are no nicely packaged solutions. Much has been written and said about esthetics, and even more about art. There are essays, articles, lectures, books, catalogs, theses, exhibits, classes, and demonstrations. But these are all about someone else's views. It is a painstaking and traumatic experience to discover one's own views, especially when so many learned people have propounded theirs so convincingly.

In his *Expressionism in Art*, Sheldon Cheney explained his warnings to students, so that his views would not just be accepted blindly. Hoping only that he could provide some clues, he would remind them: "1. *Don't believe a word I say.*" In an attempt to encourage them to think for themselves he wrote: ". . . make your life a reflection of no man's thinking or teaching." He further admonished: "2. Strive for direct response, immediate experience. Let the fact-finding mind be stilled." Finally, he recommended that they recognize and learn more of the art of the past but, more important, be open to the expressions of the art of their own time and place: "3. Accept art not as a refuge from life, but as an intensification of living."[1]

It is important to explore as many views as possible, to read and listen to different ideas, and to discuss these views and ideas with as many people as you can find to discuss them with. Above all be open to new concepts, different perspectives, and changing values. As soon as you find some explanations that satisfy you, that seem to explain esthetics, art, or dance, you must become responsible for unscrambling and clarifying your own views rather than muttering some often repeated phrase that is meaningless to you. This process is bound to make you a more sensitive dancer, discerning observer, and proficient choreographer. It might also make you unpopular with those who continue to recite the clichés.

Anyone knowledgeable about dance will agree that the discipline of regular technical exercise is a must for any dancer. The time never comes when he stops working for greater range and control of his body's movement. And, unless one is very particularly using previously choreographed movement phrases, it is necessary to explore and experiment with movement, as it may be changed and varied according to dynamic, temporal, and spatial changes.

Dancers spend many hours and use abundant energy, bottles of linament, and piles of leotards in an untold dedication to improving their technical virtuosity. Choreographers struggle, plan, and mark out movement patterns; battle with uncountable phrases of music; rehearse and plead with unprepared and reluctant dancers; shiver in dark, damp theaters, hoping for magical solutions to impossible problems. "Soon," says the dancer, "I will have enough technical skill to really dance"— as if that were the answer to it all! "Next time," says the choreographer, "I will chance on the right combination of movement design, musical accompaniment, costume, stage design, public relations, dancer proficiency, and audience response."

But less often do dancers or choreographers admit that they are not too sure what they are doing, or why—as if it were enough to proceed by trial, error, and perspiration! If comparable discipline and exploration were to be applied to understanding the nature of dance and art, many would find it valuable as well as relevant to them as performers, teachers, choreographers, or members of the audience.

It takes a special kind of discipline to think and then to clarify what you thought in words. It isn't easy to dig down and find your own views about anything. It's so much simpler to repeat what someone else said. But this kind of "I don't know enough to have an opinion," is the same as saying, "I don't have a unique way of moving, I'm just one of the crowd and need someone to tell me what to do and think."

Unfortunately we often hear loud voices repeating clichés and perpetuating easy answers to the problem. An old wives' tale tells us that dancers cannot make much sense with words and prefer to use body movement to mime what they mean. This is, of course, nonsense. Dancers are as literate as anyone who is interested and holds convictions about his work. The essential question is, "Are they really *your* convictions, based upon your understanding, your reading, discussion, and careful consideration?"

The story is told of a man who had been in prison for many years. He would walk over to the bars, shake them and then peer out, wishing he could escape down the halls, out the great gates, and into the world. But these were iron bars, and he was not a strong man. So he rattled his bars occasionally, as all prisoners must, and then sat quietly wishing he could be free. One morning a ray of sunshine crept through his small, narrow window, and he heard a bird singing. He looked about him in surprise, stood up, walked over to the cell door and opened it. He walked down the hall past the great gates into a shining world. You see, the prison doors had never been really locked; he just had never tried them.

2
What Is Dance?

Dance formulates or denotes our conception of certain dynamic patterns—only this and nothing more.
Eleanor Metheny, *teacher*

𝓜ovement is a part of man's very being. When he first moves, he lives; when he stops moving, he is dead. Sometimes his action is categorized into movements of work, play, or art. While each seems distinct from the others, there is, nevertheless, considerable overlap, resulting in innumerable variations.

To understand anything, and to communicate it to others, we think first and then try to find a way of separating the kind of thing we are thinking about from its immediate perception. We try to find something to call it, something that really differentiates it from other things, and even something to store away as memory or history. We look for a correspondence of one thing with another, or differences between them. We, for example, try to understand the relationship between a myth and the group of people who cherish it. Or we may compare what is happening here and now with what happened there and then. Sometimes, in an attempt to understand a phenomenon, we structure our beliefs on questionable assumptions.

We say, for example, "Dance is rhythmic movement," and, because we are thinking of what we call "dance" at the moment, overlook the fact that almost every movement we make is rhythmic. No one thing can be identified in terms which also describe other things as well. "Dance movement is fluid and beautiful," we hear, but so too is the flight of a gull or the leap of a high jumper. "A dancer is one who moves with grace, weaving intricate patterns through space," but so is a basketball player or a matador. What can we say specifically of this activity commonly called "dance"?

When we examine the work-play-art concept, it is obvious that somewhere there must be differences. While the movements of each are seldom random, some kinds of play, work, and art have unusual and hard to recognize form. The organization of each would seem to be determined by the particular function peculiar to the action involved. For example, the motions of a carpenter, golfer, or sculptor all have their own forms, based upon purpose as well as the idiosyncrasies of the carpenter, golfer, or sculptor concerned. The clue to the identification lies in that purpose, and in the method of achieving the result.

Beyond the readily identifiable purposes in hammering a nail so that a door may be hung on its hinges; in so hitting a ball that one wins the game; or in formulating an illusion of flight in stone for a gallery show, there are many concomitant factors including experience, craftsmanship, personal involvement, and a multitude of drives to action. The carpenter's task in hanging a door is commonly called "work" and

Photo-image of action

is considered both functional and useful in maintaining a living standard. With economic overtones of cost, necessity, and salary, work is usually "something I *have* to do in order to pay my bills," and "when I retire I won't *have* to work any more. But to the golfer who has just hit a hole-in-one, his movement serves an entirely different purpose. He has pitted all of his powers against a small white ball, the surface of the golf course, the prevailing winds, and the pressures of the contest. Then when he hits the ball (clean and hard), overcoming all the outside forces with his own power and skill, he attains a much more elusive kind of personal achievement. He is successful in his entirely nonfunctional play. By means of insight, skill, and his own creativity, the sculptor forms his image of flight to fulfill yet another nonfunctional purpose, perhaps to enlarge the viewer's perception of flight. Each of them has moved in his own way, for his own purpose.

Whether the differences are in terms of function or nonfunction, direct reality or elusive image, self-gratification or group interaction, competition or display, the carpenter, golfer, and sculptor each had different procedures and end products. What they did was determined by the movements they made in order to reach their goals. Of course there are always such variations as the professional golfer who works for money and prestige during a tournament, or the commercial sculptor who works on commissioned pieces for similar reasons. Seldom, however, does the carpenter admit to "play" as he hangs a door. He may observe that hanging a door properly is an "art," but he is undoubtedly referring to skill and craftsmanship. Work results in a real object, copying a desired model, with the end known at the beginning. Play is practiced for effect, usually pleasurable. Art creates a hitherto unknown object, the end known only after it is done. Because the words "work," "play," and "art" have so many meanings and usages it is not always easy to communicate or to understand what is meant. The same is true of the word "dance."

The Dilemma of Definition

"The dance is the mother of the arts. Music and poetry exist in time; painting and architecture in space. But the dance lives at once in time and space."[1] But the word "dance" describes many kinds of action, events, and phenomena, ranging from the patterned scurrying of ants to the overall cycle of life and death. Unusual or exotic movement is called "dance" and often refers to *any* skillfully performed action. It has even been called "life on a higher level." Such loose use of the term is disastrous, for it really means that anything can be dance, and cannot therefore be differentiated any more than boiled vegetables in an overcooked soup.

One of the basic problems is that understanding dance depends largely upon one's experience with dance. To those who know and enjoy classical ballet, *this* is dance to them. The teen-ager, brought up on rock 'n roll, will declare the latest fad dance to be "what it's all about." To those who know dance as the intricate tapping of feet, tap dance is dance to them. Dance is what you have known it to be. Dance is what you expect it to be. And anything that does not equate with your expectations just is not dance.

An average group of young college students were asked to respond to the word "dance" with some word they associated with it. The following is a partial list of their first reactions: rhythm, beauty, jazz, concert, ballet, motion, nightclub, rock 'n roll, dance of life, czardas, tango, Rockettes, Nureyev, grace, adagio, Pavlova, audition, do-si-do, topless, Kolo, Martha Graham, improvisation, design, *Swan Lake,* bellydancer, dynamics, choreography, Isadora Duncan, Charleston, studio, rehearsal. This is just a random series of lifeless words, symbolic of an immediate reaction of an unselected group of people. It does, however, indicate the wide range of function, form, and related aspects of this kind of human behavior—as the students perceived it—with their particular experiences and biases.

Sachs has written:

> . . . all supermundane and superhuman motion is dance. Turning about in divine rhythm, Siva creates the world; for the Chinese, cosmic harmony originates in the dance, planets and gods swing through the universe in dance; and late Jewish theology, indeed even Christianity, ever hostile to the dance, cannot visualize the lot of the redeemed except in a picture of an ethereal round about the shining throne of God.[2]

Dance can be work, play, or art; and just as work, play, and art can be differentiated according to purpose, so it is with the different dance forms. In a sense, the professional dancer who practices, auditions, rehearses, and finally is paid for his performance, can probably be considered a dancer-worker. Certainly those who go to the community center for an evening of folk dance are primarily concerned with fun, socializing, and play. The Hindu dancer retelling the adventures of heroes from the *Ramayana* may be performing exhaustive movement—he may be "working" hard—but his purpose is neither a functional product nor the relaxation of play. Rather he seeks to project a meaningful image, a communication through significant movement. The topless dancer in a burlesque show may be "working" hard, and "playing" with the audience, but the goal is probably something other than work, play, or art, in the usual sense of those words.

The semantic problem is magnified, and unless we try to clarify meanings the issue only becomes more confused. When uncertain about word meanings we go to a dictionary for help. According to one dictionary, dance is "to move the body, especially the feet, in rhythm, ordinarily to music . . . to move lightly and gaily about; caper . . . to bob up and down."[3] This hardly solves the problem. We still ask, "What is dance?"

Dance is movement, organized and patterned to serve its particular "dance" purpose. In another context, certain dance forms have come to have special names which describe some of their unique characteristics. While these titles may not be universally accepted, they are in fairly common usage among identifiable groups in the Western world.

Even as words may be used in many ways to fulfill different purposes, so can movement be used. Words may be so organized as to provide lyrics for a popular song, or they may be formed into a moving drama. They may ring out in political speeches or in tender love poems. In similar fashion, movement may be used for a rollicking folk dance or a sophisticated classical ballet. It may jerk and snap in hard rock, or it may sway and slink in a tango.

Though movement is the basis of all dance, it does not follow that all movement is dance. Dance fulfills different needs, and because of this, different forms have evolved. The *way* it is performed, the *reason* for the performance, as well as where and when it is performed are all important to differentiation. And because people have been concerned with these dance forms, they have participated, watched, and named them. There is general agreement among dancers, observers, teachers, and historians about these classifications. And so it is necessary to declare a *particular* dance form before any meaningful definition may be made. More complete attention will be given to these many dance forms in chapter 6, "What We Have Today."

Origins of Dance

The actual beginnings of dance can never be verified for, like music, speech, and religion, its origins are lost in the dim past. The mythological origins of dance include instances of supernatural visitation, disguised teachers, dream-trance experiences, or happenings at the eclipse of the sun or moon. The social origins may evolve from expressions of communal life, reflections on the past, immediate joys and fears, hope for the future, continual need for food and security, relation to the unknown, representation of needs and passions, and mimicry of animals either for food or totemistic benefits.

There are some traces of dance in cave paintings, stone carvings, tomb murals, mythology, and the traditional ceremonials and rituals that are still performed by contemporary primitives. But most of the evidence must be interpreted by anthropologists, historians, critics, dancers, and others who make their views available in literature or lecture.

While there is ample evidence of the life and custom of early men, there is little record of the actual movements of his dance. In fact it is confusing to know what movement qualified as "dance," or when the ceremony was considered a "dance-ceremony." The ceremony was probably made up of all aspects of the behavior of man with movement predominating in some parts and secondary in others. There are references to where and when dance took place, even references to who was moving, and for what purpose, but none as to what actually happened. The few written descriptions available are sketchy, with such phrases as, "They did a kind of a backward shuffling-hop around a wounded animal . . . ," or, as a zealous missionary described a dance: ". . . people gyrating and jumping about, making obscene gestures and indecent sounds."

But how can you describe a dance in words? It is only recently that a practical means of dance notation has been made available, and it is not easy to either read or write without considerable training. Photographs and films are enormously helpful but were not used much in early field work where important records could be made. Even with exact notation, films, photographs, and careful, skilled verbal description, the dance, as a lived experience, is not duplicated. The real dance is experienced directly, either as a participant or an observer.

In any event, dance started long ago, when one man began to relate to another, to his surroundings, and to the unknown. It has been linked to an expression of emotion, a delight in filling space with designed actions, or, most often, to express relationships with something outside of oneself. This is true of the child as he moves, sometimes to represent something, sometimes randomly, and often with great complexity. According to W. D. Hambley, it was a means of calling on outside forces to help adjust to a hostile world, of finding a way to assure the necessities of life, and of coercing the elements for social need. He described dance as "a complete expression of social and communal life, originating in the magic of animal imitation and ecstatic stimuli to get food, sex, and approach to the spirit world."[4]

Jane Harrison described ritual as consisting not in prayer or sacrifice but in mimetic dancing. She went on to say: "The mimetic dance arose not only nor chiefly out of reflections on the past; but out of either immediate joy or imminent fear or insistent hope for the future."[5]

To W. O. E. Oesterly, the origin of dance lies in "this imitative propensity of man,"[6] in relating the known to the unknown. Curt Sachs declared that, "In the ecstacy of the dance man bridges the chasm between this and the other world, to the realm of demons, spirits, and God."[7]

Ethel Urlin, in *Dancing, Ancient and Modern,* wrote of three sources: ceremonial or religious, based upon celestial phenomena; dramatic representations of man's passions; and the mimicry of animals out of beliefs in animal ancestry.[8] In *Origins of Art,* Hirn suggested that impulse to dance probably occurred when an individual or group were so affected by emotional stress, fear, exhaltation, hope, or depression that they moved in response. Gesture soon developed and meanings accrued through observation of others in similar situations, much as children do today.

> The purest and most typical expression of simple feeling is that which consists of mere random movements. These activities, whether of the whole body or of special parts—the larynx, for instance—which follow immediately upon, or rather accompany a state of pleasure or pain, are in themselves entirely nonaesthetic. Thus it is impossible to see anything artistic in the spectacle of a man leaping or shouting for joy. Yet the lowest kind of lyrical music and lyrical 'gymnastic dance' may be almost as directly connected with the original state of feeling as these purely expressional activities. The only difference is that in music and dance the movements have been limited and restrained by the adoption of a fixed sequence in time. This fixed sequence in time—the rhythm—must therefore, from our point of view, be considered as the simplest of all art-forms.[9]

In his *The Mentality of Apes,* Wolfgang Kohler described a game of spinning around like dervishes performed by all of his chimpanzees. They would often extend their arms to the side, horizontally, as they revolved about themselves and around their play area. He remarked on their resemblance to human dancers, especially as they combined more elaborate and repetitive movement patterns, such as trotting about the circle with special emphasis upon one foot.[10]

From sketchy sources, including cuneiform tablets and stone carvings, dance in Sumer, and throughout Mesopotamia, was apparently closely integrated with mythology, and rituals were performed to reproduce successive stages of the myth. The extent to which dance originated in the myth is not known, but it was obviously of enormous influence. Ishtar, goddess of Ninevah, is said to have charmed the Sea God with both song and dance.

Among other "firsts," Osiris and his sister-wife, Isis, were considered originators of dance in Egypt. Isis, as the Goddess Hathor, was patron of music, dance, and love, later identified by the Greeks as Aphrodite. From the Middle Kingdom in Egypt there are some records of dance at the Osiris festival at Abydos. Described in the text of a relief now shown in the Louvre are the masked dancers at the resurrection of the god. It was in this celebration that dance was supposed to have started in Egypt.

Coomaraswamy has clarified much of the complicated Hindu mythology of India especially that dealing with Shiva (Siva) the preserver, destroyer, and creator, the God of Dance. As destroyer and preserver he determines the rhythms of all worlds, and is shown as such in a pose of perfect harmony, surrounded by a great crown from which sparks flare up and die down. Tripurasura, the demon of the three towns of the three worlds, acts as his footstool, and it is the relationship of Shiva to him, within the triple universe, that is the basis of his dance.

One of the famous myths about the dance of the triple universe tells of the 10,000 hermits (rishis), whom the God Shiva visited to bring truth. But these hermits only cursed him and called forth a fierce tiger who leaped on Shiva to devour him. With a smile, Shiva skinned off the tiger's pelt with his little fingernail, and draped it about his neck. Then the hermits called forth a monstrous serpent which Shiva hung around his neck like a garland. Then they armed the horrible black dwarf with a giant club, but Shiva stepped on him, broke his back, and began to dance. The hermits watched him in wonder, captivated by his rhythm and grace. Suddenly all the heavens opened and gods and hemits alike threw themselves at Shiva's feet in adoration. It is this kind of dance that evokes such supreme joy in which the individual is at one with the universe.[11] "He who no sign could describe is made known to us by his mystic dancing," wrote an unknown South India poet.

The prototype of Shiva is said to be the Lord of Beasts, in horned headdress on an ancient coin seal (c. 4,000 B.C.) found in the Indus Valley. Many illustrations show him seated in the Yoga Lotus position, with exposed and erect phallus; gazelles on each side of him, and surrounded by a tiger, elephant, rhinoceros, and water buffalo. Another miniature stone torso, suggesting the posture of the later dancing Shiva, and a 4½ inch cast copper female nude, a replica of a temple dancer, both very ancient pieces, were found in the Mohenjodaro area of southern India.[12]

All of the shepherdesses in love with the God Krishna are said to have wanted to hold his hand when he danced with them, so he simply multiplied his hands so that he had enough that each could hold his hand in her own.

An old Chinese tale attributes the start of dance to great bears stamping about on stones, making sounds like thunder. Another version explains this as dancers disguised as bears.

When the infant Zeus was left on the island of Crete by his mother Rhea, the warrior Curetes performed a noisy, shield-and-weapon clashing dance to drown the cries of the wailing infant lest Cronus, his father, should find him and devour him. Several interpretations of this tale insist this is how dance began.

The Japanese myth of the origin of dance tells of Amaterasu, Goddess of the Sun and Fields, founder of the Royal House. Born from the left eye of the God of the Sea, Amaterasu quarreled with her brother one day and sealed herself in a cave, depriving the world of sunlight. Darkness and sterility covered the earth. The gods tried to lure her out, but to no avail. They sent for Ama-no-Uzeme who tied her hair with creeping plants and, brandishing a bunch of bamboo leaves, climbed on a great tub turned upside down like a drum. Amid much laughter from the audience Ama-no-Uzeme uncovered her breasts, dropped her skirts and danced on the tub. Such laughter and excitement were generated that curiosity caused Amaterasu to step out of the cave. The entrance was quickly sealed behind her and the sun came out once more. The same motif occurred in ancient Greece, when Demeter, maddened by the abduction of her daughter Persephone, banished growth from the earth until one of the gods joked with her and showed her his sexual parts.

The Hopi Indians in the southwestern United States tell the story of the youth who set out to follow the Colorado River, to get water for his people. Sealing himself in a boat made of two parts of a hollowed cottonwood tree, he floated downstream against the current. He met Spider Woman and gave her a special prayer stick with eagle feathers. Pleased, she went along to guide him, riding behind his ear. As they traveled, she taught him her great wisdom and, after many adventures, they met the Great Snake, who carried Cloud on his head. Great Snake took them to the source of water in the Kiva (ceremonial house) of the Snake people. Proving himself, Youth was initiated into the Snake Clan and learned their ceremonial dance. He married Snake Virgin and they returned to his home. Each night on the way home he built a *kisi* (altar), a shelter for his bride. They had many snake children and Spider Woman led the family to a new home on the top of several mesas, where Youth was chief. Thus was founded

Hopi Bee Katchina
(photo of Indian drawing)

the Snake Clan. He taught the people the Snake Dance so there might be rain for the crops. This was the first Hopi brotherhood and is still the most powerful clan. Each year the Snake Dance is performed even as Youth taught it to the early Hopi people.[13]

Among the early Blackfoot Indians of Montana, the buffalo were lured over cliffs and butchered on the rocks below (apparently the same method was used *c.* 30,000-10,000 B.C. when the dancing, masked shamans led the great bison to a similar doom). The beginning of the Buffalo Dance, according to a Blackfoot Indian legend, came when the people were hungry and there was no one to drive the buffalo over the cliffs. A young Indian maiden saw a herd grazing near the edge of a cliff, and promised to marry one of them if the others would jump over. Soon the animals began leaping over the cliff, and a big black bull came up to her and claimed her as wife. After her people had butchered the buffalo they looked for the girl but could not find her, and her father started a search. Coming upon a herd near a watering place he saw a magpie and begged the bird to find his daughter and tell her he awaited her. The bird found the girl and gave her the message just as the great bull awoke and bade his wife go for water. Taking a horn from the bull's head she went for water. (It is interesting to note that the Stone-Age Venus of Laussel, carved on a rock in southern France, is of a heavily pregnant woman who holds in her right hand a bison's horn.) The Indian maiden found her father, was frightened for his safety, and bade him wait while she returned to the bull with the horn of water The bull sensed the father was nearby and bellowed a terrible roar; and all the rest of the bulls bellowed back. Pawing the dirt, they all rushed out, found the man, and trampled him. The bull saw the daughter mourning and reminded her of his many buffalo ancestors who had been killed by the Indians, but promised that if she could resurrect her father, they would both be set free. Seeking aid from the magpie, who brought her a tiny bone of her father, the girl placed the bone on the ground, covered it with her robe, and began to sing a certain song that brought her father back from the dead.

The bull admitted the power of people and, before he set her free, showed her the song and dance of buffalo resurrection, in which all the great buffalo danced, slowly and solemnly, with deliberate and heavy steps. At the end of the dance the black bull told the girl to go home and teach the dance to her people. He gave her a sacred bull's head and buffalo robe to be worn by those who would dance the bulls. Returning to their camp, young men were chosen to learn the song and dance of the buffalo bulls, and these dancers made up a group whose function was to regulate ceremonial life in the community. It is said that when the buffalo herds disappeared, so too did the dance.[14]

A legend from the island of West Ceram, near New Guinea, tells of nine families who lived in a place called "Nine Dance Grounds" in the jungle. A young man named Ameta (dark) was hunting a pig that fell into a pond and nearly drowned. Ameta saved the pig and found a coconut on its tusk, though as yet there were no coconut palms. The man returned home, covered the nut with a snake-design cloth, and dreamed that he should plant the nut in the earth. The next day he planted it, and in three days the tree was as tall as he was; in three more days it was even higher and had blossoms. Climbing the tree to cut a nut, he nicked his finger and blood fell on a leaf. In three days a face appeared on the leaf, and three days later a torso, and in three more a young girl appeared. That night he dreamed he would wrap the snake-decorated cloth about the girl and take her home. The next morning he did this and named the girl Hainuwele. In three days she was a young lady, and an unusual one. Her excrement was a variety of riches, so that Ameta became wealthy. Then a Maro dance was to be celebrated in the place of the Nine Dancing Grounds; it was to last nine nights and the nine families of mankind were to dance. Hainuwele stood in the center of a ring, along with all the women, and passed betel nuts to the men dancing in a ninefold spiral. At dawn the dance ended. The next night all assembled on the second ground, because Maro is danced each night at a different place. Again Hainuwele passed out betel nuts, and when asked for them, passed out pieces of coral. The next night, on the third ground, the dance resumed, and this time Hainuwele gave precious Chinese dishes; the fourth night she gave larger dishes; the fifth night, large bush knives; the sixth night, copper betel boxes; the seventh night, gold earrings; the eighth night, great gongs. Each night the gifts were of greater value, and the people grew jealous and decided to kill her. On the ninth night, as Hainuwele stood inside the circle, she did not know the men had dug a great hole in the center. As the ninefold spiral progressed the maiden was slowly forced into the hole and covered with earth while the loud Maro song covered her cries. Then each dancer tramped the earth over her and, at dawn, returned to his home. When Hainuwele did not return, her father realized she had been killed. Taking nine branches of a magical plant used for casting oracles, he recreated the nine Maro dance circles in his home and stuck nine fibers of a coconut palm leaf into the earth at each dancing ground. At the ninth ground he drew out her hair and blood, dug up her corpse, then cut it into small pieces and buried them about the dancing ground. The two arms he took to Satene, one of the Supreme Virgins, who had come from an unripe banana. Meanwhile, the bits of Hainuwele were transformed into wondrous tuberous plants which have been food for the people ever since. Ameta cursed mankind, and Satene, maddened by the killing, built a great ninefold spiral gate on one of the dancing grounds. Standing on a log just inside this gate, Satene held out the two arms of Hainuwele and told the people she was leaving because they had killed, and they would have to come to her through the gate. As they went through the gate some of them were turned into animals or spirits, and so the world was inhabited by pigs, deer, fish, birds, and spirits, where before there were none. As the people passed through the gate they were struck by one of Hainuwele's arms. Those on the left of the log on which Satene stood had to jump over five bamboo sticks, those to the right over nine. From these two groups came the ancestors of the tribes called the "Fives" and the "Nines."

Then telling the people they would not see her again until they died, she disappeared from this world. Satene now lives on the Mountain of Death, and to reach her the dead must climb the great mountain.[15]

Early Man and His Magic

Anthropological finds from Java, China, Germany, Africa, and many other parts of the world have added to the ever-widening storehouse of information on early man. Not the least are the pre-Ice Age carvings and reproductions of animals of the hunt, preserved, in remarkably good condition, in caves and grottos throughout the world. Unusually fine relics have been found in protected caves in spite of the wear and tear of time and glacial engulfments.

From the Australian outback to the Pyrenees of northern Spain; from the frescoes of the Sahara desert to the northern plains of Russia; from the sun disc figures of northeast Italy to the fine etchings on the rock walls of canyons in Utah; from remote sections of Asia to unlikely regions of Africa there is an endless and magnificent march of powerful and vital animals across cave and canyon walls. There are monumental and minute bison, bulls, horses, birds, reindeer, elephants, and other animals of the time and place, as well as humans disguised as animals—painted in blacks, reds, whites, and the deep purple of Altamira.

The earliest of these cave paintings depict animals in their full importance. It is later in Paleolithic times that more realistic human figures were painted, and then these were usually abstracted and secondary to the majestic animals. It may be that the scarcity of representations of man himself may be due to the fear of bad luck, or "evil eye," for the paintings were obviously considered as magic.

There has been considerable controversy about the initial purpose of these paintings and carvings. One theory holds that they were a part of magical rites in the never-ending search for food. The principle of "envision the animal you seek, perform the necessary ritual: draw the picture, dance the dance, sing the song, hold the thought, and reenact the successful sequence of events leading up to the kill." The fact that the animals were often shown pierced by arrows or spears, or were shot at by these weapons after the work was completed, gives credence to the theory that this was an act of hunting magic. The animals were not just imitations or simulations but were actually the counterpart of the animal to be conjured to life.

Another theory proposes the rise of ancient artists or historians who would ensure a record of this group for posterity. This is not a very likely theory, however. It has also been suggested that these paintings were the result of playful self-expression on the part of some primitive men. But others maintain that in facing the persistent need and search for food and security of that period there was little time or opportunity for individual expression.

The fact that most of these paintings which have endured are found deep in winding grottos and caves gives credence to the idea that these were hidden sanctuaries deep in the earth—apart from the reality of the objective world. Whatever their initial purpose, the paintings that remain can be viewed simply as powerful animals, or, with very little effort, as creatures of magic—images representing more than animal forms. If you view them in their underground cave museums, by the light of a flickering torch, a semblance of magic is still there.

In a Spanish cave at Altamira are some of the most magnificent of all the huge animal paintings. Some extend over forty feet in length, and others cover small protrusions in the ceiling as if in relief. It is these smaller ceiling animals that have been said to symbolize the stars. Most of the red bison range in size from small to greater than life size. Apparently covered by a landslide, the brilliant colors in this cave seem as fresh as if just completed yesterday. In the half light, bison and smaller animals seem to gallop across the walls.

Deep in the most convoluted part of a cave at Lascaux, in southern France, are monumental, action-filled paintings in broadly outlined earth colors on pure white surfaces. Here are realistic bulls, horses, deer, oxen, bison, and even a rhinoceros, wolf, bear, bird, and unicorn. Some of the famous horses are eighteen feet long, and many of these animals appear to be wounded by arrows and spears. Some abstracted human figures are there but are secondary in size and position.

In a labyrinth grotto deep in the caves of Trois Freres, in Southern France, are over 500 animal engravings, one of them, the famous *Le Sorcier*. Painted in black, on a high ledge, he appears like a skeleton presiding over the animals below. Looking very much like a man in disguise, he has eyes and antlers of a reindeer, face of an owl, ears of a wolf, beard of a goat, sexual organs of a cat, forelegs of a bear, and tail of a fox or horse. His profile posture looks like he is doing a cakewalk dance step.

Nearby, another figure, in upright position, has the rear legs and rump of a man but animal forelegs, one with a cloven hoof. He has a bison's head, horse's tail, and is playing a bowed instrument, or maybe a pipe. In front of him on the wall is another animal figure with its head turned back. Nearest is an animal figure with the forelegs of a reindeer and accentuated female parts. Interestingly, the forelegs of this creature do not have the hooves of that species!

These half-human animals do not correspond to any known reality and may represent some mythical scene in which either god or magician is charming the animals with music and dance, or may even be depicting some ritual. While these figures may be connected somehow with magic for hunting or fertility, they are remarkably like human figures in disguise. The fact that the animals are being hunted with no weapons indicates that there are other means for bringing about the event depicted.

What were these caves that early man decorated with paintings and carvings? Perhaps they were sanctuaries or holy places, for of the many caves only a few were painted and carved. Succeeding generations repainted many of these caves, down to the Christian monks who transformed some of these to Christian sanctuaries, such as Lourdes in France. Even today many natives in the regions of the caves refuse to venture near them because of demons or spirits thought to linger nearby.

Anything deep in a cave suggests some kind of purpose, perhaps of getting closer to the seat of fertility. The fact that the paintings so often occur in remote and inaccessible parts of the cave—up to 200 to 300 feet from the entrance, and often from a passage close to the floor, where it is necessary to crawl and wriggle to get through—suggests a secret use. Here in such a dark place, or cramped vault, or at a sharp turn, the imprints of left hands, occasional footprints, and animal paintings abound. It has been suggested that some were for coming-of-age ceremonies during which the youth proved his courage and stamina as a man. Certainly it was more than chance that brought them about.

Elements of Magic

Magic is a system of belief based upon an association of ideas. It's a kind of natural law that accounts for and determines the sequence of events and relationships in the world. It's a guide for conduct, a system of justice, and a pattern for life and death. The positive aspects of magic are called "sorcery" and deal with things you should do; the negative side of magic is called "taboo" and is concerned with things to be avoided—things you should not do.

A magician can bring about any effect he wishes by reenacting it; effect will resemble cause, or like will produce like. The picture or dance is both representation and the thing represented, wish and wish fulfillment at the same time. Man gains power by representing power, and the real animal will suffer the fate of the animal represented. The real event is contained in the sample magical action, and the drawing or dance used is simply a trap. A good magician can kill an enemy by destroying an image of him. Another will tie stones about his abdomen, groaning and moving about the hut of a woman in labor, helping her as she gives birth. Some Peruvian men of magic mold a fat and grain image of their enemy's soul, then burn it, thereby "burning the soul" of their enemy. The basis of many rituals still practiced today is to move like the animal or eat of his flesh, and you will be successful in his hunt, or will acquire his desirable characteristics.

The negative aspect of magic is the basis of the many taboos in effect throughout the world. People avoid certain plants and animals lest they acquire their undersirable qualities. In some parts of the Orient the wife of an elephant hunter may not cut her hair or oil her body lest the elephant break out of his trap or slip through the nets. In past days Italian women stopped spinning their wool as they walked down a road lest the stalks of grain they passed should twist like the spindle.

Throughout the primitive world there are three basic taboos. The first tells of the necessity of separating brother and sister; second that man must run and hide from the stepmother; and third, most widespread, to avoid the wrath of the old man. Among most groups it is necessary to propitiate the old man, even after his death. Soon fear of the father passed into fear of the tribal god. In opposition to the old man was the helpful mother who advised, sheltered, and taught mysteries. The strange visitation of infectious diseases generated the idea of the unclean and accursed, especially those dying. Soon the fear of sinister places and things, as well as the dread of traps, brought about more taboos.

With the development of speech men could reinforce each others fears and begin to systemize them. Soon a common tradition of taboo was established. With taboo there was a need for a means of removing the curse. Soon there was "tell others not to," and the performance of potent acts such as spilling blood and offering of sacrifice. With taboos came restraints, new powerful ceremonies, and basic religion.

In that form called "contagious magic" the magician presumes that whatever he does to some object will equally affect a person who has been in contact with that object. Aborigines of Australia believe they can lame a person by driving a thorn into his footprint in the sand. In Malaysia, if a man's friend finds the arrow that hit him and puts it in a cool, wet place, the inflamation of the wound will subside. Among many natives, if a child's afterbirth is discarded into water the child will die of drowning. Among some other groups the child is assured of being a good swimmer. There is an old Greek saying, heeded by many today, that upon rising from your bed in the morning you must smooth the imprint of your body from the bed as a precaution against magical spells.

In the introduction to *The Golden Bough*, Sir J. G. Frazer wrote that primitive man "was a creature of superstition and terror, caught up in a great net of magic, witchery, taboo and ritual." In spite of modifications through the years of our ancestors' basic beliefs continue to haunt us today.

While some magic was performed by members of the group, the more important kinds were under the control of leaders: shamans, priests, medicine men, witch doctors, or kings. There is a distinction drawn between the shaman, whose powers come in trance from direct contact with the supernatural, and the priest or medicine man who learns a code of ritual practices from older priests. The Siberian shaman, for example, is a lone figure whose power comes from "spirit possession." Because of this supernatural contact he tends to be alienated from the rest of his community, and it is generally conceded that this shamanistic role is often assumed by epileptics or emotionally disturbed people. In many American Indian societies the shaman is set off from the rest of the community in a fraternity of medicine men. Among most groups the medicine man is simply a healer and seldom resorts to trance behavior. In Africa a shaman may assume the role of authority as a prophet who gathers a following about him. Among all groups these shamans or medicine men are regarded as awesome and potentially dangerous. Among the Bushmen of the Kalahari the shaman, or witch doctor, is a trance performer who derives his power directly from his social group. Among these people many have the power to heal and overcome the misfortunes that are thought to come from the spirits of the dead.

Sorcerers, wizards, and witches are human beings that can cause harm. To combat their evil one must seek the services of another sorcerer who is sympathetic on one's cause. This leads to a system of good and bad sorcerers, as well as a spiraling attack and counterattack through magic. Sometimes the power emanates from one's own group, sometimes from the outside.

Among many tribes there is a hierarchy of gods or supernaturals, which are both worshipped and invoked. Each of these supernatural forces has some object or animal in the real world as his representative, and to whom homage may be paid. Thus the principle of power may be personified by the elephant, bison, or bear. Fertility may be symbolized by a river, bull, snake, or ear of corn. These are called "fetishes" (objects inhabited by the supernatural), or "totems" (supernatural helpers), and are usually considered as symbols with no power in themselves. There are hundreds of fetishes, most of which are connected with different kinship groups. The child inherits the fetish from his parents, according to the type of marriage made. As soon as a woman is pregnant she consults a priest of her fetish, and he divines if the child will be acceptable. If so, time will be spent during later childhood in learning the sacred rituals and language. Each fetish or totem has its own costume, symbol, paraphernalia, language, and purpose.

Among the Pueblo Indians in the southwestern United States these supernaturals are personified as Katchinas. The Katchina may be a masked dancer who represents the spirit, or it may be a carved cottonwood doll, painted, dressed, and feathered like the dancer. The Hopi children play with these dolls, which are later housed on the sides of the fireplace or altar. As with other fetishes, the Katchinas dramatize many myths, especially those having to do with the coming and going of the gods.

Magic may well be a major phenomenon in the life of man. It certainly appears to have been an integral part of primitive life. Serving as an alternative to philosophy, science, and religion, it accounted for all of man's relationships to his world. The extent to which it is still influential is hard to say, for it has become disguised in many aspects of man's behavior. It has undoubtedly influenced the mythology, mores, literature, and art of our world. Certainly there are hidden or even unconsciously manifested elements of magic in much of contemporary life. In many parts of the world the modern primitive has elaborately evolved totem systems which have not only lasted through the years but have accumulated new involvements from one generation to another. This elaboration over the centuries has resulted in even more complex systems than those of Paleolithic times.

Masks

Probably many of the ancient masks were made of materials unlikely to survive, for stone, metal, hardwood, and more durable materials came later. Anthropologists identify them as "basic artifacts," unusually diverse in form and material. To an expert, each mask can be clearly differentiated in style, form, use, and tribal origin.

Among the thousands of masks used today, no two cultures produce identical forms. In the American Northwest the masks were of wood, while in prehistoric Mexico they were made of stone and gold. European peasant masks were often in caricature; in Tibet, Cambodia, Bali, and China there are many distorted devil masks. Africa has stylized forms, and the East Indian and Eskimo are noted for their dreamlike masks. Some are quite realistic; others are exaggerated distortions. Among the materials used are fiber, gourd, skin, bone, turtle-shell, stone, metal, animal parts, hair, clay, shells, tree branches and twigs, cornhusks, reed, bark, paper, cloth, feathers, and plants. A New Guinea mountain tribe in the Asaro River area don huge mud masks with a design like men from outer space.

Masks have been used extensively in ritualistic ceremonies as a part of magic. The wearer of the mask takes on supernatural or sacred powers, often totemistic. The mask, by a process of transformation, assumes a special quality and becomes a cherished object in itself, not to be defiled by profane hands or careless use. Its magic is profound. These "false-faces" may express folk beliefs, mysticism, other worldliness, or mythical characters associated with the different masks.

The mask affects the wearer as well as the observer. Whoever wears the mask finds freedom, because his real face is concealed. He is better able to relinquish his own identity and assume another, particularly within roles of sacred or conventionally traditional behavior. To the observer the mask represents a spirit, god, or natural force, and he feels awe consistent with the status of the one represented. The mask overwhelms the person wearing it and clarifies the nature of the ceremony. Essentially the mask is used more to identify, symbolize, and clarify than it is to conceal. Primitive man who has been conditioned by traditions and beliefs of his group, and influenced by mass response, is always profoundly affected by masked figures in a ceremony.

For us today the mask seldom symbolizes in a ritualistic way but survives for carnival times because of its potential for releasing emotion and inhibition. It provides a socially acceptable occasion for extravagance and personal freedom. Masks have also been used extensively in drama and dance, and many contemporary artists design them as works of art in themselves, capable of direct appeal to feelings common to all men.

Mythology

Myths are legends, "tall tales," fairy stories, explanations of strange and common creatures, or unusual as well as expected events. They often tell of an ancient and memorable act that is attributed to mortal, god, or hero, but usually with endless consequences. Malinowski described the myth as a lived reality, not just a story to be told.

> These stories live not by idle interest, not as fictitious or even as true narratives; but are to the natives a statement of a primeval, greater and more relevant reality, by which the present life, fates, and activities of mankind are determined, the knowledge of which supplies man with the motive for ritual and moral actions, as well as with indications as to how to perform them.[16]

The myth never breaks away from its magical circle of figurative ideas, for it is a never-ending world of illusion. The mythical world comes to rule all aspects of life and helps man to resolve many of his problems. In the *Larousse World Mythology,* Grimal wrote: "Everything in us that is not transfused by rational knowledge belongs to myth, which is the spontaneous defense of the human mind faced with an unintelligible or hostile world."[17]

By means of rituals and ceremonies, which are invariably linked to the mythology of the group, action may be taken, courage renewed, wrongs avenged, and survival assured. Mythology is the very root of primitive life, and all groups, without exception, have a mythology. And myths never die, although they are sometimes transformed when they lose their efficacy, or when they are spent in their present form.

At the time of the earliest rock engravings and paintings (*c.* 30,000 B.C.), the caves were centers for both animal magic and the rituals of men.

> They are the underworld itself, the realm of the herds of the underworld, from which the herds of the upper world proceed and back to which they return. They are of the realm and substance of night, of darkness, and of the night sky, their animals being comparable to the stars, which are slain by the sun yet reappear. The mythologies of the animal masters and shamanism, the journey to the other world by way of a ceremonial burial, men's threshold rites, rebirth, and the masked dance inspired the liturgies of this brilliant age.[18]

It may be that the lore of hunting tribes as well as children's nursery tales began at this time, but evidences of these are not easy to find. Rather those which have become traditional seem to point back to certain origins.

The northern Aranda of the Bandicoot totem in Australia have a creation myth which, like so many of the others, starts in darkness. Everyone was asleep at the bottom of a great soak. Karora, first of the Bandicoots, slept under the soil covered with red flowers and grasses. Above him was a living, sacred pole, covered with a smooth skin, reaching up to the sky. Karora lay at the root of this pole and began to think. Soon Bandicoots sprang out of his body, through the earth, and into a dawning sunrise. Karora, too, came forth from below, and where he had been became the Ilbalintja Soak, filled with the juice of honeysuckle buds. Hungry, he caught two Bandicoots and cooked them in the hot sand. Soon the sun went down and, lonely, Karora went to sleep. While he slept a bullroarer emerged from under his armpit and soon grew to be his son. At dawn both awoke and Karora gave a great call, and his son started dancing a ceremony around his father who was now decorated with feathers and blood. This was the first ceremony.[19]

Mythology is the world of gods and demons, giants and dwarfs, heroes and witches, mortals and immortals; where time stands still or goes at breakneck speed, and "once upon a time" can become present or future as well as past. Animals talk, men are transformed into gods, gods are transformed into birds, and a masked figure can easily become a device of magic. Mythological characters can be in several places at the same time and easily move from heaven to earth to underground. Far from rational, it provides a kind of symbolic order to clarify and adds meaning to life. Prehistoric peoples had a rich and varied panorama of myths dealing with all aspects of living and dying, but especially rich in topics of creation and survival. All of these became subjects for ceremonies.

Ceremony

The ceremony is made up of selected and patterned behavior of man, generally purposeful, and almost always serious. It may include bodily movement, word, or song, and it may be for solo or group performance. Undoubtedly some ceremonies are for group participation and some just for observation. In its broadest sense "ceremony" designates a planned behavior of man, animal, bird, fish, and even insect.

It tends to be repeated and becomes traditional. In a narrower sense it is qualified for human beings in terms of an immediate purpose, for example, for a religious ceremony, a funeral ceremony, a ceremony for laying the ghost.

Other words which indicate similar meaning are: rite, ritual, festival, ceremonial, or celebration. Some of these have become attached to certain events such as "fertility rite," "magic ritual," "coming of age celebration," "festival for the seasons," or "ceremonial feast." A rite, ritual, or ceremony is an abstraction of reality, not practical but *magical*. It is a matter of mimetics, of relieving emotion, of anticipation, a representation of the past, or a presentation for success in the future.

In a small chamber deep in a cave in southern France (Tuc d'Audoubert), a remarkable prehistoric remnant of interlacing curves made of footprints was found on the floor of the cave. These imprints were so clear that callouses could be seen from the soles of the feet. Most of the prints, save for some complete ones in a deeper part of the cave, were heel marks, similar to those made by some African and Australian dancers today. While there is certainly no proof of dance in this find, it does seem plausible that a ceremony of some sort was performed, and it included action by many different people.

There have been many reports of interesting finds, high in the Alps, where carefully arranged cave-bear skulls were found in small wall pockets in the walls of Paleolithic caves. Some of these arrangements were on stone slabs, with other little bones or small stones carefully placed around them. One skull had long bones passed through the eye sockets. Dated at about 75,000 B.C. it was surmised to represent some kind of a cave ritual; obviously it was no casual burial or accident. According to records, the cave-bear was probably the first "animal master," with a counterpart in Africa of the lion, and later the mammoth, and then the bison.

For whatever purpose, and in whichever guise, man performs some things in certain ways, and gradually this comes to be "the way we do it." In primitive societies this pervades the whole of life. Not a single action of any importance is performed that is not accompanied by prescribed rites of more or less elaborate form. Franz Boas suggested that rites are more stable than their explanation, even though they symbolize different things to different people—and at different times. Ruth Benedict maintained the ritual to be the most important aspect of man's life, with greater attention to it than anything else. The diversity of rites is so great, and their occurrence so universal, that many interactions, elaborations, and borrowings occur.

Most of the ceremonies among primitives today have been performed generation after generation with few changes, honoring the same gods, and have become sanctified through the ages. During World War II, Navajo soldiers returned home on leave to their Arizona reservation, where they sought out and participated in their tribal war dance. Whether these sophisticated and well traveled young men were dispelling the evil of enemy dead or just participating in a traditional rite cannot be known.

Undoubtedly ceremonies were born out of man's need to objectify those things important to him. Magical rites for survival, success in the hunt, increased fertility, safety from enemies, and the unknown were all celebrated. According to Franz Boas, the ritual, and the myths associated with it, were extensions of the need for security and also the prestige of membership in a secret society.

Today we have such ceremonies as initiation into a college fraternity, participation in a political convention, attendance at a rock concert, plus the more traditional weddings, funerals, baptisms, debutantes' balls, May Day fetes, Easter egg rolls, celebrations of Christmas, Fourth of July, and Labor day—ceremonies still, but considered refined and civilized.

The earliest ceremony was probably a composite of patterned movement (dance), vocalization (song), and storytelling (poetry), with great emphasis upon topics of dreams and divination. The point at which action became dance, sounds became music, and storytelling became poetry is impossible to surmise.

The primitive ceremony has no single purpose but can easily imitate what mythical ancestors have done, reproducing their gestures, speaking their words, and thereby having communion with them. Actually the same ceremony is often used to serve different purposes. For example, a dance done as part of a funeral ritual may also be performed at an initiation rite. Sometimes the original significance has been lost, and what is left is pattern, gesture, and sound, a symbol for an occasion, but still holding assurance of propitiation and salvation.

Many anthropologists have concluded that prehistoric grottos and caves were used for special ceremonies, and the relic wall paintings and statuettes all played an important role. The rites of passage for adulthood, marriage, and death, as well as the rites of intensification for alleviating such crises as storms, famine, and disease, may all have been conducted in such places. There has been much written of the young men being tested for courage and manhood as they stumble through the dark, damp, winding pathways where the great animals lurked. A shaman, probably in reindeer dress, directed the whole mystical experience, instructing the neophyte in his duties as an adult and further testing him for courage. Funeral ceremonies may have been conducted, highlighted with the decoration of burial mounds with reindeer and bison horns. Hunting ceremonies to insure a continuing supply of animals and to maintain man's supremacy over them must have been practiced. But no one will ever be sure of the nature of these ceremonies, only that they were performed. We can be sure of some primitive ceremonies, those which continue to be practiced today.

The following ceremonies have been selected from many parts of the world in order to illustrate the broad scope of ritual practice. These are some that have dance as a part of the ceremony.

Among the Arunta of central Australia imitative magic is practiced systematically to provide food in that barren land. Members of the Witchetty Grub totem perform a pantomime representing the full grown insect emerging from the chrysalis case. A long, narrow structure of branches represents the chrysalis case, and within this members of the grub totem sit and sing about the creature. Then they shuffle out in a squatting position as they sing about the emerging grub. In order to increase the fertility of the emu, members of that totem clear a spot on the ground and, opening veins in their arms, spill blood on the prepared space until a six-foot space is soaked. When the blood has dried into a cake they paint the sacred emu totem on it, especially the parts they like to eat: fat and eggs. The men sit around this and sing while others, wearing masks, mimic the birds as they aimlessly stand on one leg and peer off in all directions.

Among the Navajo Indians in the western United States, a purification-healing ceremony utilizes sand paintings which are prepared anew for each ritual. The medicine man chants as he paints his family of gods with colored sand. Then he bids the sick man, who ordered the ceremony, to come out, dance, and then "sit down with the gods." There is a continual chant during the ritual of admission to the path of beauty and harmony. When the ceremony ends the medicine man destroys the picture, for he would no more leave it "running" than a technician would leave an x-ray machine with its power on.

According to the Eskimo it is the Great Earth Mother who is responsible for storms at sea and also for the migration of her children: whales, walruses, seals, and all fish. When food shortages are threatened there is an elaborate ceremony during which the shaman goes into a trance and sings a special hymn while performing an amusing dance so that she may be favorably inclined toward his people. When the shaman recovers from the trance he sings a magical song recounting what Earth Mother has told his people to do. Among these people ceremonial life is richest during the long, dark months of winter when totemic legends are enacted and myths are retold by the elders.

In New Guinea there are spirit-cult rites where tribesmen don long-nosed ceremonial masks and dance about the village frightening women and children. One initiation ceremony starts with a battle between initiates and the older initiators who guard a large, peaked-roof ceremonial house. The initiates crawl into the house where elaborately disguised and costumed elders douse them with ashes and foul-smelling magic water, intended to turn them into men old enough to keep the secrets of the cult. After being shown sacred objects and instructed in ceremonial behavior, they creep out of the back entrance so that the women, waiting in front, can't see them. They run to the river and bathe, the ceremony being completed.

An interesting evidence of swift acculturation is demonstrated by an occasion in New Guinea where natives daubed in ceremonial white-face mud and paint, wearing exotic feathers and animal parts, and carrying ancient spears dance at a very modern National May Day celebration which commemorates self-government in Papua.

In an Australian initiation rite the young man dances as he embraces a pole (according to the myth, a pole arose out of Karora's head) just after subincision. There is also a ceremony at the planting of the pole, during which the great pole is carried upright on a man's back, pointing up like a flagpole. The carrier and the pole are both decorated gaily with bird down and subincision blood to symbolize the life force.

In Dahomey, the close connection between ritual and mythology is demonstrated by a man wishing to know of his future, consulting a sorcerer who dances to "draw the Fa." The Fa is both a great god and father of voodoo demons, as well as the ritual by which the god Fa speaks. To "draw the Fa," date stones are thrown onto a flat surface, some falling on convex and others on concave sides. For each position a corresponding demon has appeared, and the problem must be solved through him. Because each god has his own myth, it is the sorcerer's task to find the link. Thus a good sorcerer has studied his mythology and magic carefully and is able to solve his client's problem.

There seems to be no part of the world or any primitive group that does not have its rich ceremonial life, and there are few primitive ceremonies that do not feature dances.

3
The Unknown Past

The thundering herd that shakes the cave at Altamira, and has for twenty thousand years, was painted merely to help the hunting: so say the anthropologists. But anthropology falls prey, naturally, to scientific prejudice. A scientist would rather describe the cave pictures as attempts at magic than admit the fact that they appear to have been painted by magic.
      Alexander Eliot, *critic*

Man's dance has been so integral a part of his development that it is impossible to know exactly where and why it was first observed. Because of its very nature we can't be sure of how it was performed. Certainly it was early in man's history. Animals, birds, insects, and fish had performed "mating dances" and patterned-ceremonial movements, even as they are observed today. To know early man is to learn something of his rituals, magical rites, mythologies, and celebrations which are all basic to his dance forms.

What we know of early man is neither factual nor easily discernable. We infer from such fossil remains as bone fragments, rock carvings, stone images, and artifacts, as well as the dramatic cave and stone paintings and engravings found in many parts of the world. Another potential source for learning about early man is a study of contemporary primitive groups. It is assumed that a truly primitive people of today will have many of the characteristics of the early Paleolithic hunter. In any event, all that we have is interpretation of relics found or practices still carried on.

What Is Primitive?

The word "primitive" may remind us of a group of naked, painted and befeathered natives bearing gifts to strange gods or whooping it up around a boiling kettle. Unfortunately we are all subject to the pseudo-primitive stereotypes that prevail in so much of our experience. According to some dictionaries, "primitive" means original, first, old-fashioned, quaint, simple, and unsophisticated. In common usage the words early, undeveloped, uncomplicated, and superstitious are found. The primitive is accused of being dirty, cruel, savage, selfish, and bedeviled by senseless taboos. Consider our civilized, mature society, where so many men can be killed with so little effort, where pollution of natural resources is widespread, where members of our own group die of starvation and overdoses of drugs, where unspeakable filth and rats abound in ghettos, where hotels have no thirteenth floor, and we all avoid black cats and walking under ladders.

According to most anthropologists, primitive society is not simple. In many respects primitive man is more complex than any in Western culture. He may appear less sophisticated in terms of our enrichments and gadgets, but rather than being inferior or superior, he is simply different. In some ways he is very much like modern man, in those ways where values are parallel. But the unique difference between modern man and the primitive is in his isolation or apartness from others. As long as he lives away from and unaffected by other men he will differ from them. It is when he gives up his isolation that he loses his primitiveness and uniqueness.

With the passing years there has been less and less isolation and thereby fewer evidences of real primitive man. According to Joseph Campbell, many so-called "primitive groups" of today are more apt to be regressed Neolithic, Bronze, or Iron Age cultures because of the evident diffusion of tools, weapons, pottery, barnyard animals, cooking, and ceremonial methods, songs, games, dances, and myths. The most primitive groups include some of the natives of the equatorial forests of Africa, pygmies of Malaysian jungles, Veddas of Ceylon, natives of some Indian Ocean islands, some Amazonian Indians, aborigines of northern Australia and New Guinea, a few Eskimos of North America, and some of the Indians of Tierra del Fuego, off the tip of Southern Chile.

With real primitives there is no written language, and the words they speak serve as signals for immediate impressions rather than the expression of abstract ideas. To the Australian aborigine, for example, there is no word for fish, only a series of sounds that translate: "food in water"; and "not-being-able-to-think-about-it-anymore" means, loosely, "forgiveness" to the Eskimo.

The primitive world, prehistoric or contemporary, must be viewed in terms of its own culture and place, not from the point of view and standards, values, and morals of civilized man. If we consider culture to be a manifestation of human achievement in his interaction with the world and his fellow man, then primitives had, and still have, a culture. To refer to them as "uncultured" or devoid of achievement has no basis in fact. Atomic submarines, pocket computers, and senior citizens rest homes reflect one culture; animal totems, ritual dances, and respect for family and ancestors the other. Who can say which is the more civil culture. We can only be sure that they are different.

Primitive man, then and now, sought to control his uncertain life through principles of magic in his rites, rituals, and ceremonies. As single figures would step out of the group in order to intercede with the gods for the group, they would often assume a different character or "face." The "false-face" or mask is one of the oldest items of man's history and can even be seen in cave paintings dated back some 50,000 years.

Dance Among the Primitives

In late Paleolithic time, dances seem to have been a part of the magical rites practiced by men to gain power over animals: for success in the hunt and for protection against them. Painted human figures representing chamois buck at Teyjat; musk ox at Le Madelaine, or deer at Lourdes correspond with the imitations of hunted animals of Bushmen, pygmies, and American Indians as well. Just as dancers of earlier days are depicted with tails, antlers, or wings, so some Australian aborigines wear tails today and Hopi Indians don antelope horns or eagle feathers. In some tribes the dancers actually wear the skin of the animals being hunted or serving as totems. In some of the cave paintings men seem to be conducting a ritual around a dead bison, and today African pygmies celebrate the death of an elephant the same way.

The function and fashion of dance has remained much the same through the ages. Some of the totemistic dances of contemporary primitives seem little different from those depictions on the walls of the Spanish caves where the hunters seem to be exerting mystical power over the dead or dying animals. There is an obvious reference to magic in most cases. When pygmies act out the role of baboon or wild bear; or Andaman Islanders the turtle; the Tasmanian the emu or fish; or the Hopi Indian, the eagle, the meanings are quite clear even though there are no words to describe it.

Pictographs and petroglyphs in areas of Europe, Asia, Africa, Australia, the Pacific Islands, and North and South America all show paintings and carvings depicting ceremonial scenes with sorcerers, processions, masked men and women, patterned footprints and action symbols. There is a tendency on the part of those interested in dance to declare all such representations as "dance." How can we be sure that these are dance, not hunting, running, or simply a part of a magic formula? According to some it would not have been appropriate to duplicate a dance ceremony with a picture of the same ceremony. Sachs wrote:

> Only a very few drawings admit of definite interpretation. In most of them the conscientious scholar would rather forego positive explanations than run the risk of interpreting a battle scene as a war dance, or a man with his arms raised as a shaman in an ecstatic dance. Pictures of the dance are probably rather rare in any case. For since the Paleolithic painter usually makes wish pictures in order to obtain by this means certain effects of sympathetic magic, he will have little reason to reproduce dances which serve the same purpose by another means.[1]

The classic examples that are usually cited of dance in cave art are the "Dancing Archers" at La Cueva, the "Masked Dancers" at Marsoulas, the "Women's Dance Around the Man" at Cogul, the "Animal Masked Figures" at Lascaux, *Le Sorcier* at Trois Freres, the "Dancer by the Ibex" at Veija, and the "Animal-Like Men's Figures" at Ariege and the Dordogne Valley, as well as the hordes of often-interpreted dance paintings, sculptures, engravings, and replicas from all over the face of the earth.

In his *Tribal Dancing and Social Development,* W. D. Hambly wrote:

> ... archeological evidence shows us human figures of the old Stone Age in what are probably dancing attitudes, and these paintings are associated in time and place with pictorial representations of animal life, for man in this remote period was a hunter, and one of consumate skill. There was perhaps in the first place a deliberate invention in order to bring rhythmical motion into the daily life of the clan, and it is not improbable that these early experiments in giving rhythm a place in social and religious development emerged from imitation of animal movements.[2]

Davidson reported an ancient rock painting in the New South Wales area of Australia showing male and female figures in a "corroboree jump" (part of a special animal ceremony). Since the same movement is still widespread throughout the southern part of the continent, it is assumed that the identical position on the rock painting is of dance. A number of pictures of verified single and group corroboree dancers were found, sometimes in the characteristic black and white paint with stick beater accompanists, in central and northern Australia. Davidson surmises that they are equally as old as the European Paleolithic cave paintings.[3]

In Orange Free State in South Africa, a red-rock painting of a woman with huge buttocks was discovered, her arms oustretched on either side of a circle of human figures in animal guise. This is reported as "Totem Dance."

Campbell wrote of an engraved lion in the North African Sahara looking full-face at the viewer. In the same posture as one of the shaman dancers at Lascaux, he is so placed that the rays of the rising sun strike his figure squarely, and he seems to be in control of a whole field of engraved animals. As Master-of-the-Animals Shaman, this has probably been the dominant mythological formula basic to the magic of the Paleolithic hunter.[4]

Among primitives, dance was used in a natural way to express some purpose, and these purposes were tempered by belief and almost always accompanied by elements of magic. The dances followed prescribed patterns, and, except for some pleasure dances, were serious affairs. Nearly all of the dances were directed to or influenced by the supernatural. The intent of some are obvious, but many defy classification.

> Many of them are so old that their origin must be looked for in antiquity or even in prehistoric time. In our day the domain of ritual is restricted, but in primitive culture it pervades the whole life. Not a single action of importance can be performed that is not accompanied by prescribed rites of more or less elaborate form. It has been proved in many cases that rites are more stable than their explanations; that they symbolize different ideas among different people and at different times. The diversity of rites is so great, and their occurrence so universal, that here the greatest possible variety of associations is found.[5]

Man's dance themes are affected by his way of life, and variations in behavior result in different dance forms. But themes for food and propagation seem to be most universal. Because birth, puberty, coming of age, battles, war, death, and fertility of man, animals, and crops are so universal, these are basic for most of ceremonial dance. Through the years, with cumulative changes of population, climate, and exhaustion of herds and soil, many variations in ceremonial practices occurred. Some of these changes obscured original meanings and purposes for which the ritual was originally developed.

It is said that older Africans do not ask each other's name, village, or business, but only "What do you dance?" In the distant past there were fewer variations in dance styles, simply because man had not developed so many different ways of living, in so many different places. But as man differentiated in north, south, east, and west, with varying traditions, myths, and culture patterns, his ceremonies and dances took on changes to match. As he formulated complicated kinship systems, religious beliefs, and ornate rituals, he sought first survival and then identity.

In tribes the world over a boy becomes an adult member of the tribe through dance. When he grows old he passes on his dance to a younger man, thereby ceasing to be an active member of the tribe. Dance was not diversion or entertainment, but was a serious part of living. Power was gained from the rhythmic interaction of sound and movement, from the collective expression of emotion, and the cooperating members of the group had a strength greater than any one of the group. This was a potent force, especially when accompanied by accepted patterns of magic.

Even when men were the only dancers, the women would sit around the dancing place, clapping, chanting, or beating drums. The shape of the dance was often circular, and round and round the dancers would go, hour after hour, sometimes by day, sometimes by night, sometimes for days and nights. At other times, the dance formed into a processional led by the shaman, through the encampment, village, or around a new home, fire, or burial place. When the shaman stepped out of the group, to intercede with the gods on behalf of the group, the first actor was born.

According to Levy-Bruhl, the basis for both ceremony and dance, for participants and observer, is: "the mystic communion that binds them to the mythological or totemic ancestor. Through a mystical ecstasy generated by the dance the primitive is no longer fearful or vulnerable to the unknown; he has found his salvation."[6]

Curt Sachs wrote that:

> . . . in the life of primitive peoples and of ancient civilizations scarcely anything approaches the dance in importance. It is no art that disregards bread; on the contrary, it provides bread and everything else that is needed to sustain life. . . . On no occasion in the life of primitive peoples could the dance be dispensed with. Birth, circumcision, and the consecration of maidens, marriage and death, planting and harvests, the celebration of chieftains, hunting, war and feasts, the changes of the moon and sickness—for all these the dance is needed.[7]

> Most frequently it is not one single aim that the primitives pursue in these ceremonies. By imitating what their mythical ancestors have done in certain circumstances, and reproducing their gestures and acts, these natives are in communion with them and actually participating in their substance. At the same time they are introducing the neophytes, the younger generation which is to be added to the others, to the secrets of the sacred usages upon which, from season to season, the well-being and the safety of the group depend. And again, by virtue of these ceremonies, they succeed in multiplying and developing the totem plants and animals of the various clans of the tribe.[8]

Descriptions of dances from all across the world are becoming more readily available. Sometimes photographs and motion pictures of contemporary primitives are also to be seen. Whether right or wrong, we assume that our ancestors, who lived in caves, roamed the prairies and forests, or dwelt in crude agricultural communities, were not too unlike tribesmen of today. Reports of anthropologists, travelers, and missionaries to the most remote parts of the world have increased our understanding, but distortions of information limit a true picture of the phenomena.

Characteristics of Primitive Dance

In *Ancient Art and Ritual,* Jane Harrison wrote that, "historically or logically the dance in its inchoateness, its undifferentiatedness, comes first. It has in it a larger element of emotion, and less of presentation. It is this inchoateness, this undifferentiatedness, that, apart from historical fact, makes us feel sure that logically the dance is primitive."[9]

Generally, primitive dance is characterized by its communal nature. In a world where privacy is unknown, the group knows everyone and shares everything about each other. Dance is the main focus of social life; it is the basis for a common conscience. Elaborate rules remain within an unchanging framework. With present-day primitives this means that there has been added time for the rules to become fixed and sacred, though the original reasons and meanings are apt to be forgotten. The accumulated knowledge, patterning, and inferences are biased and narrow, but are carefully honored and practiced as long as the group retains its primitive nature. Often these dances are hidden from outsiders in order to ensure isolation. This is why there are apt to be dances for the tourists, available for all to see, and quite different dances for members of the tribe.

In primitive dance there is complete involvement of the dancers; this is not mere performance, it is a celebration of personal belief. It is a valid and important experience, inspired, vivid, artless, and naive. Here is directness to the point of clairvoyance. There is emphasis upon basic human experience, with little sophisticated or complicated patterning of movement. There is curious repetition of simple and direct action with interaction of man, sky, earth, sea, air, dreams, and fantasy. There is implication and connotation, yet with a mystical and unassuming manner, as if it were happening for the first time. There is concern for the unknown, the spirits, the dead and life after death. A kind of inevitable order is established for direct absorption of the concerned dancers as they come to be one with the unknown. This might be called a kind of image-making magic.

Because of the broad scope of primitive dance, it is dangerous to make too many generalizations, for there are innumerable variations. Interpretations change according to time and place as well as the immediate purpose of this group, in the light of their beliefs and behavior. One quite objective way of looking at dance is as a lived experience. Some dances are for doing, some are for watching. In the participation dance the dancer himself is moving with little regard for an audience. He may be called a dancer, or a performer; an animal totem, masked figure, or initiate; he may be a planter, hunter, warrior, or king; he may be a shaman, priest, or magician, but it is *he* who is moving, the one dancing, and what he is doing is called "participation dance."

If, however, the dancer is performing *for* an audience, whether the audience is the group, tribe, or in a theater, then the emphasis is no longer upon participation but upon performing for others. This may be called "performance dance." All kinds of dance can be put into one or the other of these categories.

The image making of the primitive's dance is not so much a realistic plea as a childlike belief and approach to the fulfillment of his needs. Whether abstract or mimetic, the movement and dancer's paraphernalia symbolize a plea to the unknown. The symbols become one with the import. In real life he hunted and fished and planted seeds, intent on the practical end, and in his ceremonies he *represented* his needs. While his dancing and mimicry were impractical, his needs were quite practical.

Man's first experience with symbols was probably quite emotional and self-expressive. From his original leaps, shouts, beatings on his body, and rollings on the earth he gradually moved to symbolize these explosive, emotional acts. Signs, metaphor, and symbols were used, and, over a period of time, the direct meanings became obscure. Form and pattern became more important, and the projection of images came into being. All of this formalized behavior, especially with sacred objects, masks, or other paraphernalia, may have been a dance, but beyond this it was a ritual.

Some primitive dances may be characterized by the nature of the movement; some by their shape or formation, others by intent. Most ethnologists agree that the original meanings are lost but that a kind of symbolic significance remains: the ritual. The pantomimic rhythmic action that was sometimes used to report events to a tribe often were crystalized in abstract dance. In the first place a particular event may have been reported. The action would be repeated again, on another occasion, as much for the thrill of reliving the emotion as the retelling of the event. After many repetitions, the dance was no longer about the battle, journey, or particular catastrophe. Long after the participants had forgotten the particular event they were thrilled by the emotion that stirred the original dancers to action.

From the point of view of technique, primitive dancers have a relatively simple movement vocabulary, but they tend to have remarkably strong, supple, and well-developed control of pelvic, abdominal, and gluteal muscles. Their general physical condition is apt to be good; and excellence in competitive dancing is an index of sexual vigor, aiding in the choice of a well-developed and durable mate. They move strongly and purposefully and seem to generate a charge of energy which they can release explosively, ecstatically, or with barely perceptible evidence. The quality of the movement cannot be described in words, but it certainly encompasses all extremes of dynamics, even beyond our ordinary experience.

Some classic references to primitive dance movement occur in Curt Sachs's *A World History of the Dance*. He describes "convulsive" dances, "those out of harmony with the body," where legs jerk, body trembles, songs are "panted out," and the dancers "throw themselves about with forceful flexion and extension of their muscles." Found mainly in shamanistic cultures where trance and hypnosis are a part of magical power, there may also be weaker convulsive movements, depending upon the intent of the dance. Sometimes the convulsive movement is limited, as with Malayan and Polynesian women, to their hands; Australian Arunta to the thighs; Torres Strait dancers to the head; East Africans to the larynx; Indians (from India) to the lips and eyes; North Africans and Brazilians, the breast and back; and Arabs, the abdomen and pelvis. The dances "in harmony with the body" are the opposite of the convulsive type. This form often calls upon all parts of the body to move in response to an established dominant rhythm, usually resulting in more natural action.

Further, Sachs wrote of "expanded" or "close movement," the former accenting the upward inclination of the body as represented by the great leaping dances. These seem to be found more in the totemistic and patriarchal groups. "Close movement" dances usually start from a fixed center, resulting in swinging, swaying, and suspension movement. Usually calm and composed, these dances are close to the ground and characteristic mainly of matriarchal groups, and found in the planter cultures.[10]

Another view of dance movement of primitives was made by Louis Horst in his book, *Modern Dance Forms*. The kind he called "Air Primitive" is like Sachs's "Expanded" movement, which rebels against gravity. It is the masculine movement of the hunter who leaps, lifts, and slaps, seeking to rise above the earth. The "Earth Primitive" of Horst's classification is similar to Sachs's "closed" form. Quiet and balanced, harmonious, and close to the earth, this is the women's dance or the dance of the planters, who roll, sit, whirl, and often isolate hands, abdomen, and pelvis. With this movement the dancer seems to blend into the fertile earth, to become one with it.[11]

The oldest formation in dance seems to be the closed circle, and, according to Sachs and Langer, symbolizes an important reality in the life of primitive man, "the sacred realm, the magic circle."[12] Here "great powers are loosed" while the "ordinary world is locked out."[13] Whether it separates the dancers from the observers, the sacred place from the profane, the consecrated object from the unconsecrated, is not really known. A natural extension of the circle dance is to open into a "chain-dance," which may progress like weaving, or into a spiral, labyrinthine shape, with all of its overtones of the underworld and burrowing down into the center of the earth, or conversely ascending out of the depths. Many of the later primitive, early Neolithic, and especially Greek dances were of this formation. Obviously the circling around trees, fires, sacred objects, houses, villages, and even people is one of the more obvious of the forms. Of course the very nature of the circle is such that the dancers can continue to perform easily in one place rather than moving in lines which would take them away from the focus of a group. In addition, everyone can see everyone else, a factor of safety.

Other categories have been made in terms of the intent of the dances. There are dances originating in social aims such as the birth dances of both people and tribes; initiation ceremonies that instruct new members in their rights and responsibilities, sex and cult secrets; marriage dances of sexual attraction and property endowment; war dances; and dances of welcome to strangers, as testimony of good fellowship. While some of these socially derived dances may use principles of magic, they deal mainly with objective events of concern to the group.

While there often is no difference in the kind of movement used in the strictly magico-religious dances, they seem to serve a unique function. Dances involving the worship of sun, moon, fire, river, snake, or fox may be totemistic or as placation, but almost always they are utilitarian. Using mimicry, and through magic, these are highly serious affairs of a ritualistic nature. Food, fish, and game are needed, rain must come, the floods must recede, a warrior is sick, a man is dead. This is dance to sustain life, to lay ghosts, to ensure survival. Sometimes the dances resemble each other closely, then again they may be markedly different. Some of the religious dances are stately, others are spirited; some war dances are solemn, others forbidding and nervous; some ecstatic dances are fiery and out of control, others seem frozen in one place. Not only do they vary from group to group, they often differ according to the occasion in the same tribe. Among some, the same dance, identical in every detail, serves many purposes.

Robert F. Thompson, in a remarkable account of dance entitled *African Art in Motion*, has synthesized accepted criteria for dance excellence in some contemporary West African dance groups. Foremost is the strong power of youth which enables the dancer to "step inside" the rhythms with balanced control and steady dynamics. The intensity generated by a conscious attack on time and space accounts, in part, for the buoyance and drive of the action. All parts of the body are supple and interacting.

There is an elusive "simultaneous suspending and preserving of the beat," a deliberate play with the phrasing, which is essentially African. The so-called "get down" movements, where the dancer bends his knees and crouches close to the earth, are important, sometimes occurring on a heavier drum beat, as a climax for the dance or even as a solo for the dancer.

Another important aspect of African dance is the special attention to the complicated movement superimposed upon multirhythms. Such multiple-meter in dance affords enormous vitality and requires phenomenal control. It has been reported that some African dancers are able to combine two rhythms easily, and some can even combine three at the same time. Four or more rhythms carried simultaneously are rare, though some East Indian dancers seem so equipped.

Thompson, in identifying criteria for good dance in West Africa, wrote that the accomplished dancer moves with style, conviction, and a serious appreciation of his ancestors, from whom the dance came. "Looking smart," and aware of his skill, he is able to "show off" with the grace and strength of a splendid wild animal. Another criterion of excellence is the exactness with which the dancer begins and ends his dance, the timing of the action, and the interaction with the drummers and singers.

Most of the good West African dancers are balanced and symmetrical in their action, and with this stability there is a great premium placed upon a serene face. Value is given to moderation in size, costume color, tempo, phrasing, and complexion color. Dancers are said to be "cool" when their action is clear, brilliant, and smooth, "moving with a kind of ancient magic."[14]

The rhythms of primitive dances are sometimes simple, but usually complex. They range from a hypnotic repetition to complicated polyrhythms; from the four-square rhythms of the Occident to the elusive 3, 5, 7, and 9 combinations of many-toned drums; from a throbbing monotony to wild syncopation and melody. Accompaniment for primitive dance cannot be tied down to a neat explanation. With many dances a "call and answer" of song, drum, and dance occurs, often improvised; native instruments unique to the place are used, and often the self-accompaniment, that is the sounds coming from the dancers themselves, is even more exciting than all the rattling gourds, clacking sticks, ringing bells, and slapping strings.

Thurston Knudson, expert in native drum techniques, reported a remarkable similarity in basic rhythm patterns around the world. "The real differences," he said, "are to be noted in the way the drums are played—the fingering, the attack—not in actual rhythmic patterns."[15]

Categories of Primitive Dance

The evaluation of a culture imbued with scientific method is apt to find many of these dances strange, impractical, and even ridiculous. But the tribal group, moving in the unison of dance, or exposed to the sincere dance of performers like the shamans and medicine men, did gain power and assurance. In a terrifying world where savage beasts, storm, fire, and unknown terrors would strike at unprotected individuals, this group action was important for survival. From a heightened pulse and energized body, each was pervaded by a sense of well being. With many bodies moving as one, from an insistent rhythm of drums and movement, groups were knit together, beliefs were strengthened, and family and tribal ties made stronger. The collective generation and expression of emotion formed people into a group stronger than any of its parts. While group rhythmic action still has a potent effect upon man, contemporary man does not use it as effectively as did the primitive.

The following represent the major occasions for primitive dance. *Initiation* dances were performed to celebrate both birth into the world as well as acceptance into the tribe. Almost all primitive groups celebrated, and still celebrate, both of these. The dances for birth often accompany the entire labor and delivery as a magical aid. Both mother and baby are thereby assured strength and wisdom, and more particularly, are free from evil spirits who come at this time. The other "birth" or initiation into totem or tribe usually occurs at puberty and marks a high point in the life of the individual. Here is the time of a new name, new dress, different hair style, special decoration, responsibilities, and status. Often the birth process is reenacted, as, for example, with young boys before circumcision in the Kikuyu tribe in East Africa, who are reborn of their mothers, crawling from between their legs, are washed, cry, and then dance into new tribal relations. The boys are no longer "women things," and the girls are potential mothers. Midway in these ceremonies both boys and girls are taboo, and finally both will have acquired full sexual powers.

These puberty, or coming of age, rites are almost universal, but always are performed for the boys who are usually tested for courage, stamina, and skill. Sometimes the ceremony takes place in a circle with the initiates in the center, in order to draw power from the circling adults. In other groups, the elders are encircled by the initiates, who attain adulthood by dancing around them. Sometimes the ceremony occurs in a special place: a house, cave, or where the sacred objects are kept.

Among the Arunta of Australia, both boys and girls, after subincision, dance to meet the spirits of their tribe, to learn of their ways. An Achomawi Indian girl, taboo at her first menstruation, dances for ten full days into womanhood. The Andaman Islanders do frantic dances after a long fast, then break fast with a giant feast marking the acceptance of the new members into the tribe. The induction ceremony of the Bantus involves old and new members circling around two fires and gradually joining forces until all are circling one fire, thereby becoming one group. In many parts of Africa and Asia, scarification accompanies these ceremonies. Elaborate tattoos and skin carvings are made on different parts of the body. Sometimes the purpose is for spilling blood, sometimes just for decoration. Ash or astringent rubbed in the fresh cuts cause welting of the skin, which serves as a badge of completion.

Food dances differ from hunter to planter culture, but both maintain elements of magic either to lure or placate the animals or the gods who control rains, storms, floods, and plenty. From the time of the most primitive of early men up to the Middle Ages, when guilds and farmers used their songs and dances as symbols of their work and performed dances mimicking animals and the actions of sewing and reaping, planting, and caring for the crops, man has literally sung and danced for his food.

Marriage dances were an important part of the earliest ceremonies, which often included the act of mating. The exhibition of sexual prowess, personal charm, strength, and endurance have been called "obscene" by some lay observers, but few of these dances are merely erotic, rather they are magico-religious and traditional among many tribes. The founding of a home and the generation of children and a family were most important to early men. Among some African Bushmen, the bride sits in a shelter on one side of the village, the groom on the other. Tribesmen start a circle dance between them and, as the dance progresses, encircle the two, and, bringing them together, all encircle the new homesite.

The ancient ceremony of "dancing the bride out" has survived from early days up to the present time with the popular shivaree or charivari of pioneer days. Among the Teutonic Europeans and many Orientals this ritual still occurs. Polynesians danced to make personal attachments, which often resulted in pregnancy, and was ultimately followed by marriage. A popular axiom in those islands was: "the basis of marriage is dance." The Oraons of Chota Nagpur, in India, have a celebration during which maidens present germinated barley seeds to villagers and to young men they want to dance with. This is said to be the remnants of a magical rite to increase the fertility of the bride as well as the crops. Other magical rites survive in the traditional sword or arrow dances among the Bedouin Arabs, American Indians, and Scots as they perform special dances at weddings to ward off evil.

Secret Societies, or Totems, all include dances in their celebrations to prove veneration to totemic affiliations and fraternity with other members of the group. Sometimes it was sun, moon, plant, or tree ancestors that were worshipped, but more often it is a ratification of the individual's relationship to his animal totem. Animal ancestors, or even a reincarnation from some animal, are celebrated. The obvious animal sounds, habits, and character are all basic to the action performed, even to masks and sounds of accompaniment. The Eskimo prepared their sacred totem poles, displaying the shape, face, or symbol of their ancestors. The dances performed about these poles sometimes extended up the poles as well. In the Ivory Coast, in Africa, some dozen masked men, one for each totem group, made enormous jumps across the dancing space, and with raffia costume trembling and long pointed sticks banded with jangles, led totem ancestors in a dance, later to be led off by children of the group. The famous Hopi snake dance ceremony is a celebration of the relationship of the snake clan to rain. The American Indians, among others, have particularly well-known dances for clans such as eagle, antelope, rabbit, bear, butterfly, dragonfly, crow, and bear. These are just the ones that have survived through the ages and give something of the picture of what used to be performed.

Indian drawing of Hopi Katchinas

48 *Dance: From Magic to Art*

War dances are probably the best known and universally performed of all. They were done among all the hunters and many of the planters to build courage as well as assure victory over enemies. The war dance was usually part of a larger ceremony for strength and cohesion among members of the tribe. According to Hambly, the war dance was remarkable,

> . . . in its faithful portrayal of every incident of combat, pursuit, mutilation, rape, and cannibalism. On the artistic side, the best one can say is that war dancing represents a perfected form of primitive art and tragedy. With regard to the social importance of the war dance it may be justly said that no other is so essential for strengthening communal bonds and arousing the right mental attitude for aggression and defense.[16]

These dances assured self-preservation and established both tribal and personal prestige by collecting scalps, heads, or enemy tokens. The display of skill, strength, and stamina were often basic to sexual selection. Undoubtedly there was increased emotional state among the dancers that aroused others to action for defense or attack against enemies.

The Arunta use the war dance to increase virility, the Navajo to dispel the evil of one's enemies. The Dakota, Sioux, and Apache, great warriors of the American Plains Indians, reenacted the heroic deeds of tribal hunters and warriors in their dances. The Maoris of New Zealand imitate all of the aspects of war in their dances; and among some of the earlier hunters, the warriors' wives danced to insure the success of their husbands who were in battle.

Geoffrey Gorer described a frightening war dance at Loudina, in West Africa, where young men, all armed with bows, slings, hatchets, and cutlasses danced in a ring around the drums. Each wore the most bizarre of costume, some in animal skins and some naked. Dancing around, shouting, grimacing, and waving their weapons, they had extremely realistic fights among themselves and finally seemed to lose control and become ecstatic.[17]

Communication dances often took the place of storytelling, with an occasional narrative or chant to clarify the action. Legends, myths, and histories, as well as educational models for behavior and responsibility, were enacted in dramatic dance form. Children were taught very special dances related to ancestral belief, custom, and practice. Often these performances helped the young to learn and develop acceptable habits and understandings.

Worship or religion pervades almost every act of primitive peoples; inseparable from everyday life, it seems a natural occurrence. Of course, in his egotistical way, early man associated his deity with the power of good and evil, to be appealed to for satisfying his every need. Representation of his needs and desires would, according to the tenets of magic, result in the satisfaction of them. In his book *The Sacred Dance*, Oesterly suggested the purposes of worship dance to be primarily to honor supernatural powers. In the pre-animistic stage these powers were vague and undefined; but later, in the animistic stage, they developed into actual spirits of good and evil in the guise of gods and goddesses. Dances were performed to honor them, especially through imitation and sacrifice.[18]

Worship dances were also done in order to show off to a higher power, and to acquire power and prestige by imitating the gods. Thus through a form of sympathetic magic the dancer found union with the gods. By dancing himself into unconsciousness he would make his body a fit abode for the gods who would take his body to contact the group. These dances were also performed to consecrate a victim for sacrifice or to appease the spirit of a slain enemy victim. Homage to the gods might occur through an elaborate initiation of maidens to their service, or an ecstatic ceremony by shaman or chief. The astral motif, the rhythmic action of celestial bodies, action in cardinal directions, and trance-like action were all to be found in the worship dances of early man.

Dances for Life include that part of the ceremony in which dancers seem to combat the forces of disease and death. Because both were due to magical causes, those with supernatural abilities were called upon. Magicians, medicine men, and shamans could be considered the first doctors as well as the first choreographers; certainly they were the first dance therapists. As a magical operation, dance was important for every conceivable end. Beneficial to individual dancer, group, and observer as well, strength and harmony were said to be established.

Sometimes the sick person danced to exorcise the demons within him, and sometimes the chief or medicine man danced. The sick person might be placed in the center of a ring while the dancers moved about him. This kind of a dance was often performed in an ecstatic state, especially until the spirit of the sickness was driven out.

In northwest Australia there is a dance-drama of death and resurrection, very much like some of the modern passion plays. The dancers sink into the ground slowly and hide their heads under the boughs that they carry. At a given signal everyone leaps to his feet and with loud shouts and persistent chanting, celebrates the resurrection of his soul. In Malaysia an old and very sick man will squat in the middle of a "spring-floor," and to the accompaniment of a chanting group, led by one man playing a nose flute, the young children of the village dance solemnly around him. In the Celebes a procession of men and women with red flowers in their hair dance around the sick person who lies in the middle of a circle. Arabs used to get the patient into trance and then force the evil spirit out in dance.

Funeral dances differ little in form from those for food, war, and fertility except in tempo and solemnity. Sometimes the exact pattern, steps, and song are used throughout these rites, but obviously for a different purpose. It has been suggested that this is possible because of the magical property of the dance act, regardless of the purpose. The majority of funeral dances are performed in the "magic circle" around the corpse, shaman, food for the dead, actual bones, tree destined for the coffin, or village of the deceased. Remnants of these rites remain in the Irish wake and the traditional Chinese funeral.

According to Oesterly, there were five main categories of funeral dance:

1. To drive away the ghost of the departed, particularly if he were an enemy or had an evil spirit.
2. To keep the ghost from roaming through the villages and environs, to "lay the ghost."
3. To frighten away all of the evil spirits which always hover about at any death.
4. To impersonate the dead in hopes of reviving him.
5. To honor the dead, to assure him affection, and to reassure him he need not linger behind to molest the living.[19]

Among the natives of the central Cameroons, the funeral dancers wear horned antelope masks and carry images of food offerings, helping the dead to "find the road." The Andaman Islanders perform a "dance of tears" on the occasion of a child's death. The mother wears the child's skull, decorated with tiny shells, around her neck as she dances. Among some of the southeast Asians, bits of bone that remain after cremation are carried on bamboo trays. The dancers lower the trays to show that the bones are dry, with no liquid. Young girls carrying brass vessels turn them upside down to prove that they are "empty vessels." Thus a procession moves through the villages concerned. Among the Tarahumares of Mexico there are usually three funeral feasts, then cactus juice is sprinkled over the dancers to drive away the ghost of the departed.

Political dances are hard to differentiate, since almost all occasions were essentially political, in that they were concerned with the welfare of the tribe. The Arunta welcomed neighboring tribes, as they came to visit, dressed in full battle regalia, complete with swords, shields, and boomerangs. The northern Ashanti have a yearly ceremony at which time they abuse each other in word and action. This is considered an emotional catharsis of personal and political hatreds where they can get even with leaders and important members of the tribe. The actual dance is done with dolls, the dancers imitating animals and competing in feats of skill. In some African kingdoms, tribal leaders are selected, and assume office, in a dance ceremony. After induction, tribal laws, edicts and proclamations are given in song and dance. In Mali, West Africa, Dogon dancers, with towering headdresses, flail the air with fly-wisks as they dance for visiting dignitaries. Male dancers, masquerading as women, wear cowrie-shell masks over their rustling fiber skirts.

Pleasure dances may be a degenerate form of what was once a communal celebration. They are usually supplemental to a feast and include an exhibition of personal charms. Undoubtedly these are forerunners to the typical entertainment dance forms of today. It has been noted that the further a group moves from the naive belief in magic, the more he enjoys the purely pleasure dances. Usually happening at feast time, "pleasure dances" range from the frantic dances of the Andaman Islanders to the circling couple Squaw Dance of the American Navajo Indians.

Ecstatic dance is usually found in the hunter culture, especially in those with shamanistic belief. Many observers have suggested that the typical convulsive movement of ecstatic dance makes the performer more adaptable to trance, which is apparently the aim. This kind of dance often occurs at times of great need or disorder, such as war, famine, or disease. Essentially the ecstatic state is said to make it easier to contact the supernatural, so shamans, medicine men, and even chiefs seek to attain it. Haitian voodoo, and the hypnotic state of Polynesian dancers, Flagellantes of Mexico and the American Southwest, and the famous hypnotic dancers of Malaysia all employ this mysterious and often sadistic technique. The Maoris have their great "crying feasts," the Middle Easterners their "Dervish turning dances," and the Ceylonese their "Devil dances." The ecstatic dance is often an important part of healing ceremonies as well.

FUNCTIONS OF PRIMITIVE DANCE

The following involve dance either wholly or as a part of the ceremony:

Rites of initiation	*Birth, puberty, tribal membership, for leadership role*
Marriage	*Fertility rites, mating, founding of a home*
Secret society	*Initiation, periodic ritual, totem worship*
War	*For victory and courage, for strength, placate dead*
Communicative	*To describe, tell legends and history, educate*
Worship	*Honor gods, elements, fetish-totem, ancestors and tribal heroes, priesthood, for protection*
Food	*Hunting, fishing, animal mimicry. Fertility rites. Later agriculture, harvest, rain, plenty*
Life	*Exorcise demons, cure ills, effect longevity, resurrect*
Death	*Burial, dispel and "lay the ghost"*
Political	*Choose ruler, welcome friends, frighten enemies*
Pleasure	*Feast, fun, competition, celebration*

Dance in Early Civilizations

There is little factual record of dance in the early city states, save for the remaining paintings, murals, and sculpted pieces that suggest dancing postures. Some of the cuneiform writings of Mesopotamia and the hieroglyphics of Egypt tell of ceremonies in which processions and dances occurred, but no descriptions of dance action remain. There are many interpretations of what might have happened, and each adds something to our view. By the time the great civilizations of the Near East, Egypt, and India had reached maturity, the primitive ritual had been replaced by ceremonies with faithful adherence to form and tradition. The refining influence of growing religions, and the devout traditions of its priestly caste were responsible, to a great extent, in drawing dance beyond the purely emotional phenomenon of the earlier forms. Nomadic life was a memory for these men of the great cities. While these changes were taking place, outside the borders of the great cities dance continued, unchanged by the concentration of progress, even as primitive groups today remain relatively isolated. These primitives unconsciously retained the basic qualities of dance, while the great civilizations distorted its substance in order to control meaning and develop a new ceremonial form.

With this new civilization, power no longer was thought to be in a tree, mountain, river, or rock, and man was beginning to speak, move, and think in abstractions. A limited and fixed symbolism was developing, and even the gods took on more human attributes. Dance as a profession was founded by the practicing priests and priestesses. But whatever they called it, magic was still paramount, controlled chiefly by the priests.

From ninth century B.C. cuneiform tablets in Mesopotamia, Assyria, and Babylonia come records of *The Poem of Creation,* with reference to solemn dance rituals and processionals.[20] These took place for the Babylonian New Year, as they celebrated the renewal of nature in order to assure the perennial return of cosmic order. The ceremony lasted twelve days, at the critical period of the farmer's year when agriculture was at a low ebb. From a plaque in the temple of Ningal, at Ur, a sacrificial ceremony is shown, with a priest and female attendants moving before a seated king.

Marduk, King of Babylonian gods, had a yearly festival with chanting and dancing priests, magic ceremonies, purifications, and sacrifices. The entire course of life was regulated by the gods, so their life, death, resurrection, and marriage were all celebrated. At the first of every year the Festival of Zagmuk took place while the gods gathered in the Sanctuary of the Fates. Later kings were crowned there amidst processions, dances, songs, and other appropriate ceremonies. In the text of the Assurbanipal, a ring dance is described around an idol, following the signs of the zodiac; and as each sign faces out into space, so do the dancers in the ring. Apparently the Babylonians either believed in, or practiced, a ring dance in which the twelve constellations moved in harmony with the celestial spheres.

Early Sumerians, in the third millenium B.C., had harps, drums, pipes, and lyres for music to accompany their sacred songs and dances. Religious processions were said to be an important part of their worship ceremonies. Early Assyrian processions were led by men playing harps, and at fertility festivals wine-crazed dancers slashed and mutilated themselves to the accompaniment of drums, cymbals, and droning oboes.

In a culture so rich in poetry, ornamentation, pottery, musical instruments, carvings, mythology, and burial ceremony it is inconceivable that there was no dance. But evidence is sparse. If, as in other groups, they followed the mythology, then they did indeed have many dances.

The earliest traces of dance in Egypt date from about 2545 B.C., when hieratic dances were led by priests to express the immutable order and harmony of the stars. The dance was especially designed, perhaps with the original plan given by adept astronomer-priests. Ranging around a fixed altar, which represented the sun, priests clad in brilliant costumes made signs for the zodiac with their hands, while turning rhythmically from east to west, following the course of the planets. After each circle the dancers stopped, immobile, to show the constancy of their earth. By combining movement and mimicry, the priests told of the harmonies of the astral system as well as the laws of the universe. Plato thought the dance must have been designed by a god because of its "divine ingenuity." One of the reasons why we have no records of these dances, save for occasional references and mural paintings, is the secrecy with which the priests guarded their dances so as to increase their mystery, transmitting their rules by word of mouth.

Other religious dances in honor of Egyptian gods like Apis, the sacred bull, and Bes, the fertility god, were popular. A carving at the Metropolitan Museum in New York City shows the gods Anubis and Horus kneeling, their arms completing a pose seen in contemporary Spanish classical dance. Dance pictures of the New Kingdom (after 1500 B.C.) show young girls dancing, probably, as in other cultures, indicating the virgin maidens in the service of the gods, performing devotional dances. Sachs has suggested that present-day Dervish dances have undoubtedly retained something of their pre-Islamic influences, back to central Asian shamanism. The ecstatic state of the triple circle of whirling men with arms outstretched shows probable astral influence, and with the frescoes of whirling figures at an excavated tomb near Giza, both lend credence to the supposition that whirling dances were performed in early times.

There are hieroglyph names for many dance figures or positions which really give little information about the action, but do indicate something of the variety. The attitude of two male figures, each standing on one leg, face to face, was the hieroglyphic sign for dance. It is said that slaves danced such a one-legged advance-and-retreat dance around 2500 B.C. The old Egyptian word "hbj" means dance, and also refers to the "bridge," a backbend which is seen in several of the paintings.[21] Sometimes this position of hands and feet on the ground, navel pointing to the sky, is considered a symbol of the over-arching sky of night, or an expression of the wind swaying the reeds of the Nile. There are the figures called "calf," "the capture of the boat," "the leading of the animal," "the rape of beauty," "the taking of gold," and "the colonnade." The positions vary from a woman being hurled through space by two men, to what seems a rapid turn. Another picture shows a position similar to a ballet entrechat in which the feet cross and beat in the air. If it is possible to reconstruct action from static pictures, then the feminine dances were slow, with vocal accompaniment, emphasizing their figures with tight, transparent, and sometimes pleated costumes. There seemed to be solo, duo, trio, and groups of semi-gymnastic dancers who somersaulted, tumbled, and made "bridges" with their backs, like our circus performers. Two reliefs show men executing "splits" equal to the ending of the can-can.

In the reliefs, the hands never show spread fingers but seem to be conventional flippers. Apparently there was much sleight-of-hand and juggling, feats of balance, and other acrobatic feats. The bellydances of present-day Cairo may be one of the remnants of the muscular controls these early dancer-acrobats had.

The profile silhouette of so many of the Egyptian figures was the result of a plastic limitation, for rules of perspective and foreshortening on a flat plane had not yet been discovered. The resulting cliché of flat, single-plane figures with angular arms and legs would never be recognized by their models, and certainly is no indication of how Egyptians really moved.

In a land where greatness was associated with the aristocracy and sacred images, there was a kind of deathwatch over everything. The grandeur of Egypt was dedicated to chronicles of the king, his court, and testimony to his achievements and exhibitions of power and wealth. Preparation for death and resurrection was a major part of the lifework of the kings, and so dance served these same purposes. Sachs wrote of the funeral dance of pre-2000 B.C. Egypt and described two characteristics: the life charm of the "long stride" and the "leg throw."

> In the sixth dynasty of Ancient Egypt (c. 2500 B.C.) the women dancers who are accompanying the coffin throw their legs in a wide spread over the heads of the dancers in front of them, and their descendants of the Middle Empire dance toward each other . . . with a long tilting step.[22]

Funeral ceremonies proceeded with much lamentation and sacrifice, but none were more important than Abydos festival as shown in a relief now in the Louvre, in Paris. Marking the origin of really spectacular dance, priests and other performers portray the death and resurrection of the great god Osiris. Men with fantastic masks and ornaments perform dances, and falcon-headed souls welcome the risen deity with joy.[23] On the night of his divine passion there was a festival of lights throughout the kingdom, with oil lamps commemorating both the dead Osiris and all the ghostly company who lived with him for all time. The purpose of these ceremonies was to represent in dramatic form, through dance, music, song, and pageantry, the search for the god's dead body, its joyful recovery and assembly, followed by its resurrection. In Osiris, Egyptians saw the promise of eternity, and they confidently believed that they too would inherit eternal life.

On the Feast of Eternity a procession in which an image of the deceased was carried by dancers was a popular ceremony. Their action was slow, gliding and measured, with arms raised overhead, palms turned out. Women with grease-smeared heads, covered with ashes, leaving eyes and mouths conspicuous, moved with twisting and balanced steps, their eyes half-closed. Each dancer performed the entire dance at least once through, repeating it oftener the nearer she was related to the deceased. Some Greek authors wrote that a friend also joined in the procession, personifying the dead man, imitating his expression, gestures, faults, and qualities.

On a Twelfth Dynasty (c. 1900 B.C.) wall painting of the Middle Kingdom, in southern Egypt, three women perform "The Wind," according to the hieroglyphics. One stands upright, waving an outstretched arm above the trees, another bends under this arm like a palm, the third is seen in a "bridge" backbend. This is thought to be a weather charm in which the dancers seek to enchant storm, wind, and rain.[24]

There is no real evidence of any social dance among the aristocrats, but peasants apparently still danced their old fertility dances as shown on a Giza relief about 2700 B.C. There were rites of baptism which took place in the presence of fire and water: three times the one being baptized would jump through the flames of the sacred fire, after which water would be dashed over his head from a tree branch dipped in water. Dancing women called *awahim* (wise or learned), implying that once they may have had status but later become prostitutes, performed in transparent gowns, "beating on drums and castanets in quick time" as they danced. Often wearing a short apron and jewels, they later became a part of harem entertainment.

Priests were thought to invent dancing, because, with their obsession for ceremonial, they were conscious of the carriage of their bodies as an attribute of majesty, and the hieroglyph for dance also means "carriage" or "bearing." In one inscription there are detailed directions on how a newly-appointed minister of state should enter the Audience Chamber "dancing," so that he would project the qualities of devotion, loyalty, grace, tenderness, and energy. The king would reply to the minister with another "dance" and the entire affair would end with a procession of court dignitaries, priests, and musicians. Thus, choreography, the actual notation of dance action, is said to have begun in ancient Egypt.

The earliest Indian art, of which there is reasonable information, is Vedic.[25] The Vedas are sacred books that describe, among many other things, the process and end of art, as well as the tenets of the religious esthetic of ancient India. Earlier Dravidian cultures had elaborate fertility ceremonies, and some of the early statuettes and coins seem to refer to ancestors of the god Shiva in several of his characteristic postures. As civilized cities, Mohenjodaro and Harappa were well advanced by 2300 B.C., but records are scarce and the writing system has not yet been deciphered.

Faubion Bowers wrote that theater in India is supposed to have begun with the god Brahma himself commanding the first dramatic action. According to old holy books, good and evil lived side by side in heaven and the gods fought and destroyed the evil. Brahma asked that the battle be reenacted and the demons fought again to interfere with such a representation. Again the demons were beaten, this time with a flagstaff. Brahma decreed that such performances were for the amusement of all and that they should continue. In order to protect future theaters a sacred pavilion should always be built and marked off by the sacred flagstaff. This is still a practice in many villages of Asia. The stage area is enclosed and high; the audience sits on the ground, in the open air, a bamboo pole with a banner on top marking the place.

After the creation of the world, Brahma confided all his secrets of dance and drama to Bharata, a sage. This came to be the massive *Bharata Natya Sastra,* canons of dance and drama for all of India. Recorded in the fourth or fifth centuries A.D., after centuries of oral transmission, it details the rules of choreography, performance, costuming, makeup, and production.[26]

Of all the gods of India, Shiva is perhaps the most interesting to the dancer. But Shiva is no mortal dancer, rather he is an actor-dancer in a cosmic theater where he is both performer and audience simultaneously. There are many dances of Shiva, yet they are all similar in that they manifest primal rhythmic energy as to be seen in "the choral dance of the constellations, and in the planets and fixed stars, their interweaving and interchange and orderly harmony."[27]

In *The Dance of Shiva,* Coomaraswamy described three of his dances: first, "The evening Dance in the Himalayas," performed by Shiva with two arms, for the Mother of the Three Worlds. All the gods gathered around, Brahma holding the time-marking cymbals, Vishnu playing a drum, Indra the flute, Sarasvati the vina, and Lakshmi singing. Everyone dwelling in the three worlds still assembles each twilight to see Shiva in his celestial dance and to hear the music of the divine choir. "Tandava" is another well-known dance of Shiva's, the one he performs in cemeteries or burning grounds. Here he usually has ten arms and moves wildly with a multitude of imps around him. This dance, of pre-Aryan origin, represents a half god, half demon who revels with death at midnight. Another of Shiva's dances is the "Nadanta," the dispute with the hermits, performed before an assembly in the Golden Hall of Chidambaram, the center of the universe. Images of Shiva as Shri Nataraja show him to have four hands. One right hand holds a drum and the other is lifted in the gesture of "do not fear." One left hand holds fire and the other points down to the dwarf Muyalaka, who holds a cobra. His left foot is raised. His braided and jeweled hair whirls in the dance. In his hair is a coiled cobra, a skull, and the mermaid figure of Ganga (Ganges). Upon his head rests a crown of cassia leaves and a crescent moon. In his right ear is a man's earring, in his left, a woman's. He wears necklaces and a jeweled belt, anklets, bracelets, and toe rings. His breeches are tight fitting, and around his waist is a fluttering scarf with the sacred thread. He usually stands on a pedestal from which springs an eternal fire.[28]

Summarizing the significance of Shiva's dance, Coomaraswamy wrote,

> First, it is the image of his Rhythmic Play as the Source of all Movement within the cosmos, which is represented by the Arch: Secondly, the Purpose of his Dance is to Release the Countless souls of men from the Snare of Illusion: Thirdly the Place of the Dance, Chidambaram, the Centre of the Universe, is within the Heart.[29]

Coomaraswamy continues,

> But like everything human, like language and laws, myths become spent and lose their efficacy. There comes a time when myths play a lesser part in the lives of individuals. But myths do not die; they are transformed.[30]

4
The Known Past

Infinity is a notion which most people find hard to conceive of. Creation myths were accordingly constructed to show that man and the universe did have a beginning. Once created, they thought, things were established forever. Before the idea of universal change was thrust upon people by evolutionary science, whether they liked it or not, change was regarded with misgiving. . . .
       Theodosius Dobzhansky,
       philosopher

The coming of agriculture and food production heralded the Neolithic or New Stone Age. There was great regard for fertility of the earth through the snake symbol of the soil, and other phallic associations, in most of the ceremonies and much of the pottery decoration. Wall murals, pots and potsherds, coins, sculptures, decorations, frescoes, and even jewelry tell part of the story of these times. Out of Mesopotamia (Iraq) and the rest of the Near East, to Egypt, India, China, and Central America a new world was forming.

Early Paleolithic man was concerned with tangible realities of his world and his magic was of a simple one-to-one relationship between him and his immediate surroundings. In the late Paleolithic period there were indications of increasing complexity in life, social relationships, and ritual. Even the cave paintings went beyond simple representation into basic abstractions. It would appear that man was realizing more in life than sheer survival. He was finding time, energy, and opportunity for richer and more comfortable experiences.

Nomadic hunters had followed herds of animals as a matter of course. This was the way life was. Perhaps one hunting band remained near a herd that served as a living larder, fought off poachers, then one day realized the potential of staying in one place and caring for the herd. This all started at the intersection of the great hunting trails and an arc of flat land called the "Fertile Crescent." Here in the rich soil many edible plants were to be found, harvested, and soon considered basic elements of diet.

So civilization dawned here in this area extending from the Nile, up the African coast to Syria, then down through Iraq and Iran to the Persian Gulf. The general dates 7500-4500 B.C. are set for this period that marks the cultivation of plants, domestication of animals, possession of land, rise of kings, division of people into classes, start of the exploitation of lands and people, conquest of nature, and the rise of acts of worship, with belief and religion, which would in time, take the place of the old magic and sorcery.

The Natufians (7500-5500 B.C.), who lived in Palestine and Iraq, harvested primitive grains with sickles and consumed pigs, goats, sheep, and oxen which later constituted barnyard stock. According to current evidence it was the Natufians who marked the transition to an economy of stock breeding and wheat and barley farming.[1]

There is growing evidence of planting cultures in many equatorial villages at an even earlier time, with yams, coconuts, taro, bananas, and breadfruit. Additionally, gabled houses, snake and crocodile worship, palm-fiber cloth, and a rich mythology and art have also been documented. Late excavations in southern Turkey and at Jericho (Jordan) also indicate similar settlements as far back as 6000 B.C. It may be that further archeological investigation will set the dates for the first farmers and urban settlements at an even earlier date and in locations farther apart.

From 5500-4500 B.C. there was increasing village living, pottery making, weaving, house building, and tool making of bone and flint. The so-called "mature cultures" were emerging throughout the Middle East around 5000 B.C., and in India and China some 1,000 years later. The time span of 4500-3500 B.C. is called the High Neolithic period and covers the formation of geometric fields and patterned villages. There was symbolic decoration of pottery, a sophisticated mythology, casting of human statuettes, and the probable use of idols. Neolithic culture appeared in the Aegean, the Balkans, and in southern Europe from about 4000 B.C., then spread west through the Danube basin and the Mediterranean and Atlantic to the west and north around 2500 B.C. The great Sumerian (Iraq) cities flourished around 3500 B.C. The first dynasty in Egypt began around 2800 B.C., China in 1600 B.C., and the Americas as late as 500 B.C. Characteristic of the maturing cultures was the hieratic city-state, with a rising kingly and priestly class and all of the basic traits of civilization: writing, the wheel, mathematics, the calendar, royalty, taxation, bookkeeping, funeral rites, colored pottery, metalwork, and jewelry.

With the end of prehistory came the move from isolationism, the start of literacy, and the rise of specialists with the accompanying class systems, according to ability and status. As men became farmers and herdsmen, they no longer simply followed their herds, and their sense of direction and perception improved. While tending their flocks they noted the migration of stars, and certain of these were personified, even as deities. It was soon observed that certain stars ruled the heavens when it was time to plant seeds, when the rains came, and when it was time to reap and to store fodder. Stories were told about the people and their groups—their taboos and fetishes, their world— and a tribal mind came into being. Now man could be trained and told what to do, and what not to do. This new power gave rise to a new and rich mythology and tradition.

Many temples were built so that shrine and entrance faced east, to the direction of the sunrise, particularly at the equinox or on the longest day, when the rivers flooded. A link was made between the moving of the celestial bodies and the power of the shrine. This orientation of temples served to fix the great annual festival of the New Year. On one morning, in a temple oriented to sunrise of Midsummer Day, the sun's first rays would blaze down through the gloom of a long alley of pillars and light up the stone god, or other symbol, in all of its splendor. This practice was widespread in Egypt, Assyria, Babylon, and the Far East as well as in Greece and at Stonehenge in England.

The First Great Cities

Around 4000 B.C. there was an expansion south to the delta of the Tigris and Euphrates rivers in Sumer (Mesopotamia), and the first of the great Sumerian city states came into being. With them came agriculture, pottery, metalwork, and cuneiform writing. Here on the fertile mud flats such kingly cities as Ur, Eridu, Erech (the first known empire), Kish, Lagash, and Babylon flourished. Mud-dried bricks were used to construct the first known temple, which was for the marriage of the Earth Goddess to the Sky Lord. From evidence of the following years, the queen of each city was identified as the Goddess and the king as God. The palace of the royal couple, topped by the ziggurat temple tower, was the center of a hieratically organized city where everyone had his place and followed the rules of this model of paradise. According to Campbell, this ziggurat temple was the prototype of the Hindu-Buddhist World Mountain, the Greek Olympus, the Tower of Babel, the Aztec Temple of the Sun, and Dante's Mountain of Purgatory.[2]

While the life of the hunter was rooted in shamanistic belief, the maturing cultures of western Asia, Europe, and Africa were progressing beyond the objective world and recognizing cosmic order. No longer was an animal dance sufficient for ceremonies. Now it was more often a pageant of the spheres: planets, stars, sun, and moon, all representing universal law. The earthly representatives of this cosmic order were the king as the moon, which was the pivot about which everything else happened; the queen as the sun; and the virgin priestess as Venus, who was with the king at his death. Ministers of the king were the treasurer as Mercury, the minister of war as Mars, the prime minister as Jupiter, and the lord executioner as Saturn. Everyone sat around the king in the great throne room and, when the moon was full, the king revealed himself; otherwise he remained veiled so as to shield others from his radiance. In this way the king and his court represented heaven on earth. Sometimes the rules changed and the queen was moon and the king was sun, but always they were the royal gods. This great sophistication happened in a relatively short time, but it had obviously been building for much longer than the usually identified time span.[3]

The concept of one king, one state, and one law came into focus. The land and the people beyond all of this splendor were considered barbaric and illiterate. So began the dynasties of the Divine Kings, supreme rulers with great power and wealth who took with them, at death, whomever they chose. And this was a widespread concept across near and far lands. Not only were the kings considered godly creatures, but they were kings because they were chief priests of the temples. Among the Sumerians there were many lesser priests, honoring special gods, each jealous of other priests and gods, and all in conflict with each other. It was in Egypt that the Pharaoh had even greater singular power, above that of any king-priest; indeed he was considered an immortal god.

A highly complex mythology was developing, and with it the arts. A new awareness, a quickening of human dreams and hopes, and all kinds of new realizations and relationships were triggered. With the art of the kings came sophisticated masks, flags, coats of arms, symbols of power, special costumes and robes, cosmetics, jewelry, and gladiatorial and priestly vestments. Pottery was extraordinarily fine and ornamentation was complicated, with geometirc design being dated as early as 4000 B.C. Nowhere is transition clearer than in some of the petroglyphs of the late Paleolithic ages where the vivid impressions of animals gave way to geometric scrawls.

Especially fine pottery designs with swastika, Maltese cross, bird wings, stylized figures of women and gazelle, among many others, were found in Samarra, on the Tigris River in Iraq, and south to the Persian Gulf. Along the Euphrates River in Syria, statuettes were found of woman, dove, cow, ox, sheep, goat, and pig. These same forms turned up in Crete, Egypt, Africa, northern Europe, and later came to be the foundation of the Greek tradition. It was from Syria that the cult of the dead was transferred to Egypt in the fourth or third millenium B.C. According to Campbell, it was out of the symbolism of this period and place that the mythology of Ishtar and Tammuz, Isis and Osiris, Venus and Adonis, and Mary and Jesus came.

> From the Taurus Mountains, the mountains of the bull-god, who may already have been identified with the horned moon, which dies and is resurrected three days later, the cult was diffused, with the art of cattle-breeding itself, practically to the ends of the earth; and we celebrate

the mystery of that mythological death and resurrection to this day, as a promise of our own eternity.[4]

Rituals based upon the interaction of death and sex to foster and complement life were practiced among Paleolithic primitive peoples, but they really had their flowering as a part of the cosmic imagery in the hieratic city-states of Neolithic times. Indeed, cult sacrifices were important ceremonies for ensuring the well-being of the community.

According to Campbell, it was the remarkable finds of Sir Leonard Wooley, uncovering the royal tombs of Ur, in the sacred Sumerian city of the Moon God Nanna, that threw light on the customs of 5,000 years ago. First he found decayed brick, clay sherds, and rubbish. Then on the first level he found the "Standard of Ur," a mosaic of figures in mother-of-pearl on a lapis lazuli background, showing a picture of life in Ur, with a banquet entertainment scene, sacrifice of animals, as well as warriors, slaves, and chariots, all clearly displayed. Under the first layer of digging, Wooley found graves of commoners as well as royalty. In one tomb lay guards wearing copper helmets and holding spears in their bony hands. At another site lay nine court ladies with elaborate gold headdresses. At the entrance to this were two carts with the crushed bones of drivers, donkeys, and grooms. On top of the groom's bones was a silver double ring, once attached to the reins, and on it was a golden donkey. Nearby was an inlaid gaming-board and a collection of weapons and tools. In Queen Shub-ad's grave, court ladies lay in parallel rows, each wearing headdresses of gold, lapis lazuli, and carnelian, with elaborate bead necklaces. A man's skeleton, a court harpist, lay at the end of one of the rows. His arm bones were still across his broken harp which was ornamented with a gold and lapis lazuli calf's head. The queen lay in the remains of a wooden bier, with two women crouching nearby. The upper part of her body was hidden by gold beads, with silver, lapis lazuli, carnelian, agate, and chalcedony strings hanging from a collar, forming a cloak to the waist, and bordered with a wide band of tubular beads of gold, carnelian, and lapis lazuli. Covering her crushed skull was a headdress of wide gold ribbon looped over a large wig. Golden willow and beech leaves, alternating with golden rings hung down from it. More gold leaves and flowers were attached above. A five-pointed comb, decorated with golden flowers and lapis lazuli inlay was stuck into the wig. Spiral gold wires decorated the temples of the skeleton and heavy half-moon earrings hung from the queen's ears. Beside her was a second headdress made of thousands of lapis lazuli beads. To this solid blue mass of beads, little golden animals were attached: stag, bull, gazelle, and goat alternating with clusters of pomegranates, pods, and rosettes of gold and bangles of carnelian, all on twisted wire. She wore three amulets in fish form (two gold, and one lapis) and another gold amulet was decorated with two seated gazelles. All of this was apparently a carefully planned sacrifice to the king-god. With King A-bar-gi in his chamber were three people, and in a nearby pit were sixty-two. With the queen there were twenty-five people.[5]

The ritual death of the king, with the accompanying sacrifice of his court and family, became an honored practice in the Near East civilizations and spread to Egypt, Sudan, Rhodesia, and the rest of Africa; to Crete, Greece, and the rest of Europe; to India, China, and the rest of Asia; and finally to the Maya and Aztec in America.

Paralleling the Sumerian beginnings was a similar series of events in Egypt, though it is generally conceded that Sumer was first.[6] West of the Nile delta in Lower Egypt was a culture of reed and pole-hut villages, inhabited by people who made plant fiber textiles, ivory, shell, and bone ornaments, and who practiced special burial rites in which the corpse was placed in a contracted "embryo" position. In upper Egypt there were hunters and fishers, with some cultivation of grain, domestication of animals, decorated pottery, and similar burial practices. The first Egypt was a nation united only by war between upper and lower Egypt, and for this reason it was called The Land of Two Kingdoms. The First to Third Dynasties were marked by the carving of hard stone and ivory, fine woodwork, metalwork, carpentry, and complicated architecture epitomized by the magnificent step pyramid at Saqqara, which served as a burial vault for King Zoser. The main building is a six-level pyramid in the midst of a great walled compound of subsidiary tombs and ceremonial structures formed like the original royal court. Facades were of white limestone blocks with occasional fluted pillars like bundles of papyrus stalks. Embossed hieroglyphs, blue-green tile, and incised niches confirm Imhotep as one of the world's first great architects. This monument for King Zoser marked a climax to the trend toward deifying the Pharaoh. No longer was he a fortunate mortal but a god on earth, to be worshipped as the generator of prosperity and stability to the Two Kingdoms.

The Old Kingdom (2900-2270 B.C.) covers the First to the Sixth dynasties and is the period of Classical Egypt. Marked by geographic isolation and plenty, the country was at peace, and people throughout the land lived the same way, paying homage to the same natural forces: sun, moon, stars, river, and earth. Each year the Nile rose and flooded the fields and then subsided, leaving rich soil. Gradually ceremony developed, celebrating the sanctity of the God Pharaoh, who was considered directly responsible for the fertility of the land and who was therefore the great provider and protector of the people. Traditions and basic cultural forms were established, and a magnificent display of art and craftsmanship is seen on tomb reliefs, sculptured pieces, pyramids, dams, and monuments to the king and his court, as well as lesser gods.

During the Seventh to Tenth Dynasties there were over thirty kings, and by 2100 B.C. the Old Kingdom had passed away with only a lingering royalty at Memphis. The Middle Kingdom, encompassing the Eleventh to the Thirteenth Dynasties, was dominated by the Theban princes and saw an even greater increase in agriculture and ceremony. By 1555 B.C. the New Kingdom was ushered in with much political grandeur. During these Eighteenth to Twentieth Dynasties the Caesaristic Pharaohs controlled great wealth and many splendid buildings. And with Amenophis IV (husband to Nefertiti), great religious reforms were initiated—he changed the capitol to the desert at Tell-el-Amarna. Tutankhamen, stepson to Amenophis, transferred the royal residence back to Thebes, and with Ramses II built the colossal monuments at Abu Simbel, Karnack, Luxor, Abydos, Memphis, and the great mortuary temple at Thebes.

The Twenty-first to the Twenty-fourth dynasties were filled with turbulence and change, and Egypt came under Ethiopian rule for some time. In the Late Period (712-525 B.C.) Egypt was conquered by the Assyrians and then the Persians, and finally came under Greco-Roman rule when Alexander the Great conquered Egypt. Founding Alexandria, he established the quarrelsome Ptolemys as rulers, and the fall of Egypt was assured. In A.D. 640 Egypt was under the influence of the Arabs and Turks for a time and then entered the European sphere after the conquest by Napoleon.

Perhaps no country on earth has had so much archeological study, or exhibits more complete architectural and artistic relics. The studies, books, photographs, and so on available about Egypt are staggering, and most museums in the world have Egyptian artifacts on display. The British Museum in London has rooms, floors, and buildings filled to overflowing with these national treasures, and is second only to the Egyptian National Museum in its scope. Literature dealing with Egyptian mythology and art grows larger each year, and the situation becomes more exciting and fabulous as time goes by.

The discovery of the tomb of Tutankhamen in 1922 marks a peak of archeological success. According to Ceram, it was especially remarkable that so little of this area had been disturbed by tomb-robbers. In the antechamber were an exquisite, brilliantly painted wooden casket, animal-sided couches buried among luxury objects, and four huge chariots hammered with gold and inlaid with color. The first sealed door led to a solid gold shrine with inlaid panels of blue faience showing magical symbols to protect the dead. At the other end of the burial chamber, through a low door, was a golden shrine-shaped chest with four lovely protecting goddesses nearby. Behind three shrines was the sepulchral room with an even more brilliant gold shrine by an immense yellow quartzite sarcophagus with protecting goddesses inlaid on it. Under a massive slab lid was a radiant golden effigy of the boy ruler, with face mask of pure gold, eyes of aragonite and obsidian, and brows and lids of lapis lazuli. Beside his head was a tiny withered wreath of flowers, still tinged with color after 3,300 years. Finally, within two more coffins, each with effigies of the young prince in richly ceremonial dress, was the cadaver of Tutankhamen.

Contrasting with the dark and shapeless mass of the mummy was a golden mask covering the head and shoulders of the king. This was the only known, untouched mummy in the Valley of the Kings for the past 33 centuries. Within the linen windings were amulets, magic symbols, and some 143 pieces of jewelry. The embalmed body had been carbonized, but the head, resting on a pure iron amuletic headrest had a refined and well-formed face with clearly marked lips. This eighteen-year-old Pharaoh was literally wrapped in several layers of gold and precious stones.[7]

One of the greatest temples is Abu Simbel, which serves to unite the great gods in a pantheon of gigantic scale. Amun, Lord of Thebes; Ptah, Lord of Memphis; Ra, Lord of Heliopolis; and Ramses, Lord of Egypt, are seated back from the entrance but so placed that the rising sun illuminates each in full glory. Approaching Abu Simbel by water, passing a smaller temple to the Goddess Hathor and Ramses' queen Nefertari, the sixty-seven-foot-high colossi command attention. Their thrones show gods of the Nile binding the Two Egypts, and above are hieroglyphs and a group of baboons. Around the huge figures are members of the royal family. Above the entrance stands the Sun God being worshiped by a king. Within the great hall is a double row of eight huge images of the king, facing one another across the main aisle. The walls are covered with reliefs showing scenes of Ramses' campaigns and ceremonies for worshipping the gods. Beyond this great hall are many relief-decorated rooms and sanctuaries for ceremonies.

Valuable historical records were found inscribed on the walls—tablets and stele—which clarify much of the history and mystery of this land.

Sumer on the great rivers Tigris and Euphrates, Egypt on the mighty Nile, and Mohenjodaro on the broad Indus were the famous centers of the developing city-states. Village tribes from what is now Pakistan moved south to where the Indus flows into the Arabian Sea, built dikes, drained the fields, and, before 2500 B.C., started to build a great city. It is probable that some of the requisite skills were learned from Sumerian traders. Mohenjodaro, on the lower Indus, and Harappa to the northeast, were splendid cities with wide streets, rectangular blocks, and efficient drainage systems. Mortar was used with kiln-dried bricks, and many of the foundations are still intact. Both cities had a central plan with a raised ziggurat citadel in the center. They were obviously governed by strong and prosperous leaders. The citadel at Mohenjodaro had a platform 50 feet high with a 400 by 200 foot base. This may have housed government officials or served as a refuge from flood or as a grain storehouse. There was a brick-walled public bath nearby.

The toy and jewelry relics are remarkable, with copper, bronze, precious stones, gold, silver, and clay predominating. Many religious forms, such as the fig tree, a three-headed figure who may have been a forerunner of Shiva, and statues of fertility gods and goddesses have been unearthed. Sophisticated animal toys and figures, many with movable parts, have been found.

The people of the Indus Valley had a form of writing, weights and linear measures, and a brisk trade with the outside world. There was a sheltered harbor, and beyond the city, rich wheat and cotton fields. At its height, the Indus influence spread from modern Bombay to Karachi, inland north, and to the west.

After about ten centuries this civilization disappeared. Whether it was caused by erosion of the soil, invasion by outsiders, or engulfment by rivers of mud, the major centers dwindled and came to ruin. A thousand years later the Persian empire included this area in its holdings, but Mohenjodaro, city of the dead, was gone.

The basic concept of these archaic worlds was centered about the king as archetype, the protector, the sacred farmer, the builder, the teacher, and the deified god. In each of these places there were characteristic myths, legends, rituals, and, of course, dances. The celebrations, festivals, and developing traditions could be no other than part of the new social order, reflecting the beliefs of the people and the will of the king.

Mythology

Myths and rituals associated with fire came mostly from the Eastern world because this is where fire was discovered. Some of the oldest had their start from Africa, Arabia, the Near East, and India to Southeast Asia, Indonesia, Melanesia and, most ancient, from the Admiralty Islands off the New Guinea coast, where Paleolithic culture seems to have lasted longer than elsewhere.

Campbell reports that the story of the Great Serpent is found in the mythology of all the early planters, as early as 7500 B.C. One day a young woman went into the forest and met a serpent who wooed and married her. After she bore him a son and daughter the serpent sent her away. He fed the children and they grew. One day he sent them for fish which they brought to him. "Cook it," he said to his children. When the sun rose, it warmed the fish and they ate it raw and bloody. The serpent said: "You eat your food raw, perhaps you will eat me." Then he bade his son crawl into his belly and gather fire from it, and told his daughter to gather coconuts, yam, and taro. The boy brought forth fire from the belly of the serpent and they lit a fire and cooked their food. When the serpent asked which food they liked best, cooked or raw, they answered "cooked."[8]

It is possible that this myth developed out of an earlier foundation where the serpent is seen in cave paintings, plaques, and female figurines, and from the same tradition that produced the legend of Persephone and Eve.

Another old myth tells of the moon brother and the sun sister. As a young woman she was visited by a lover whom she never saw. Curious, she blackened her hands in the fire before he came one night and, embracing him, left handprints on his back. The next day she saw the prints on her brother's back and ran away screaming. The moon has been chasing her ever since. When he catches her there is an eclipse. This myth is known to North American Indians and North Asian tribes.

It was in the Western world that many large stone axes were found. They were all too large to be used by one man, and so it has been assumed that they were to be used in rituals. Linked to thunder, the myths of Thor's hammer and the thunderbolts of Zeus and Indra probably originated in the West.

The myth of the Thunderbolt has long been associated with a man, and fire as the gift of a goddess. One of the descendants of this is the Ainu goddess of the hearth named Fuji, goddess of fire, also the name of Fujiyama, the Japanese sacred volcano. In Hawaii, Pele is the goddess of the great volcano where the old gods are still said to play. Japan has a sun goddess, and the pronouns for sun in French and in German are both feminine.

The realm of mythology is the world of "anything can happen." Nothing is limited by positive reality; gods can appear simultaneously in several places, with equal impact in each. Paraphernalia, especially masks, are experienced as an apparition of the god or demon and often treasured as both symbol and reality. The extent to which the mythology of any group has molded its character is impossible to determine, but the impact is powerful. The mythology of Neolithic man broadens its scope because of the very changing nature of man and his world. This is especially noted with the introduction of agriculture and the rise of religious and political organizations. According to Campbell: "Religions, philosophies, arts, the social forms of primitive and historic man, prime discoveries in science and technology, the very dreams that blister sleep, boil up from the basic, magic ring of myth."[9]

Myths are mostly concerned with gods and forces of nature; legends with heroes of old—of fabulous tales about the relationship of human beings and extraordinary beings. These unusual heroes and gods were inevitably associated with magic, ritual, and sacrifice. It is inconceivable that these myths were not influential in the evolution of human thought from magic to religion, science, and art.

It has been suggested that the interplay of sovereignty, force, and fertility were the three great functions to be found in many of the myths of mankind, and on the cosmic level are embodied in personal deities, while on the human level as priestly rulers, warriors, and farmers. Mythology looks at man in his cosmic surroundings and unfolds patterns of disaster and triumph, of daring and courage by spiritual and mortal beings, sometimes in conflict, sometimes helping each other. The myth, says Ernst Cassirer never escapes "the magic circle of its figurative ideas." Above all, mythology is a world of illusion: ". . . aesthetic visions, rooted in time, but they look out over the mysteries of human conduct and belief."[10]

Interestingly, there are many similarities among characters, themes, and details of the mythologies of countries widely separated by time and space. The likenesses, for example, among myths of Sumer, Egypt, Greece, Rome, India, Scandinavia, and the American Indian are so marked that it scarcely seems possible they are not related. Whether there was borrowing from one culture to the other; a common ancestry or heritage, or common solution to basic problems is not known.

But myths and legends have been passed down for centuries, long after the original cultures have blended into the past. To a marked degree they represent the magic, religion, art, and ethnic story of a people; and to know their mythology is to understand the spirit, art, and life of these people. Indeed, there is even relevance to the contemporary world which is fashioning its own mythology.

MESOPOTAMIA. At the time of the founding of the hieratic city-states, the "round dance of the planets" in the heavens provided a basis for the developing mythology as well as the organization of the society. The extent to which the sun's rays influenced temples, ceremonial chambers, and decoration can be verified by relics. In many primitive societies important ceremonies occur at dawn, for in the hunting mythology the sun is the greatest of all hunters. He is the lion, the eagle, the great orb whose early rays "scatter the herds of night stars." The Sumerian motif of a great eagle catching an antelope in each claw corresponds to the hunter sun, the arrows being the sun's rays and the antelope one of the star herd. By means of powerful magic, the night renews the stars and dawn brings the sun again.

One of the greatest figures in Babylonian mythology was Ishtar, the capricious and imperious mother goddess whose symbol was a star. Moved to pity at the hardships of her earthly children, she descended to the underworld to visit Tammuz, her brother-husband. Sorry to have caused his death, Ishtar, daughter of the Moon God, went below and bade the queen of the underworld to let her enter. Through many gates Ishtar was deprived of crown, earrings, necklaces, breast ornaments, studded girdle, bracelets, and anklets, and, finally all of her clothes. As she entered the presence of the Dark Queen a great battle ensued. But the great god Ea knew that if Ishtar lost, all generation of men and women would cease, so he created a magnificent man to go to the queen of the underworld and please her. Ishtar was then free to return to her own realm, receiving her robes and ornaments as she passed from door to door.

The epic of *Gilgamesh* includes both the story of a brave and strong king of Sumer, as well as a flood, which is identified in time with the Biblical deluge. Gilgamesh, part man, part god, was handsome, brave, and strong. He loved women, and none were safe in his presence, but no one dared challenge him in combat. Beseeching the great Mother Aruru to make another man to match him, the people watched as she molded a man in clay while reciting prayers to the gods. As she worked the South Wind blew on the image and Enkidu came to life. He was fashioned with hoofs, thighs, and tail of a bull, but from the waist up he was a strong and graceful man, beloved by animals.

Gilgamesh, piqued and curious, sent his most accomplished courtesan to lure Enkidu away from his animal friends. When he had lost his innocence, the animals shunned him, so Enkidu returned to the city with the courtesan and learned the ways of the court. Gilgamesh had a horrible nightmare about a warrior who was destined to conquer him and reported this to his mother, Ninmah. She explained that the dream meant he would fight with a stranger but from this he would find great good. Soon after this there was a fierce wrestling match between Gilgamesh and Enkidu. During the fight Gilgamesh realized he had found a man as strong and as brave as himself, released his hold, threw back his head, and laughed because the prediction had come true. From then on Gilgamesh and Enkidu were inseparable friends.

But Enkidu missed his life with the animals that roamed free across the deserts. One night he had a terrifying nightmare in which a black monster swooped down on him and carried him off to the underworld realm of the King of Eternal Darkness. Here he stumbled along over the dead and dying, whose only food was mud.

Wise men bade Gilgamesh and Enkidu to sacrifice to the Sun God, after which a message came to Gilgamesh that he must seek out and slay the monster of Cedar Mountain, fell seven cedar trees, and thereby deliver the land from evil. The two friends set forth, overcame the monster, and fulfilled their mission. Ishtar, goddess of love, appeared to congratulate them but was spurned by Gilgamesh. Ishtar planned a dreadful revenge, persuading her father to send the Bull of Heaven into the City to trample the people, destroy the temples, and slaughter the warriors. Together Gilgamesh and Enkidu killed the bull and threw his bloody pelt into the goddess' face, and so Ishtar was again insulted.

Ishtar put a curse on Enkidu and he fell ill. After thirteen days he died in the arms of his friend. Frantic with grief, Gilgamesh realized that Enkidu was in the House of Death with only mud for food, and so he sought out the one man who had the gift of immortality. After many trials and battles he found the king who had won immortality, heard of the Great Deluge where one pair of all the birds and creatures of creation had been gathered together, how it rained for six days and nights, and how the flood waters receded on the seventh day. "Thus," said the king, "did I receive my immortality." Exhausted, Gilgamesh fell asleep at the foot of his throne. The queen urged her husband to help, so they awoke Gilgamesh and directed him to find the Flower of Youth that lay at the bottom of the sea. Hurrying to the sea, he plunged into its depths and plucked the flower. Without tasting of the flower himself, he hurried back to his people, enjoying the perfume of the flower he carried. One afternoon, hot and dusty, he carefully placed the flower on a rock near a lake where he bathed. Coming out of the lake, he saw a snake snatch the flower and disappear. Brokenhearted, he returned to Ureck, his city, where none could console him. He had lost his friend to the House of No Return and had brought eternal life to a race of serpents.[11]

EGYPT. Ancient Egypt is famous for its cults of the gods and the dead, as evidenced by the tombs, temples, and wall carvings and paintings devoted to both. Even a cursory view of Egyptian mythology introduces hawks, jackal-headed gods, winged scarabs, human-headed animals, horned and winged suns and moons, hissing serpents, sacred cats, celestial cows, smiling crocodiles, and gods and men crossing the River of the Dead in a variety of boats. Even in the later periods of Apis, the sacred bull, the winged disc of the sun was placed highest in honor. Many gods provided reason for the rituals that were practiced throughout the land.

Greatest of the gods of Egypt was Osiris, son of Geb (Earth) and Nut (Sky), brother-husband to Isis, and father of Horus (God of Light). Osiris, principle of good, was both Sun and Moon God, generator of fertility, and great benefactor of all Egypt. Represented sometimes as man, sometimes mummy, he held contradictory roles as God of the Dead and Source of Renewed Life. Long before the Pharaohs, the great, dark King Osiris ruled in Africa. He was tall and slender, so that his body fit easily his immortal soul. His black naked body, from ankles to wrists, was decorated with beautiful crimson-painted flowers. On his head was the white plumed crown of Upper Egypt, with an ostrich feather on each side—for these feathers are as light as truth. He wore a fine plaited beard as befitted a great man whose fertility caused life to swell in the desert. Around his neck and shoulders he wore a white collar of ivory, precious stones, and symbolic beads. Wherever he stepped, a lily blossom appeared in commemoration of the water lilies in the lake at the edge of the world where he was born. Those who obeyed Osiris might find the Isles of the Blessed.

Isis, queen of all gods, goddesses, and women, was patroness of healing and motherhood. She ruled in heaven, on earth, on the seas, and in the underworld where she dispensed rewards and punishments for all mortals. Isis's symbol was the cow, which was sacred to her. On monuments and in wall carvings she is usually depicted as a young woman, seated, with Horus on her lap. She wears horns on her head with a moon orb between them and holds a metal rattle in her right hand. Associated with her are the moon, the lotus, the serpent, and ear of corn. Her festivals were symbolic of both joy and grief and served as prototypes near and far. She was especially honored in Greece and Rome as well as Egypt. Isis and Osiris were widely loved and worshipped by all Egyptians, and there are many tales told of their adventures.

One of the tales is long and complicated, involving many other gods. Essentially it tells of the eternal combat between Osiris and his brother Set, God of Darkness and principle of evil. Set arranged a trick whereby he had Osiris locked in a coffin and thrown into the Nile. Later Set opened the coffin and cut Osiris's body into fourteen pieces and scattered them throughout Egypt. Devotedly, Isis collected all of the parts except one and buried them in different parts of the land, which accounts for the confusion as to just where Osiris is buried. But, according to another myth, the prayers and cries of Isis, and the rites she performed, aided by the gods, caused the pieces to join together and Osiris lived again. By means of magic formulae, Isis brought Osiris back from the dead. So it was that Osiris became the God of Resurrection and Eternal Life, Lord of the Underworld, and Great Judge of the Dead.

INDIA. Mythologies of India are different from those of other lands. They do not represent a shadowy past or imaginative folklore but are very much a part of everyday life and belief. The adventures of Rama are as real to Indians as scriptural history is to us. Offerings to Agni are as meaningful as the Roman Catholic Mass. Through their myths the Indian people of today learn moral, philosophical, religious, and spiritual teachings as well as the history of their country and people.

The alarming complexity of Hindu mythology precludes any broad coverage of the gods, demons, sages, and heroes. Outsiders often call the tales childish and fanciful but they deal with past and future, visible and invisible, in ways that make sense to the Indian. Reality, in all of its aspects, is represented by millions of gods, each with many different functions and names. Similar functions are assumed by different gods; many gods beget other gods, interacting like electricity and heat. There are few of the gods who do not assume directly opposite roles and operate equally in each, such as Shiva who is creator and destroyer, God of Dance, and God of the Burning Yards at the same time.

Hindu mythology is based upon the concept of an unchanging Absolute, represented by Vishnu the Protector. In one myth, Vishnu lies motionless on a thousand-headed cobra, floating on an infinite and immobile ocean of milk. The ocean represents totality, uniformity, nondifferentiation, and nonmovement. The serpent, Ananta, is eternity or the absence of time. According to the *Rig-Veda,* the Lord created the seas and put a seed in them. From this seed came a golden egg which, after a celestial year, split open through the power of thought. The upper half was divine and the bottom was material. Between the two, atmosphere formed above and the earth floated below on water. From the egg came the first being with a thousand thighs, feet, arms, eyes, faces, and heads. He was all that has been and all that will be. From him issued gods, goats, seasons, cattle, earth, workers, sun, moon, atmosphere, sky, and so forth. After this sacrifice he entered into himself, with himself.[12]

Another reason why the cycle of mythology in India is so complex is because of the intermingling of the many gods and heroes of Hindus, Buddhists, and Jains. In addition there are the myths of the Central Indian people who live outside the caste system. The Tamils of South India are the source of yet another mythology, concerned more with men than gods. There is some intermingling of tales but many are sacred to only one group. The most ancient people, the Jains, drew heavily on the ancient Dravidian tales which have been influential to all.

Early Dravidian rites were performed to ensure a good harvest, and, following the dictates of the myth, celebrated the harvest with complicated festivals. Human victims were consecrated, feasted at a great dance festival, and later sacrificed in a particularly slow, gruesome, and horrible death. The remains of these victims were divided among the villagers, who buried small bits in their field in order that their next harvest would be bountiful.

One of the oldest Dravidian legends tells of early man who was 6 miles tall with 265 ribs, born as twins, and becoming man and wife with his sister. They kept reproducing, each time producing twins, and as they matured they kept getting smaller in size. By the time each was twenty years old they were eighteen inches tall, had eight ribs, and suffered hot days and cold nights, diseases, and storms. In time they all found their end in the Ganges.[13]

Brahma, Vishnu, and Shiva are the chief gods of the later Hindu period and form a holy trinity; actually they are three forms of one supreme being. All are concerned with forms of energy. *Brahma* is a red god, four-headed and four-handed. In one hand he holds a copy of the *Vedas*, in the second a spoon, in the third a drinking cup, and in the fourth a string of beads. In the beginning he had five heads but Shiva cut one off. Brahma rides in a great swan cart accompanied by his wife, Saraswati, Goddess of Poetry and Eloquence.

Vishnu is a blue god whose vehicle is a great bird, half man, half eagle. Like Brahma, he has four hands in which he holds a shell, quoit, club, and lotus flower. Lakshmi, his wife, is Goddess of Wealth and Beauty and is playfully called Daughter of the Milky Sea. Vishnu sleeps on Ananta, the serpent that lives forever. When the present age ends Vishnu will remain in that position and a lotus flower will grow out of his navel. The waters of the world will cover everything, but on the very top of the stalk Brahma will appear to start creating the new world. Vishnu preserves energy as Brahma creates it. Like other gods, Vishnu appears in many animal and human forms, often visiting earth to correct evil.

Shiva, the third phase of Brahma's energy, is the White God. He is known by many names, lives high in the Himalayas, and is often called Lord of the Mountain. As with the others, he is both a kind and an angry god; he is God of Arts, Knowledge, Dance, and Gaiety. He has from two to ten arms and three eyes, one of which has the power to kill. He holds a trident in one hand and a rope in the other. Aided by his wife Bhavani or Parvati, he rides in a white vehicle drawn by a snow-white bull. This third god of the trilogy destroys energy as Brahma creates it and Vishnu preserves it. The reader will note the dual nature of these Hindu gods.

The time of Buddha dates from 563 B.C. but stories of his previous existences are numerous. Born of miraculous conception to Queen Maya, Buddha appeared first in the guise of a beautiful white elephant. At the instant of his birth the rivers stopped flowing, trees and plants flowered, musical instruments played, and ponds were suddenly covered with lotus flowers. The child, who talked immediately, was received by Brahma and the other gods. Wherever his feet trod, a lotus bloomed. By taking seven strides in each cardinal direction, he took possession of the world. The same day were born Yasodhara Devi, his wife; Kantaka, his horse; Chandaka, his squire; Ananda, his friend and disciple; and Bodhi, the great tree under which he was to have illumination. The young prince was named Siddhartha and, after his mother died, was watched over by her sister.

When the young prince was twelve the king locked him in the palace so that he might not look on age, sickness, or death, but before

Siddhartha married he had to prove his ability in the arts of his caste. Winning all of the events, he married his princess and lived a carefree life with no problems. Visiting a nearby town, he saw old men, disease, and finally a wretched beggar who told him he had left the world to pass beyond suffering and joy in order to attain peace.

Siddhartha vowed then to follow the same path. Leaving his palace, wife, wealth, and young son, he cut his hair, exchanged his robes for rags, and went out to a hermitage where the Brahmans accepted him as a disciple. As the monk Gautama, he sought wisdom in Yoga, but did not find it Only after six years of isolation by the great river Uruvilva did he find a balance between this world and transcendent asceticism.

Siddhartha then sought the tree of wisdom, Bodhi, the sacred fig tree, and sat down under it to wait. Mara, the Buddhist demon, tried to disturb him with voluptuous maidens, devils with a thousand mouths who drank blood and spread darkness, and finally threw his great disc, but it turned into a garland of flowers suspended over Siddhartha's head.

The following day Siddhartha had complete illumination; he had become Buddha. Choosing to become a teacher of men rather than retire to Nirvana, Buddha set forth on his greatest work as prophet, leader, and example to all mankind.[14]

Ceremonies

A social order establishes and continues its cultural pattern by action and feeling about those actions. Conformity to behavior of people within the group, especially if there is any degree of intensity, tends to be repeated. If it is important it will be transmitted from one generation to the next. And ceremonial expression continues to grow and flourish, with its rules, out of totem, taboo, and magic, developing into rites which consistently become more complex. But with the complexity there are also inconsistencies, though after a while no one notices them.

More and more, man seemed disposed to make and use images derived both from his common experiences as well as his dreams and fantasies. Most of these were related to life and life giving, such as phallic symbols; but there was also considerable emphasis upon death and the dead. Other great themes of early rituals were the gods as emblems of creative, destructive power, as Shiva; fetishes and animal totems such as the snake hidden in the earth; the bull, strong in passion; the long-lived crocodile who kills so quickly; and the early rising cock which watches over the flock.

Out of the first "Leap-Shout-Rolls," developed a form demonstrative of both feeling and knowing, and finally a symbolic occurrence, which, in movement, is called "gesture." When the formalized behavior took place in the presence of a sacred object, this was the real ritual. Often this was a celebration of "Right Attitudes," but soon enough the source and meanings were forgotten and the repetition of the form became automatic.

NEAR EAST. In Persia (Iran) there are sparse relics showing a motif of a lion and prince fighting, and on a carved stone relief there are huge Lords of Medes carrying lotus flowers as they climb up to the place of royal ceremonies. Bronze ceremonial wrestlers, with what look like jars on their heads, were found in ancient Mesopotamia, east of Baghdad. It has been surmised that they could be replicas of Gilgamesh and Enkidu because they were near the clay tablets upon which the epic of *Gilgamesh* was written in cuneiform letters.

Records tell of a ceremonial procession in Babylon with the participants passing down a center street, under the mammoth Ishtar Gate, moving near the seven-staged Tower of Babel and the famed hanging gardens. An annual procession of the gods occurred at the New Year. Statues of the principal deities were carried through the Ishtar Gate to the outskirts of the city, where they were put on boats and taken up the river to the Garden Temple. Then would come the consummation of the sacred marriage of the principal god and goddess, on which the fertility and prosperity of the land depended. The joyous return back through the Ishtar Gate was highlighted by the gods on boat-carriages, each decorated with gold, lapis lazuli, and carnelian. The king and a parasol carrier would be in one boat-carriage, his priests in another. His consort, with her crown tipped by a six-pointed star, would ride in yet another boat-carriage. The Sun God and other deties would follow, each in their own specially decorated boat-carriage. The complete record of this festival was discovered in a series of carvings in Malatya, in the north. Apparently each major city celebrated in much the same way.

EGYPT. In the annual festival of Amun at Thebes, a great procession moved along the sphinx-lined avenue carrying the sacred bark of Amun, with banging tambourines, chanting priests and burning incense filling the air. Barks of other gods joined the parade and then all of these were loaded on a flotilla of real boats on the Nile. This festival lasted twenty-seven days and was so designed that it convinced people of the god's greatness and the splendor of the life to come.

The *Book of the Dead* refers to a number of papyri (160 more or less) on the wanderings of the soul after death, its trial before Osiris, and the doctrine of resurrection. Central to each of these is a section called the "negative confession" of the dead and the weighing of his heart before the supreme judge of the underworld.

When a king or an official died, his mummified body in its painted coffin was ferried across the Nile and dragged to its final resting place in the Valley of the Tombs of the Kings. Paid mourners, musicians, and acrobats distracted the crowd, but at the door of the tomb the priests were laying out food, ungents, flowers, and apparel, while reciting magic formulae intended to allow the dead man's Ka, or "double," to enjoy the offerings. Then talismans were put at the four corners of the burial chamber to protect against evil and the funeral ceremony was over.

Meanwhile the Ka, wandering through the dark, looking for the Judgment Hall of the Dead, calls himself Osiris, and seeks resurrection. Finally he reaches a great hall where a giant statue of Osiris sits at the far side, wearing the white-plumed crown, arms folded, holding a staff of justice. The suppliant faces a great shrine upon which there is a pair of scales. The jackal-headed Anubis and the hawk-headed Horus stand by with the ibis-headed Thoth to record the result of the weighing. On the shrine is a creature, part hippopotamus, lion, and crocodile, devourer of the dead. To escape this monster he must make forty-two negative confessions to satisfy forty-two judges and then weigh his heart against the feather of truth. If the man passes these tests he will dwell forever in Osiris's favor and will bear his name.

Apis, the sacred bull, worshipped at Memphis, was considered to be a reincarnation of Osiris. He would always have a black hide with a white triangular spot on his forehead, a half-moon spot on the right side, and a knot under his tongue. When such a bull was found in Egypt it was treated as a god until it was twenty-five years old, when, with great ceremony, it would be drowned in the Nile. His death was considered a national calamity, and all Egypt would mourn until another bull with the correct markings was found, when joyous celebration would prevail. The new god would be provided the purest of water, the most beautiful cows, and splendid apartments. After each bull was dead his embalmed remains would be buried in a great stone sarcophagus.

INDIA. Very little is known of the early history of India which, until the sixth century B.C., was the story of the Aryan expansion in the great Indus and Ganges valleys. The original civilizations of India were related to those of Mesopotamia, with Harappa and Mohenjodaro on the lower Indus delta as great commercial cities that prospered *c.* 2300 B.C. Conquering invaders moved to the east and formed feudal principalities.

Most of the Indian ceremonies can be linked to the religious and warrior heroes from the *Rig-Veda*, and the two great epic poems, the *Ramayana* and the *Mahabharata* (described in greater detail in chapter 6). The extraordinary richness of these sources accounts for the great popularity and variation for ceremonial content. Throughout the villages and countryside, people sit in circles enjoying the recitations, songs, and dances depicting all parts of these great stories. They are found in every language and dialect throughout India and southern Asia. Even the great theater of China and Japan was influenced by these epic poems.

5
Link to the Past

The task of the present generation is to construct a history of things that will do justice both to meaning and being, both to plan and to the fullness of existence, both to the scheme and to the thing. The purpose raises the familiar existential dilemma between meaning and being. We are discovering . . . that what a thing means is not more important than what it is. . . .

George Kubler, *historian*

Through the years dance has served the social group of which it was a part. In some cases it changed very little because the people remained much as they had been. The action, design, and reason for dance continued much as before. In other groups, where changes in the relationship of people were taking place, some of the old forms remained but became just symbols of the original intent, a traditional "thing that we do." With others, new responses occurred as new ideas, events, and personalities came into focus.

Recurring Primitive Dances

Wherever primitive groups remained isolated, they continued to practice and value the old dances, ceremonies, and rites. The traditional life-style, language, dress, and tribal relationships apparently remained much the same as they had been since the Stone Age. Only in the most remote parts of the world, however, were people safe from contact with the outside, so some change was inevitable.

The primitive dances still being done today are sometimes characteristic of the hunter culture, sometimes the planter, and more and more—with the intrusion of tourists and cameras—a blend of both, and a resolution into entertainment.

The descriptions that follow have been reported during the past 100 years and, according to written accounts, will not continue unchanged for long.

Hunters

The hunters are preoccupied with all aspects of the tracking, confrontation, killing, and appeasing the spirit of animals. They also tell of the skill and success of the strong, brave hunters. These are all materials for dances, as is everything else concerned with the hunt. Most of the ceremonies for assuring food include mimetic animal action so as to influence them either as prey or guides to the larger herds. Whatever man hunts, and especially what he favors, is what he dances about. If there are many animals, then he dances about many, if there are few, he dances about the few. Even today among several South African groups there are from eighteen to twenty-two different animal dances still performed. With the passing of the buffalo herds of the American plains, most of the buffalo dances of the Indians also passed, except as commemorative affairs.

According to a report by George Schweinfurth, from what is now North Zaire, Munza was a great dancer-king, known throughout Africa.

> Dancing there in the midst of all, a wondrous sight, was the king himself. Munza was as conspicuous in his vesture as he was in all his movements . . . he had now attired his head in the skin of a great black baboon . . . the peak of this was dressed up with a plume of waving feathers. Hanging from his arms were the tails of genets, and his wrists were encircled by great bundles of tails of the guinea-hog. A thick apron, composed of the tails of a variety of animals was fastened round his loins and a number of rings rattled upon his naked legs. But the wonder of the king's dress was as nothing compared to his action. His dancing was furious. His arms dashed themselves in every direction, though always marking the time of the music; whilst his legs exhibited all the contortions of an acrobat's, being at one moment stretched horizontally to the ground, at the next pointed upwards and elevated in the air. . . .[1]

Spencer and Gillen described a furious Central Australian dance at the burned village of a dead man—representative of a hunting group among whom both life and death is a violent experience. With wailing mourners all about, a wild dance accompanied by shouts, beating on the ground, and battling among dancers took place. This was to "lay the ghost" and make sure that he did not return to frighten anyone. The Aborigines of Australia live on two interrelated planes. One is the necessary daily event, including food gathering, eating, drinking, social intercourse, marriage, and death. The other plane consists of ritual, symbolism, and faith. To those who can "see," the rocks, trees, rivers, and hills are "dreamings" that mark the exploits of heroes and serve as abodes for the spirits. Everything has its "shade" which remains when the material shadow is gone. The inner shade or soul is distinct from the material shade or body. The result is a rich symbolic representation in art and ceremony. The ritual implies art to the aborigine, and ritual is the ordered arrangement of symbols and symbolic acts. Man expresses inner "shades," and this is as evident in the dance as it is in the rich rock carvings and paintings.[2]

An early report by A. N. Tucker on dances of the southern Sudan included a description of one dance called "Bul." The dancers were oiled and brilliantly painted, wearing elegant headdresses. The male dancers, carrying long spears and shields in one hand, clubs in the other, marched around an open space. As the drums sounded louder all would dash forward, as if toward a foe or prey. After this, girls would choose partners and, in couples, perform a dance made up of two jumps forward and one jump back, accompanied by a song. After this the men's dance was repeated.[3]

An Eskimo dance-song refers to the hunter's bow, and the many stanzas tell of the use of the bow. Dancers reenact and illustrate the use of the bow while singing about bending and straightening the bow in order to send the arrows straight.[4]

Indians of the Central Amazon in Brazil are a vanishing tribe of some 100 members, the last of a once famous tribe of hunters. They are avid dancers and their accompaniment is by huge bamboo flutes. The characteristic rhythm of their Spear Dance is three steps followed by a pause in which the foot slaps the earth. The dance is done in a circle, and is practiced for weeks before the frequent competitions with other village groups.

The Yanomamo, living deep in the jungles of Venezuela and Brazil, have numerous inter-village feasts and display their wealth, food, decorations, and dance. To prepare for these affairs the men go on great hunts. The women who remain at home sing and dance to bring good luck to the hunters. They do a curious asymmetrical stamp and slap while they perform intricate hand gestures. The visitors always dance-parade, brandishing spears and weapons. Two dancers circle in opposite directions and return to be replaced by two others until each visitor has circled the space. The action consists of four steps forward, stop, throw arrows on the ground, prance around them, pick them up, and advance four more steps, and so on. Finally all visitors prance in single file, clashing weapons overhead, form a circle in the middle of the village, and pose in satisfaction at their great display. The host group then performs, moving in a closely-knit group, clashing their weapons overhead and dancing around the edge of the village. Feasting is followed by raucous competitive chanting and bartering. All of this is repeated soon at another village, with new hosts and visitors.[5]

Among the American Plains Indians the Gods of Sun, Earth, Moon, Morning Star, Wind, Fire, and Thunder are powerful totems to whom many kinds of dances are dedicated. With the Pawnee, the sun is considered most powerful. An important sun ritual each year lasts almost a week and is made up of processions, self-mutilation, and symbolic dances. The deeds of the heroic and the young are mimed, tribal affairs are recalled, and rededication to the Sun God is repeated.

A recent article in *Natural History*, by Richard B. Lee, described the Bushmen of the Kalahari Desert in Africa as among the last of the great hunters. As Bantu medicine consists of sorcery and witchcraft and European medicine with pills and hypodermic syringes, their medicine is in the pit of the stomach of each Bushman. This medicine may be transferred from one to another, thus the Bushman trance dancer effects cures by rubbing sweat and laying on of hands. The medicine sleeps within the stomach and can only be activated in the heat of dance. As the medicine heats, and finally boils, its steam rises through the spine and into the brain, at which time the dancer is in trance. At night a fire symbolizing the medicine burns. Around the fire sit the singing women; around the women the men stamp and circle, first clockwise then counterclockwise. Songs telling of animal or natural happenings begin the ceremony. A few men, bent over, shuffle heavily in phrases of seven counts, carrying rattles and fly-wisks. The next dancers develop into a trance, sweat heavily, stagger, and fall. Other dancers come to their rescue until they leap into "half-death." When one dancer is in trance, the other dancers rub his body to keep it warm, making it shine. The one in a trance may call out and tremble. Soon he rises and begins his "cures." Through the deeply-pitted dance circle he moves, and then starts rubbing the patient with trembling hands as he groans and cries out. Moving away, as if to recoup his powers, he returns to the patient. Each sick person receives this kind of treatment. After some hours of trance, the dancer falls down and sleeps, and then other trance performers will come forth and the dance may continue from one evening to the next day or night. This and most other dances of this group occur at the full of the moon.

A semi-sacred dance was reported among a hunting tribe on the African Ivory Coast. With only three performers, one young boy in a purple antelope mask, covering a dappled material over his body and head, straw tail, jangles on his legs, moved with body crouched over, knees bent, always looking down at the ground, but the mask set so that it looked up. Other dancers stuck a tuft of grass in the center of the dancing space and then moved off to the side. The antelope came timidly out and sniffed the grass, jumping at every sound. One dancer-hunter clacked his knife and the antelope ran away. Cautiously it came back, sniffed, and retreated again. This was repeated many times. Suddenly it saw the grass, straightened its legs, and made for it, bolting away quickly. Back again, greedily, it sniffed and grabbed for it. The dancer-hunters pulled their bows, and the antelope fell wounded and was still. The hunters came out, cut off its tail, and left.[6]

At the birth of a child, the Gabon Pygmies have a special song which welcomes the child into the world and, in giving him his name, wishes for him beauty and a long life.

> A man-child is born,
> A man-child is born,
> May he live and be beautiful.
>
> A man-child is born,
> A man-child is born,
> May he become old, very old.
>
> Joy, joy, praise, praise!
> Ngongonabarota, know it, is his name.[7]

While this song is being sung the father dances to the sound of drums, while the rest of the family makes a circle about the child.

An Australian rite from Arnhem Land deals with coming of age in which the boy's uncle performs the circumcision. The boy, of the kangaroo clan, lies on the ground. His uncle leaps savagely on him and performs the deed with a sharp stone. The flow of blood is likened to the sunset which tells of the end of one day and the coming of another. The young kangaroo is about to become a full-grown one. Mimetic dance then takes place and the boy must participate with the rest of the clan members.

On the death of an elephant, the African pygmies emasculate it and put a flower garland around its neck. The private parts are also draped with flowers and then buried in the depths of the forest. Singing of how they did not wish to harm him, and assuring him that it was no hunter that had killed him ("your time had come") the hunters perform a victory dance around the fallen beast.

A remarkable group of African dances is included in the book *African Art in Motion*, described by Robert Farris Thompson, from a collection by Katherine Coryton White. The Gle Gbee dancers of the Dan people of West Africa are believed to have emerged, as spirits, from the water. Even witches fear them because of their great power. They wear tall, conical headdresses (trimmed with leather strips, cowrie shells, and animal fur), featureless masks, long fiber tails, and a belt of bells around the waist; their arms and legs are covered with brightly striped blue and white cloth. A short raffia skirt hangs over tightly-bound stilts, which are covered with the blue and white cloth made into pants. Obviously this dance demands amazing feats of balance, in which the performer seems to jump, cross his stilts, appear to be sitting down in space, twist, and look down ten feet at the people below him. Sometimes he sits on the roof of a house, sometimes sliding down the thatch. Moving as a heroic figure, his action seems to be a sacred act.[8]

In *Africa Dances*, Gorer describes the dance of the Nesshoue (river fetish), in West Africa, performed by slim and elegant dancers who wear wide belts of cowrie shells, to which a piece of antelope skin is attached like a tail, thick necklaces of cowries and white beads around their necks and foreheads; their eyes are rimmed with black, and all is topped with bright red-pointed hats. Cowries and bits of metal hang from knees and elbows, clashing and jangling with their frenzied movement, which, regardless of its speed and drive, is very precise and controlled.[9]

From east of the Volta River in Africa (Ghana) an old Anlo war dance was described by Odette Blum. Today the dance is performed as entertainment on special occasions The procession moves around the village with the dancers bowing to the dignitaries. In the main dancing area the drummer introduces all of the rhythmic themes to come. Four dancers, in an even line, move directly toward the musicians, as if they were the enemy. They wheel to the left, circle counterclockwise, and return to the starting place. They repeat the same pattern with another step. Then dancers approach each other and compete in performing their favorite steps. Only at a certain drum signal may a dancer leave the circle.[10]

The Kwakuitl Indian war dance is usually performed by a woman wearing rings of hemlock branches. Moving in short steps, resting on one foot and then making a short step on the other, she holds her elbows close to her body, forearms stretched forward with palms up. This means that she is trying to gain supernatural power from the underworld. Entering the dance space, she circles it to the left and then the right, around the fire, with her short steps. She circles four times then moves backward, looking at the floor. Suddenly she closes her hands, having caught the power. She then throws the power out to the audience who fall down to escape, for it might cause disease should it enter the body.[11]

Another dance described in *African Art in Motion* is of the Ejagham, who live in southeastern Nigeria. The famous leopard dancers are costumed in a skin-tight knitted costume that completely covers the body, from conical hood to ankles and wrists. A raffia ruff covers a hole in the chest of the dress where the dancer enters. Around wrists and ankles is the same kind of raffia ruff that means danger in the forest. Striped in brown, orange, and white, the costume means "terror." The brown stands for terror, the orange for people dancing, and the white for peace and purity. A heavy bell is attached to the waist by two sashes, one red and the other white. These are mourning sashes and refer to the fact that this spirit has come from the dead. The dancer carries a staff and a bundle of leaves with which he "throws greetings." The leopard dance is a long and complicated series of encounters with different members of the tribe, many changes in drum and singing accompaniment, and very special relationships among cult members. Throughout the action the leopard continues with characteristic pelvic movements forward and backward, which rings the large bell hanging at his hips. The syncopated sound of the bell creates a startling sound that coincides with his other actions.[12]

The Yoruba, called the "makers of civilization," of western Nigeria and eastern Dahomey have a remarkable dance performed by very strong, athletic dancers who carry heavy wooden images on their heads and whips in their hands. While the elders dance around in a forest circle, the young men carry their burdens, demonstrating their skill and endurance.[13]

In Mali, West Africa, during the funeral ceremony, the hunters crouch to one side when the drums beat out the hunter's special rhythm, and then stride menacingly into the dance arena to reenact the hunting prowess of the newly dead man. Starting slowly, the drums quicken and the masked dancer lopes ferociously around in circles and finally spears his imaginary victim. The hunter, victorious, then drops exhausted to the ground.

Franziska Boas described a Pacific Northwest Kwakuitl Indian initiation dance consisting of four parts, with four song stanzas. One person makes up a song and gives it to someone else, asking for words to be sung to it. The song then belongs to the man who made up the words, and he is usually the dancer. The first dance was usually performed naked, with a neck and head ring, girdle, wristlets, and anklets of hemlock branches. After each stanza the dancer went into a sacred room to get new decorations. The second dance, performed by a helper, is an exhibition parade of the mask. In the third dance, done in circles, the initiate is dressed in blankets and cedar-bark neck and head rings. In the fourth dance he wears the mask. The characteristic dance posture is with the body bent forward slightly from the hips. With small steps, weight on the entire foot, and close to the ground, the weight transfers to one leg as the other knee straightens, and the knee bends as the other leg lifts. This causes a marked downward accent. Then alternately the accent is up, the weight being transferred as the knee bends, and the knee straightening as the other leg lifts. Sometimes the knees lift high, but the characteristic knee action always remains.

The elbows are close to the body; the women have one hand at the side, at shoulder level, the other in front, waist high. Then they lower their arms and swing from side to side, with the head moving in opposition. The palm of the lower hand is forward. The men use the same arm movements. Rhythmic variation occurs only in the leg action. Another characteristic is the quivering of the entire body, including the hands and lower jaw. This marks an ecstatic dance. The shaman's fingers quiver. Anyone making an error in dance step or in drum beat was seriously penalized, from donating blankets to forfeiting one's life in the old days.[14]

Franz Boas reported that every aspect of life of the Kwakuitl Indian hunters is accompanied by some form of dance. The infant in the cradle is rocked as the mother sings dance songs; and as children they have play dances. Young and old dance, especially with movement of their upper bodies. One of the most important of their dances is of the cannibal dancer, who is supposed to bite bits of flesh off the arms of onlookers. He first jumps down from the roof of a house, his face blackened and wearing rings of cedar bark on his head and around his neck. Covered with eagle down, he crouches down and circles the fire. He disappears into a sacred room, and when he comes out he is standing tall and moving with high steps. Many different songs are sung for him, for example:

> I went all around the world trying to get food, all around the world.
> I went all around the world trying to get skulls, all around the world.
> Food is always being put into my mouth, put into my mouth, therefore I am supernatural.
> I am always swallowing life, I am always swallowing life, my food is alive.

The dancers mime these words and are only restrained from attacking the audience by the assistants who hold the ring around their necks.[15]

From West Africa, Gorer reported a formal, sacred dance, stylizing a human sacrifice. Accompanied only by drums, a boy circles the dance arena, waving a tiny white flag, and goes out. He returns with two young men dressed in white drawers and shirts, each carrying on his shoulders a little girl in a yellow wig, red coat, blue trousers, and covered with cowrie shells and bells. An old witch follows, naked to the waist and wearing a white skirt, waving an empty calabash toward the dancers. The flag bearer circles the dancers as the young men do a complicated step. The little girls wave their arms and heads until, as the speed increases, they are hanging upside down and are thrown out like rag dolls. At the end the little girls are thrown out toward the drums and held by their ankles while being swung around and around until they nearly touch the ground. Suddenly they are lifted over the men's shoulders and borne out. The old witch follows, carefully holding her calabash as if it were overflowing.[16]

From Gorer's *Africa Dances* comes the description of a fertility dance of hunters from the southeastern Ivory Coast of Africa. This took place in a large area in front of the village, with the first group of young men, naked save for loincloth and rattles which they held, dancing in a small circle near the drums. On completion of each round, the steps were elaborated. The rest of the villagers stood in a larger circle, singing, to which the dancers replied. Soon everyone joined in the circle, doing a syncopated shuffling step. When everyone was in the circle, a group of strangely dressed old men rushed into the center and mimed the copulation of animals. After this everyone formed a new ring around the drums. Four little girls, naked except for a necklace of red seeds and a small apron, broke through the ring from the four points of the compass. Slowly, and in perfect rhythm, they moved zigzag, almost squatting, to the center of the circle. They held their aprons in one hand and scattered imaginary seeds with the other. When they arrived at the old men, they knelt and were blessed, then carried out of the ring. Meanwhile the rest of the dancers had been circling and singing.[17]

In New Guinea, tribesmen perform many spirit-cult rituals. Remnants of white man's materials, like red plastic, sunglasses, mirrors, and hats blend with cowrie shells, bird feathers, flowers, ornamental bamboo necklaces, and armlets for costume and decoration. Wearing bright facial and body paint, the dancers' dances include mock fights in which the initiates "attack" the elders during initiation ceremonies.

In New Britain the lizard-skin drums sound out for the New Year Sing-Sing (pidgin for song-dance festival). Participants come from miles around, and many of the groups living near the sea wear costumes and carry paraphernalia that is obviously from the Western world. Gauze bandages, cardboard headdresses, religious medals, and even bits of nylon goods enhance their dyed fibers, feathers, and tree branches. In their war dances these people shout defiantly from behind their beautifully patterned wooden shields. Wearing white masks above their bone-pierced noses and pig-tusk ornaments circling below the ears, they shout and stamp belligerently, shaking the circles of seashells about their wrists.

For the Andaman Islanders dance is a social affair, being a means of both enjoyment and ceremony. There are few special dances, but instead one dance for all occasions. Usually held in the center of the village, around the fire and after the evening meal, most of the villagers participate. In the early days a dance was always held before a fight, and the peace ceremony was also a dance. One of the more characteristic features of these dances is the accompaniment furnished by a "sounding board," a heavy board placed over a hole in the ground. When the dance leader hits the board with his foot it makes a hollow, drum-like sound.[18]

Rafael Karsten reports that most dances of the Amazon territory are magical in character, being a kind of conjuration. Accordingly all ornaments and decoration for the dances have magical significance. The Indians believe that by certain body movements, as well as through chants which accompany the movement, they can conjure evil spirits. The Nahotti Dance is apparently performed for amusement, but the name refers to "evil spirit," and in early times was done to cure the sick by driving out the demons who possessed them. In this dance the performers formed a ring around the patient and began jumping up and down, chanting loudly and marking time with rattles and bells held in the hands.[19]

Porteus, in *Primitive Intelligence and Environment,* reported a dance ceremony among the Bushmen of the southern Kalahari in Africa. After feasting, the women stood in a close circle and began clapping a strange, broken rhythm. An older woman lifted her voice in a high-pitched cry, followed by a shrill chorus. Then the dancing began, first with young boys and later older men. They moved close to the earth, arms swinging, their breath exhaled in animal-like grunts. Their eyeballs gleamed in the firelight as they shuffled around the fire, heels kicking up puffs of dust. Boys dashed out with bells on their ankles, holding sticks and oxtail wisks. One girl broke away from the singers and danced alongside the men with provocative gestures, then returned to the women. This continued until a tremendous hypnotic state was generated. The fixed, staring eyes of the dancers verified the fact that this was a trance dance.[20]

These are just a few of the many dances of the hunters, all of which are quite different from those of the planters, even as the dances of the planters are different from the dances of the city-states. But in one thing all are similar, and that is in the deep regard felt for dance as a part of almost every ceremony.

Planters

Dances of the planters were preoccupied with the cultivation of the earth, sowing and germination of seeds, and with the maturation and harvesting of crops. With great reverence for the earth, rain, rise and fall of rivers, influence of good and bad spirits, and the procession of moon and stars, some dances were mimetic of the planter's action, others with the seed and its germination, or even the role of a particular god or totem held responsible for success or failure of germination.

The solar seasons are important in the calendar of celebrations of all planting cultures. Spring is planting time, compassed by the equinox; summer is the growing time, marked by one solstice which we know today as Midsummer Night or St. John's Eve; autumn is the time of harvest; then there is winter, the season of the dead, with its sleep and rebirth with the sun. Each of these important seasons have corresponding dances. For example, rather than take a chance on the return of spring, with its renewed life, there were rites to insure this. There are literally thousands of forms, but the essence was in sacrifice. Perhaps the earliest of the ceremonies included the killing of an individual, couple, or group, usually in the prime of their lives—strong, important individuals. These people symbolized the vitality of the tribe, and by such sacrifice, insuring that the tribe would become stronger. Sometimes an animal, a young and vigorous beast, would lead the procession or dance, as a sign of rebirth. Small children would also perform during the dances. In time, animals, effigies of old age, or other symbols of death and decay were sacrificed, magically supplanting the old symbols. This death and rebirth practice occurred many times in many parts of the world and has entered mythology and religion even to the present day.

Ruth Benedict wrote, of the American Zuni Indians:

> The Dance, like their ritual poetry, is a monotonous compulsion of natural forces by reiteration. The tireless pounding of their feet draws together the mist in the sky and heaps it into the piled rain clouds. It forces out the rain upon the earth. They are bent not at all upon an ecstatic experience, but upon so thorough-going an identification with nature that the forces of nature will swing to their purposes. This intent dictates the form and spirit of Pubelo dances. There is nothing wild about them. It is the cumulative force of the rhythm, the perfection of forty men moving as one, that makes them effective.[21]

Among the Swahili of Africa, many of the harvest dances are leap dances, and it is said that the higher the leap, the higher the corn will grow. In an Australian corroboree dance, aborigines, wearing tall hats and with knees lifted high, jump in supplication for rain. The head priestess of the African Ashanti, covered with white clay, shuffles about in a stooped posture, singing and dancing thanks for the fruit and yams piled high nearby. The Oroans of India mime a reaping motion, as if to coax the earth to bear abundantly, while other dancers imitate the picking of the fruit. In New Guinea, pigs are sacrificed near mango trees so that the trees may hear the squealing of the pigs. Meanwhile there is a quiet ritual dance around the tree so as to increase its yield. Captain Cook and other adventurers and early explorers in the Pacific described great harvest dances in detail. Sacred hulas were performed to the boom of great drums, sonorous gourds, and organ-pipe bamboos thumped on the ground. Complex chanting and singing about the heroes and gods were also an important part of these ceremonies. Most of the harvest festivals were performed before the rise of the moon, but after sunset. As with so many of the other dances, there is little record of actual dance steps, only that they were similar, if not identical, to many of the others.

In the southern Sudan, the Nubas still cover themselves with ashes to ward off evil spirits and perform their celebrations at harvest time. They sing, wrestle, and dance until moonrise, when a great sound from the sacred Kudu horn sends them to their homes. Plains Indians, in times of drought, are led by a medicine man in a vigorous and lengthy dance around a sacred hill or tree. When the dance has reached its climax, the medicine man climbs to the top of a hill or a tree and repeatedly pours water on the ground or on the dancers' heads. The spirit who enjoyed the dance will realize that rain is needed. If there is no rain, then they repeat the dance again and again until it does rain.

Some contemporary tribal men live as if this were the New Stone Age. Some, like the Camayura Indians of Brazil and the Ainus of northern Japan, cultivate meagre gardens. Some New Guinea tribes plant in one place, and when the soil is exhausted, move on to another. Some have advanced to irrigation systems and even use metal tools. Among those people who still cultivate the soil and herd cattle and sheep in the same ways they did before cities were established are the Berbers (Greek, "barbarian") on the southern Atlas Mountains in Morocco. Living north of the Sahara and isolated in their mountains, these people have changed little through the centuries. Probably descendants of the first white settlers in North Africa, they came from the Middle East about 7000 B.C. and still perform their ancient dances as they have through the years.

In West African Mali, where grain is a sign of wealth, tribesmen in conical hats dance and chant praises of their creator Amma. This festival is held every sixty years to renew the Dogon way of life. Through the day they dance while waving one-legged stools, calabash bowls, and fly wisks, each of which has religious significance. At a Doma ceremony on the death of an elder, the Kanaga dancers (men in masks topped by the outstretched arms of Amma) begin a series of swooping arcs with their bodies as they progress in a straight line. Then they circle the dance place three or four times, swooping down to touch the ground with Amma's creating hands, and then off to repeat the action.[22]

Young Bororo men of the animal herders of West Africa smear their faces with red paint, dress in all their finery, and dance for a week before girl judges in a kind of a male beauty contest. Standing in a line opposite a semicircle of observers, the handsome youths chant a long sustained note and sway hypnotically from side to side. Each wears a long ostrich feather in a deep blue headband over a blond hair wig. Many fine pearl necklaces cover their light-brown glistening skin. Long narrow skirts hang from their waists, held close to their legs by small chains, just below the knees. Two old women march up and down before them, jeering at those less handsome than the others. Soon the sustained note-song dies out and the young men begin to jump in time to the all-over sound of small metal buckles on their left ankles. The old women give shrill cries and move about jerkily as the crowd starts to yell. This is continued with no rest for some five hours. Then the dancers begin to strut about while they again voice the endless, piercing sound. They roll their eyes, show their strong, white teeth, and grimace horribly. A column of five young girls finally enters and kneels before the boys. They wear heavy gold rings on their ankles and gold tubes that cover their backs. While the men still hold their shrill notes, the girls move to the men of their choice. The song stops, the dancers disappear, and the magic ceremony is over. Everyone is reassured, for as a celebration ushered in the rainy season, this one has marked the time to move on with their herds for the next eight months of the dry season.[23]

The Zuni, Hopi, and other Pueblo dwellers of southwestern United States are all very group-oriented and have long practiced a rich ceremonial life centered in the community of their masked gods. The whole group participates in these ceremonies which are conducted at very special times by trained priests and members of the totem. These people are excellent farmers and depend wholeheartedly upon their gods for rain and abundant harvests. Perhaps the most famous of the Pueblo Indian rain ceremonies is the Hopi Snake Dance. Lasting for nine days, from the preliminary rituals to the final dance, this ceremony func-

Drawings of Hopi dancers

tions to emphasize the relationship between the snake and the members of the snake fraternity and to deal with scarcity of rain. Young members of the Snake Clan are initiated at this time. After many complicated rites preliminary to the final event, the priests of the Snake Clan start their sacred chant. Soon initiates and elders, dressed in simple kilts and bodies rubbed with ashes, trot into the rectangular dancing space with the sacred altar of cottonwood branches at one end. Deep below are the many snakes which have been brought from the sacred kivas, after being gathered weeks before. In groups of three—initiate, leader, and gatherer—the men trot around and around the arena. Soon one of the initiates reaches in the *kisi* altar and drags out a snake, which he puts between his teeth. Moving back into the line of the dance, he continues trotting while he holds the snake in his mouth. The leader keeps him on the right path, and with the gatherer, is ready to stroke the snake with prayer feathers if his fangs get too close to the boy's face. One after another of the initiates follow, each getting his snake. As the snakes are let loose, the gatherers sweep them up and coil them

Link to the Past 97

about their necks until everyone seems covered with snakes. The entire ceremony then moves over to one end of the arena where the women in full ceremonial dress are sitting. A large circle is marked off with cornmeal, the snakes are loosed within this circle, and the women sprinkle sacred meal, from ceremonial bowls, all over the snakes. Then suddenly all members of the clan rush in, gather up as many snakes as they can, and run to the four cardinal directions, to let the snakes go to the gods, off the high mesa top. The ceremony is over. And the rains come, if not to the top of the mesa, then to the farmlands below.

Ethnic Dance

Out of the magic, ritual, and mythology of the primitive and early civilized groups came a form of dance dedicated to the reenactment and dramatization of the legends of culture heroes and gods. Appropriate ceremonies were being developed for the new relationships between men, their leaders, and their gods. Periodic celebrations of important events and observations were becoming traditional affairs. Particularly there were solemn occasions for the "rehearsal of right attitudes." As the tribes and more formal groups discovered commonalities of race, religion, environment, and need, they found their essentially ethnic character.

One of the most outstanding examples of ancient ethnic dance is the early Buddhist, later Hindu, religious ceremonial dance of India. Temple and shrine dances were important to the religious life of the people. As with all artistic, theatrical, religious, and social life in India, dance was influenced by the tales of the heroes and gods in the *Mahabharata,* the longest epic poem in the world. This is the real encyclopedia of early Hinduism, being about seven times the length of the combined *Iliad* and *Odyssey.* Coming from the shadowy period of the *Rig-Veda*, the *Mahabharata* refers to names of priests, warriors, and heroes of the late Vedic period around 900 B.C. Through the years the poem has grown in size and drama. The divine hero, Krishna, who seems to be the main character today, was apparently added in later years and was not a part of the original story.

The *Mahabharata* is a complex tale of a bitter quarrel that developed into a war of extermination. The five sons of Pandu were unjustly deprived of their ancestral kingdom by their wicked cousins. After great battles, in which all of their enemies and many of their friends were killed, they regained their kingdom. The whole atmosphere of the story is of a society emerging from tribalism. The heroics of bravery, loyalty, and truthfulness were all encouraged; none refused a challenge nor was capable of cowardice.

There have been endless additions to the original narrative, dealing with ethnics, religion, and even politics. The *Bhagavad-Gita*, the most influential Hindu religious poem, is a part of this great epic poem, and is one of the best known works in all of Sanskrit literature.

The *Ramayana*, another later and shorter epic poem, tells of the adventures of a supernatural hero, Rama, incarnation of the god Vishnu, who took human form to save mankind from the demons. Among dozens of popular versions, the core of the story revolves about Rama, the ideal Hindu man, and Sita, the obedient and respectful wife, willing to give up her life to defend her virtue. With many variations on the theme, Rama, with his army of friendly monkeys, fights to rescue his kidnapped wife from the evil king of Lanka (Ceylon).

These two epic poems have served as the basis for traditional festivals, ritual dances, sculptures, paintings, music, dramas, songs, and folk arts of the entire subcontinent of India as well as Cambodia, Thailand, Indonesia, Burma, and all the rest of Asia. The persistence of these great stories as recurring themes has discouraged realism, and the legends, myths, distortions, and exaggerations continue to flourish, especially in music, poetry, and dance. The concept of *abhinayam* evolved, whereby through suggestion, the thoughts and feelings of characters in relation to their causes and effects were communicated. Professional dance performers, teachers, and dance centers emerged and became an influential force throughout the land.[24]

The earlier Kerali dances were both folk and classical, religious and secular. From the third and fourth centuries A.D., the classical Indian dance-drama developed many of the facial expressions, hand gestures, and stage conventions that have become a part of the later ethnic dances of Bharata Natyam, Kathak, Manipuri, and Kathakali. While each of these used common elements and had common content, each is rooted in its own local folk tradition and enjoys a unique and separate existence today.

While other parts of Asia had their rituals and ceremonies, such as the Ceylonese devil-dances, Burmese and Indonesian spirit-dances, and the music-dance-drama fusions of Chinese opera, only Japan had a rich and classical dance form. Oldest of all these was the classical Noh, which grew from indigenous materials into a precise form in the fourteenth century. One of the great arts of the world, it is as subtle as the tea ceremony and the play of "listening to incense." This is an art based upon the god-dance, or some legend of spirit apparition: an

Kathakali dancer (Chet Milar)

art of noble posture, dancing, chanting, and acting that is not mimetic but highly abstract, as if in "half-shadows." Some Noh performances lasting up to five days were performed at initiations, marriages, and Buddhist memorial services for dead Shoguns. This form was directed to aristocrats only and was never popular outside the courts. Through the years, style and form have changed little. Costume, masks, stage settings and props, accompaniment, even to special make-up and wigs, remain as they were centuries ago, a truly tradition-bound form of expression.

The popular Kabuki and doll theater did not appear until the sixteenth century, but the content of all these derived, as in the Indian dance, from the legends and myths of heroes, warriors, kings, and gods. As with the Indian dance, these are still performed and represent the real classical theater of each land.

There is little in the Western world that can approximate the Indian and Japanese dance forms, but the dance of Greece was of particular importance in influencing the rise of the chorus and the development of drama in the Western world. Indeed, it was the Greek influence that marked the start of the great differences between the views and arts of the East and West. The Greek blend of music, poetry, and dance was the nucleus of the developing tragedy form, and many dramatic songs were especially written for dance. The warrior, funeral, snake-handling rituals, processions of the first fruits, maze dances, and dances of young men as they were performed in Crete are all documented in Lawler's *The Dance in Ancient Greece*,[25] but we learn little of the action, simply that they were done. On mainland Greece there were mourning dances and ceremonies to honor the gods. Animal dances were predominant and often of a quite primitive nature. Dances at shrines and festivals occurred as early as the sixth century B.C., and some survive to this day. But there is no direct line of Greek ethnic dance as it exists in India and Japan. Only the folk dance forms remain relatively intact.

Since early Occidental history, the dances of Spain have been famous. As far back as Carthaginian days, Cadiz was considered the center of Spanish dancing, and when the Romans took the city they found classical dance there. In the eighth century the Moors added their flavor and scope to all of the Spanish arts, particularly dance. Through the years there has been a long and notable history of classical performance dance in Spain, a true ethnic form. Another survival from early Catholic days is *El Baile de los Seises,* a dance still performed at the high altar of the cathedral of Seville on Corpus Christi

Spanish dancer (Chet Milar)

Day. Two lines of six choir boys promenade through the streets, up the steps, and down to the center of the church in a solemn and traditional dance.

Some of the early Biblical dances, and later dances of the Jews, might be considered a kind of ethnic dance. Records from the Bible and Talmudic writings provide sparse references but no actual descriptions of dance action; certainly there is nothing here of a traditional performance form.

Folk Dance

The most persistent dances probably developed out of the ethnic form combined with the primitive ritual dance. There was obviously little difference between ethnic and folk dance in the beginning. But folk dance branched off as a participation dance of the people, while ethnic forms became more of an entertainment, a spectacular performance, celebrating ethnic traditions of the people. With the development of different nations, language, dress, music, folk arts, and dance—along with political, social, and economic characteristics—became a means of identifying national differences.

Many of the original folk dances grew out of, or were similar to, primitive dances of magic. Long ago, the reasons for these dances were forgotten but the movement patterns and accompanying story, song, and music lived on. There are many mimetic animal movements and work or worship gestures in dances for hunting, planting, reaping, working, fighting, courting, praying, and having fun. At the time of the medieval guilds there was great emphasis upon specific dances and songs in which the action of weavers, tanners, bakers, blacksmiths, and other guild members were rehearsed. Some of these are still done today, but hardly for the same reasons.

Folk dances have usually been fairly simple, with relatively easy step patterns and body action. They were sometimes performed in groups, in a circle or lines, often as a man-woman couple, or as a trio of two men and a woman or two women and a man. While the action was not complicated, people of different groups and cities or nations developed nuances and styles of performance. A basic two-step, for example, might be done high into the air and in a brisk tempo in one area, and in a stately and reserved fashion in another. Just as with certain costumes, dialects, singing style, and food choices, so did ways of performing simple folk dance steps evolve.

Social Dance

Not until the transition of folk dance into the court dance of Italy and France take place did what we think of as "social dance" come about. But when the change did occur, it was reserved entirely for the aristocrats. Nothing could illustrate better the close connection between the dance of people and the kind of society in which they lived. The lusty folk dances of the peasants were transformed into the mannered and precise dances of the courts of kings. It is from these adaptations that our social dance has evolved. Special music was written by court musicians and preclassic music, and dance was born.

In medieval times there was little difference between social and folk dance. Peasants would romp through the countryside, all equal, with no lead couple, in open ring formation. The thirteenth century *estampie,* round, and *carole* were popular then. The aristocrats, in their heavy, long costumes, and the women with towering headdresses performed in more limited space, with restrained steps. By the fourteenth and fifteenth centuries, they moved indoors into special rooms, and some important man and woman led the procession of other couples, arranged in descending court rank. The solemn tread and stately bows of these originally sprightly dances came to mark the dances of the courts.

France became the dance center of the Western world, and the courts of the Louis's set the dance style, etiquette, morals, and behavior of aristocrats for all of Europe. In 1588, the classic *Orchesographie,*[26] by Arbeau, appeared, describing and discussing the dance and music of the times. It was out of the many court social dances that the ballet was formed, and, for a time, the king and members of the court performed in these ballets. The transition came in the seventeenth century when the ballet moved from the courts onto the stage of the royal theater. Social dances again stressed the participation aspect, even though there was an unusual emphasis upon display and the personality and technique of the dancers. This was a reflection of the character of the courts. England, Germany, Austria, Spain, and Russia all borrowed styles and manners from the French courts. But in all of these countries the vigorous folk dance of the peasants still prospered.

In 1651, John Playford wrote his famous *The English Dancing Master,*[27] in which a wide variety of social dance forms were described. There were many changes in the eighteenth century. The Industrial Revolution was stirring, and the French Revolution wiped out the

French aristocracy, as well as its dance. *La Carmagnole* was the dance of freedom in which the participants danced around a tree topped with a cap of liberty. There was even a Ball of the Bastille, on the freeing of political prisoners from the great prison in Paris. Country dances were imported from England to the continent, and another kind of revolution—one in social dancing—began with the waltz. For the first time, as a spirit of naturalism invaded social dance, bodies touched, as men frankly held ladies in closed dance position. Gone, except as period pieces, were the formal and stiff preclassic dances. In Pemberton's *Dancing Master*,[28] published in 1711, there were directions for teaching the minuet to school girls, a possible evidence of resistance to these changes for the young ladies of England.

Toward the end of the eighteenth century, after the French Revolution, powdered wigs became unfashionable, tight breeches were replaced by looser trousers, and dark cloth coats replaced the colored silks. Men's hair was no longer tied, but worn in a short bob. Ladies wore hoops, high-heeled shoes, silk stockings, and their hair in tight curls. In the United States, George Washington opened his inaugural ball with his favorite dance, the minuet. By 1815, the minuet had vanished, and the waltz, galop, and polka came into favor. The lancers, mazurka, and schottische followed as popular dances for balls, while rural areas continued their country dances: rounds, jigs, reels, and squares.

The nineteenth century in New York City, Washington, D. C., and Boston saw the introduction of formal balls for the Prince of Wales, President Lincoln, General Grant, and high society. The last decade, known as the "Gay Nineties," enjoyed waltzes, and, with John Philip Sousa's *Washington Post March,* did the two-step. There were polkas, quadrilles, Virginia reels, mazurkas, schottisches, and galops. The waltz and the polka were performed in closed dance position and were considered sinful and obscene by some clergy, and decrees were issued forbidding glides and turns in the closed dance position. In Europe, where these paired dances were banned, noblemen built private ballrooms so that they might waltz and polka as they chose. In 1885, Allen Dodsworth wrote *Dancing and its Relations to Education and Social Life*.[29] Among many descriptions and directions, the author attributed the moral decline among people to the polka. *Dancing*,[30] a volume in *The Badminton Library of Sports and Pastimes,* was published in 1895. The author, Lily Grove, discussed special problems of guests and hostesses at balls as well as the kinds of dances being done.

Gradually this form of dance was considered a socially acceptable activity for ladies and gentlemen, and dance halls, ballrooms, and dine-and-dance places became popular. While the elite still favored their great hunt and debutante balls, the lower and middle classes were enjoying their own dances in less glamorous surroundings.

6
What We Have Today

> ... man's need of ritual existence is today as strong as ever, and so is his drive toward common movement which is as old as man himself. We do not like to admit that what separates us from primitive man is a rather thin veneer of culture which can so easily crack and a skin-deep civilization which, at the slightest provocation, can be lacerated. Our tribal instincts still run amuck and, speaking figuratively, we continue to dance wildly to evoke the spirit of victory as well as fertility.
>
> Walter Sorell, *critic*

During the Golden Age of Greece, dancers were actors, singers, and acrobats, and almost always mimes and poets as well. Performers in classical Chinese, Indian, and Japanese theater were equally proficient in acting, singing, and dancing. But until recently, dancers limited their activity to dance alone, indeed, to only *one kind* of dance. The stereotype calls for quite specific and specialized things that a dancer is expected to do; and as the scope and variation of dance has increased, so dancers have become even more specialized. Differences in purpose, kind of movement accompanying paraphernalia, and actual design and form of the action have been allocated to different categories. Where it once sufficed to say "I am a performer," and mean, among other things, "I am also a dancer," now one must differentiate with, "I am a dancer of: folk dance, social dance, square dance, tap dance, classical ballet, modern dance, jazz, American Indian dance, Jugoslavian Kolos, classical dances of India (even to a section of India, for example, Manipuri), Ceylonese devil-dances, Japanese Kabuki, or rock 'n'roll." And this is just a small sample of the many categories within the family of dance.

Unfortunately, a dancer within any one of these groupings often studies, rehearses, composes, performs, and even teaches with little regard or knowledge of other kinds of dance. There is often misunderstanding and even animosity among dancers, as has been evidenced between some dancers of classical ballet and modern dance.

Westerners know little of the dance of Asia, even as few Asians go beyond their traditional forms. Folk dancers turn away from tap dancers, devotees of the waltz shun the burlesque stripper. Most dancers will tell you that they are interested only in their favored form. While some teachers and choreographers seem convinced that a broad experience and knowledge of many dance forms enriches anyone's experience and ability in dance, many others demand a single-minded dedication to *the* one dance form. Just how much habit, personal skill, security of the known, and fear of the unknown affect us is hard to assess. Almost any dancer will agree that if there is a choice between moving styles, he will do the one he knows best and can perform with the greatest skill.

Choreographers are aware of the intrusion of action they have used before, occurring again and again in movement design. While this may be considered the persistence of a personal style, it may also be the result of too little exploration into the wealth of dance experiences available to us all.

A Multitude of Forms

A historical view of dance is more than a matter of dates and innovations. What has happened in its development reflects changes in the lives of nations, peoples, and, in retrospect, often seems inevitable. Many concepts, as well as problems, still seem familiar to us today, and we are interested in the "modern" points of view of some of the old records and writings, for example, the words of Noverre in *Letters on Ballet and Dancing*,[1] written in 1760. These seem very pointedly directed to dancers of today. Furthermore we are often surprised at the recurrence of certain styles in content, technique, accompaniment, or interaction with other arts.

The dance that we know today is the direct result of all the adaptations of the earlier forms to our contemporary world. Some seem to be new but are really extensions of older ones; many forms are old but appear in new dress; some, like the ethnic, and a few of the folk dances, are very old and steeped in rigid tradition.

The dances described below are presented in alphabetical order for easy reference.

Acrobatic Dance

Acrobatic dance is that movement performed by solo, duo, or group, during which the dancers defy normal range of action and, with flexible joints and well-toned muscles, do movements that most of the spectators deem impossible. Back bends, body rolls, balances, leg splits, sinuous writhings, double-jointed manipulations, and action that seems to turn the body inside out are some of the acrobatic tricks used. Accompaniment by dramatic music and drum rolls always increases the excitement. They may dress like snakes, fish, or birds, or, frankly, like well-trained gymnasts. The audience usually claps when the action seems unusual or complicated, or, especially, beyond their capabilities.

Aerobic Dance

Aerobic dance refers simply to a system of exercises performed to music, the length and speed of which are increased according to the overload principle. This is not dance but exercises for improving physical fitness, particularly appealing to those who are overweight and lacking in muscle tone. It is probably called "dance" to make it more palatable and exciting.

Another kind of pseudo-dance that is practiced and taught in some community centers, recreation departments, and schools, where the aim is to involve people in movement experiences, is called "Ladies' Dance Class." Usually directed by a teacher, this may feature limbering exercises, weight control, fad dances, gymnastics, trampoline, belly dance, folk dance, and a potpourri of "things to do" because "doing movement is good for the figure," and sometimes is even fun to do. While any of these may be commendable, they are not dance as such, but rather a form of movement therapy. It is possible that participation in a regular dance class might be equally beneficial, but many people are repelled by the fear that a dance class is beyond their capabilities.

Ballet, Classical, or Traditional

This is that form of dance that grew out of the sixteenth and seventeenth century social dance of the Italian and French courts. From the time of Louis XIV and the great French dancing master Beauchamp, and from others, especially in Italy and Russia, a standardized code of action was developed. With five fundamental positions of the feet and legs and associated positions of the arms and hands, the vocabulary of ballet is objective, precise, and unchanging. Small units of action combine with others and result in longer patterns, each with its characteristic rhythms and names. These movements, always described in French, are the same in any land in the world, though the style and dynamics may vary. Sheldon Cheney described ballet as "a type of dance bound up in a strict code of technical regulations, designed exclusively for a small class audience."[2]

Ballet is unnatural and abstract, its movement demands an erect spine, turned-out hips, symmetrical and balanced action, and carving fluid lines. The rise onto the point, the elegant lifts, and the noble leaps are all part of the illusion of the dancers who appear to be immortal, who easily defy gravity.

Dances are choreographed by combining dance steps and combinations, fitting them to or with music, and, somewhere, identifying the action with written words or libretto. Pantomime is often used to further clarify the action. The form of the dance may vary but, if it is in classical form, will always allow for an adagio, a *pas de deux*, or *quatre*, with male and female dancers performing together, then each doing solos and then repeating the first figure.

There is a close connection between staging, costuming, decor, and theatrical effect in the ballet, each of which blends into the whole.

Some of the greatest musicians have composed music for ballets, and so, too, have great painters produced scenery and costumes. One of the most basic laws of ballet is "aplomb," perfect balance and stability, which can only be acquired by thorough and constant training and practice. Elevation, line, and lightness are other bases for the ballet dancer. He must know the technique of classical ballet and must then acquire maturity and mastery of expression. There is a perfection of craftsmanship, a tidiness and deftness of movement, as well as the streamlined exactness, which is particularly valuable for the classical ballet dancer.

Ballet, Contemporary, or Modern

The extent to which modern dance has influenced ballet is phenomenal, and it is sure to influence it further through closer collaboration. And this is reciprocal, because many modern dancers are recognizing the advantages in studying ballet technique and in understanding the point of view. Some choreographers use a modern dance approach and add ballet embellishments, some use classical ballet in one part and modern dance in another, but the happiest combination has been in an unself-conscious use of both to further the intent of the choreographer. When the action, be it balletic or modern, is inevitable rather than contrived, then the result is often good. But the "traditionalists" in each field still resent any change in the "pure" form they favor.

The combination of the two forms has been especially triumphant in musical comedy. Occasionally it is said that modern dance would benefit from the discipline and objectivity of the classical ballet while ballet would gain depth and scope for choreography by manipulating some of the invincible laws that limit expansion.

Character Dance

To some this dance means the practice and adaptation of folk dance steps to the movement vocabulary of classical ballet. While simply dressing a competent ballet dancer in the appropriate costume might provide an illusion of time and place, it lacks validity. Essentially it would lack the "character" of the source, hence "character dance" for the ballet dancer. Another view is that this form is based upon actual characterization such as a Spanish countess, a frontiersman, an Indian chief, or an Irish washerwoman. While characterization is often used as impetus or even as thematic material for literal approaches to dance, "character dance" is different. The "characters" of "character dance" are usually based upon stereotypes, and that means emphasizing the clichés that are supposed to represent any category. Often a standard set of gestures, movements, and antics result. Costume, decor, and paraphernalia repeat themselves, and the very sight of the character, even before he moves, comes to symbolize the whole of his character.

Children's Dance

Includes many kinds of experiences, ranging from specific "steps" to be learned to situation in which the children may develop their own creativity in movement; from "do as the teacher does," to "what can I do?" Of course the problem is to understand what is expected of the program. Parents, teachers, and the children concerned may have a variety of ideas about what should happen.

The difficulty for any teacher of children's dance is to reconcile these differences in goal, as well as to plan and carry out a balanced, interesting, and, hopefully, an educationally sound series of lessons. Unless those concerned seek to make dancers of the children and "teach them some dances," it is necessary to consider the age, interest, and experience of the children as well as suitable kinds of activity. According to the guidelines for children's dance set up by the Dance Division of the American Association for Health, Physical Education and Recreation (now the Dance Association), the following movement-centered experiences are considered basic, and should be available from early through later childhood:

> Experiences in awareness of changes in body shape and elements of time, space, and force.
> Explorations and improvisations of movement in terms of familiar experiences and properties of sound, sight, and feeling.
> Experiences for synchronizing movement and musical structure.
> Experiences with basic locomotor and nonlocomotor action, leading up to combinations and traditional dance steps.
> Relating dance activities to curriculum in school.
> Experience in singing games and movement songs.
> Additional middle-years dance experiences in folk dance, dance techniques, ethnic dances, fad dances, and chances to perform for classmates and parents.

Such suggestions imply that the teacher must renounce some of his own dance background for the unique and everchanging form of the child's. The teacher provides an environment where the child is free

112 *Dance: From Magic to Art*

to discover how his own movement feels, especially in his early dance experience. So the "learning principles of discovery, perception, and actualization are thus applied to the child's increasingly discerning use and mastery of his own body's movement."[3]

Often the teacher compromises his students because parents, community, and children have been conditioned by what they see on television or what their friends are learning in "ballet," "tap" or "acrobatics." Sometimes such studios are financially successful and popular with "stage-struck" children, but when parents become more interested in their child's self-discovery, opportunity for movement exploration, and elements of creativity than with fostering mediocrity, exhibitionism, and the inevitably stereotyped dances and dancers, then the teacher concerned will change the emphasis.

Dance Drama

This is not so much a form of dance as it is a story action that uses any of the appropriate dance forms. The dramatic expression is resolved by dancers who perform a choreographed story which may rely on libretto, pantomime, or abstraction of a natural happening. Clearly this is more of a choreographic approach than a distinct dance form.

Dance Therapy

This is the adaptation of dance experiences to the emotionally disturbed, and has become an important adjunct to their treatment. When directed by a psychiatrist or specialist, the dance therapist has been helpful in dealing with psychotic patients. It is commonly agreed that in man's development, language was preceded by nonverbal communication. In today's word-centered world, movement has been repressed as a way of communicating yet unconsciously operates to express emotion. It is in tapping this deep-seated impulse to move that is so effective.

Since movement is so basic a human experience, it is sometimes possible to reach a patient with movement even though he will not talk, listen, or respond with his other senses. Often the therapist will simply move near the patient and, for example, stand near him and sway from side to side. Sometimes he can interest him in grasping a rope, picking up someone else, and then all moving together, sometimes in opposition or together. Sometimes it is the drum beat, singing, or music that helps to involve him.

Among primitives, dance therapy was an accepted procedure. Whether it was to drive out the demons or keep death away, it was a successful practice. The extent to which the traditional ritual was believed, and even cherished as therapy, was probably important. And a group of one's friends and family, or the designated medicine man moving, chanting, and repeating an insistent rhythm were powerful aids.

There is evidence of good results with dance therapy among all age groups and, with time and patience, with most problems. In addition to involvement and background in dance, the dance therapist should have additional training and understanding of a broad range of emotional abnormalities as well as normal behavior. And, above all, he must be aware of his limitations. He must, like any other therapist, work under direct medical supervision. Each year there are more centers for specialized work for potential dance therapists. Not all dancers are successful in this field, because it takes a very special skill and personality to deal with such problems.

The movement of dance therapy serves an entirely different purpose than dance as a performing art in that it is very personally geared to the needs of the patient.

Dramatic Dance

This dance, sometimes called "theater dance," often augments or highlights dramatic performances presented in theaters. It has often been said that when words lose their dramatic impact it is time for movement to take over. This has been ably shown with opera ballet, musical comedy, some drama, mime, and dance-drama.

Opera ballet adapts movement to the story line of the opera. While opera's real substance is singing, it really is a complex of music, drama, decor, costume, and libretto. In the early operas of Lully and Rameau, ballet was the pivot of the entire composition, but in time it became an auxiliary. In some instances it is simply an interlude, with no apparent connection with the opera. In its highest form it is part of the development of the entire action, varying, of course, with the opera content and period.

Here is an example of ensemble emphasis upon the music and singing, with the ballet dancers secondary to the music. Seldom do the singers dance; usually a separate group of dancers is employed to undertake this specialized action. If the choreographer is really concerned with forwarding the progress of the opera, he will use the theme as nucleus for forming ballet action to the appropriate sequences. The alternative is to simply fit ballet steps to the music, with no regard for the drama of the piece.

Educational Dance

This involves all kinds of dance, as wide in scope as the rest of education. While each of the forms of dance may be a part of the educational picture, it is usually folk, social, ethnic, some theatrical forms, modern, and ballet that are included. But they are only educational if they are approached "educationally." The more students know and participate in a wide range of dance experiences, the more they will know of dance as a form of human behavior rather than a particular technique, especially if the teacher is sensitive to the student's need to "learn" rather than to "be taught."

If by education we mean meeting and increasing the potential of the student, helping him to find relationships, encouraging him to broaden his views, and providing opportunities for enrichment and creativity, then the dance experience will stress the *process* of searching, learning, experimenting, improvising, organizing, creating, and sharing, rather than simply performing as the *end* product of the dance. Obviously there are positive educational benefits associated with dance performance, but only after the preliminary process of self-discovery. When the teacher is more interested in concert, recital, or display of student talent than with what is happening to the student, then you may assume that this is not wholly educational dance. It is necessary that teachers and administrators understand clearly the principles associated with educational policies.

Much of the current controversy about "where dance belongs in the schools" could be solved if the basic issue could first be solved. WHAT IS TO BE EMPHASIZED, PROCESS OR PRODUCT? It may be that fine arts or performing arts are better equipped to deal with the fostering of dance performers, choreographers, and critics. But with such goals, they are not necessarily better able to emphasize the development and integrating process of students who do not plan to become dancers.

Is dance just for dancers? Is music just for muscians? Is painting just for painters? Where then is the audience, the spectator? Actually it is impossible to be sure in which department this stress upon the developmental aspect will occur. It may happen in physical education, maybe in drama, maybe in performing arts. *Where* is of less importance than that it *does* happen somewhere. This depends upon

University dance majors and high school students in a day of dance.

the philosophy of the administrators, the goals and experience of the teachers, the curriculum, and, mainly, the opportunities for student growth.

I am sure of one thing. The relatively common occurrence of two or three dance specialities and philosophies within one school shows a sad duplication of effort, talent, and opportunity. It is evidence of inconsistent points of view, diverse objectives, unreconcilable personality clashes, and obvious disregard for students. The "opponents" do not even care to know what happens outside their environs. How unfortunate that dancers, dance teachers, and leaders can't reconcile their differences and recognize the assets and advantages of reciprocal classes and discussions for both process and product.

Esthetic, Natural, Creative, and Interpretive Dance

These are names given early modern dance forms. With Isadora Duncan's break from ballet, and with the new expressionism in all of the arts, these terms were used interchangeably to describe a free and relatively natural movement experience. Isadora Duncan had depended enormously on music and, with her loose Greek tunic costume, bare feet, and spiraling imagination, opened the gates of "significance in the movement" rather than in the form. Fortunately there was a form imposed by the music. But in contrast to the strict movement code of the ballet, this provided a new surge of freedom in action.

Ethnic Dance

This is an artistic, presentational spectacle performed by highly skilled and sensitive dancers, within a strictly theatrical setting. Always surrounded by the shadows of culture gods, heroes, and manners, the dances may tell complex stories, as with the Indian and Japanese classical dance, or weave intricate designs and rhythms, as with the Moslem-influenced classical dance of Spain. In each of the forms the dancers perform highly stylized actions which are understood best by members of the same cultural heritage. Others may enjoy the spectacle but the real meanings are disguised in unrecognizable symbolism.

Ethnic and folk dance had the same roots and celebrate many of the same occasions. But ethnic dance is a performance dance, and folk dance is a participation event. Most of ethnic dance is an art form, and folk dance is purely social and recreational, having given up its magical properties long ago. According to La Meri,

> . . . the ethnological dance does not include the folk dance, the former being an art dance and the latter a communal dance. But I believe it is safe to say that all ethnological dance arts spring from communal dance.[4]

Ethnic dance has been influenced by all of the elements and relationships that make up an ethnic culture. This is more than national or language orientation, for, as in the case of Asia, the dance of the Hindu, along with the myths of the *Ramayana, Mahabharata,* and all the hero figures and legends, have spread from India to Bali and Java, and to Burma, Japan, Cambodia, and Thailand. This is *the* great ethnic influence of the Orient, in art, religion, and life-style. The dance from India eastward sprang from the gods, and dance was sent as a precious gift to enoble the heart of man and inspire him with his ideals and ethics.

The rules for Indian dance were very strict; indeed, they are still strict. The *Sastra*, which details canons of dance, allows certain costumes, makeup, movement, plots, and style. The *rasa* (feeling) allows ten moods: heroism, fear, love, laughter, pathos, wonder, terror, contempt, sorrow, and sublime tranquility. *Bhava* (cause and effect) gives variety to the plot. For example, the *rasa* might be love, the *bhava* could be husband and wife as cause, and undying devotion as effect; or two strangers as cause and doubt as effect.

Basic principles of classical dance techniques are similar in European ballet and Thai, Cambodian, Indonesian, Balinese, or Indian dance drama. The spine is erect, shoulders are level, with feet positioned according to the five positions and half-toe of European ballet. Additions to these are *somapada*, feet together and parallel; *ancita*, foot resting on the heel, showing the sole and toes; the quiet placing of the feet in the Kathakali; the slow Japanese Noh walk, and the Javanese walk where the dancers seem dreamily suspended on strings, like puppets. The hundreds of *mudras* (hand symbols) used are precise and beautiful, each one understood by most of the spectators. Originally they were priestly gestures accompanying the *Rig-Vedic* hymns, much as the Jewish rabbi and Catholic priest use ritualistic gestures. The vocabulary of this language is exhaustive and exact. Finger and wrist gestures submit to a rigid code. If the spelling or pronunciation of the *mudras* are incorrect, the dancer misses his point and is ridiculed. When the *mudras* are correct the spectators know the season of the year, time of day, who the hero is, what family he comes from, what river he is crossing, and all about the birds, animals, fish, joys, despairs, loves, and hatreds in the drama.

By the late 1800s, many of the early temple Nautch dances, and even the ancient Devidasi forms, had been reduced to entertainment by prostitutes, and laws had been passed to ban them. Some say that Pavlova, on one of her visits to India, was influential in reviving the Indian classical dance. It was brought once more into favor and soon was recognized as an art form. There are four basic forms of classical dance. In the south are the Bharata Natyam (most ancient and classical) and the exciting men's dance, the Kathakali. In the north is the Kathak, the old Nautch dance, and the Manipuri, least difficult and most social of all. Dancers in the Western world can only approximate the degree of muscular skill of the average Indian classical dancer. For example, an uncanny control of facial muscles allows for a change from deformity to beauty, from youth to old age before your eyes.[5]

There are many other ethnic dance forms that have grown out of the culture and life of a group, and they are performed in traditional style so as to assure the perpetuation of the form. The Japanese Noh play and Kabuki theater are both classical forms, mainly dance but including acting, singing, and chanting-speaking. Kabuki, the latest form, cherishes the old characters and stories, but, in addition, has added more contemporary materials, altering much of the classical style.

The ethnic dance of Spain has drawn from the north, central, east, and south of the country, including the Moorish-Eastern flavor, blending the classical and gypsy flamenco into a neoclassic art dance, a true emotional experience of all Spain. Each of the influential forms has been affected by the people, their clothes, manners, worship, economic status, and physical characteristics. Toes turn in in Japan; forward in Burma, and outward in Java. Feminine thighs close, and male thighs open in most of ethnic dance. In Java, men's arms lift up and out, women's are held close to the body. Hand actions differ widely, and are important to nearly all forms, as the *mudras* in India and finger snapping and castanet playing of the Spanish flamenco. Head, face, and eye movements are often complicated and carefully choreographed.

Many ethnic groups are searching their mythology, legends, music, and history in order to find a true nucleus with which to build a lost tradition of dance among their group. This has happened in Israel, with the actual commissioning of artists and choreographers to select from Yemenite and Hebrew ritual to produce authentic and meaningful material and choreograph ethnic dance forms for the nation.

Folk Dance

As ethnic dance mirrors the traditional culture of a people, folk dance is geared very particularly to its national characteristics. Ethnic dance is a performance-display, a retelling of the legends and tales of a culture; folk dance is a communal, sharing, participation activity in which the people all join. It is closely related to folk song, folktale, folk costume, folk craft, language, work habits, weather, environment, food, and politics. Anything important to people, especially as they relate to each other, is both material and excuse for folk dancing. There are dances for celebrating current as well as traditional events, and few holidays pass without their complement of folk dances.

There are remarkable similarities among folk dances, yet the formations of the dances, the characteristic style of movement, and even the way a simple walk is executed, varies from one nation to the other, sometimes province to province, as does the rhythm, music, costume, and relationship of men and women. People who value folk dancing foster occasions when groups dance both for pleasure and display of national characteristics. Some nations rely on the folk music, dance, and gay costumes to symbolize their nation—indeed, travel posters with their pictures lure tourists to a land that cherishes the old tradition.

But the illusions of such advertising are soon shattered when we realize that not all people in Holland wear wooden shoes, or that the people of the exotic countries we visit do not wear their colorful costumes every day. Certainly the great masses of people do not leave their television viewing to dance folk dances any more than we do.

The stereotype of a particular dance step as "belonging" to a nation, such as the waltz to Austria, the schottische to Sweden, or the polka to Poland, has long been disproved. Combinations of steps belong to people in general. Because men have two legs and progress through space in much the same way, there are only a few things that anyone can do, regardless of nationality. One can progress alternately from one foot to the other, as in a walk or run; one can jump from two feet to two feet; or hop from one foot to the same foot. Other than crawling, rolling, or unusual action like sliding or knee and hand walking, man can only progress through space, in our atmosphere, by walking, running, jumping, and hopping, with their combinations and variations. Walks, runs, jumps, and hops abound in folk dancing, as they do in combination, such as a polka, which combines a hop and steps. Done in a broken rhythm, the fast hop is followed by three steps: hop, step-slide-close, step. Another basic folk dance step is the schottische, which is a combination of three steps and a hop, all in an even rhythm. Though they may be called by different names, or even pronounced differently, the polka, schottische, hop, jump, run, and walk are thoroughly international. Style may change but the mechanics are the same.

The experts say that knowing the steps and patterns of a dance is not enough, for this is not understanding the spirit of the country concerned. Those who value authenticity in folk dancing must study, search, experience, and even travel to the country concerned. Then there are those who simply enjoy the vigor and superficial excitement of a "foreign dance." It is quite possible to enjoy a session of folk dancing with little concern for style or spirit. Of course it blends in with all the rest of the recreational dance forms that serve a purely social-fun goal but it is no longer folk dance in its true nationalistic sense.

There are many active folk dance groups and clubs to whom authenticity is important. These, with special performing groups, and with those dancers who have learned from their fathers, form a nucleus to perpetuate folk dancing today. In many American cities there are national group meetings where the old country traditions are kept alive: a Polish wedding, a Greek baptism, or an Armenian picnic, where native language, music, songs, food, traditions, and dance are a natural occurrence.

Jazz Dance

Jazz, as a word, refers to music in which a melody is played against a steady background beat. Whoever plays the melody phrases it to his design and, staying with the beat, tries to fill more notes to a measure than were originally written for it. There were no rules for early jazz, and many of its black originators did not even read music.

Jazz dance first appeared in 1917 as "dance-songs" accompanied by jazz music One of the early songs was:

> First you Mooch to the left and you Mooch to the right,
> You do the Shimmie to your heart's delight,
> And then you whirl yourself around and 'round
> Goin'down, goin'down, till you're near the ground,
> Now you sway at the knees like a tree in the breeze
> Now buzz around just like the bumblebees,
> Then you do the Sooey around the hall,
>   That's nothing' but Scratchin' the Gravel, that's all.[6]

Some of the early steps were called: eagle rock, the buzz, shimmy-she, scratchin' the gravel, mooche, black bottom, Charleston, truckin', lindy, and jitterbug. Whether performed by blacks or whites, the early dancers revised and varied these basic steps, always leaving room for improvisation and addition of common movements like the sensual hip rolls, shoulder shakes, and isolated action of other body parts.

But always jazz dance follows the insistent beat of the music, sometimes parallel to it, sometimes syncopating the beat and embellishing it with complex rhythmic structures which only finally coincide with it. No longer is it the crude and relatively simple folksy form developed out of the action of black street people. Now it has all the sophistication that is inherent in the musical form called "progressive jazz." It has become more of a style than a distinct dance form.

Modern Dance, Classical

This is a term which is used increasingly to describe the early modern dance from the period of the Denishawn days and the sequential break from that group by Martha Graham, and then Doris Humphrey and Charles Weidman. Along with Tamiris and Hanya Holm of the New York Wigman school, these great dancers and choreographers shaped modern dance in the formative period of the late 1920s and early 1930s. Even as Isadora rebelled against the ballet, these moderns rebelled against the fairly superficial character dances of Denishawn. They explored the body in action, and gave consideration to choreographic materials that reflected social anxieties and, finally, something outside the dancer's self. Themes of universal mythology, dramatic conflict and fundamental ideologies abounded. They explored new dance paths, with the potentials for movement from contemporary life. They sought to give "physical substance to things felt," to reveal human behavior and emotion.

It is easy to identify the start of classical modern dance, but where it stopped being classical and became contemporary 1970s is hard to say. It may be that we are too close to the transition and a greater perspective is needed. There are still many dancers and choreographers who resent and resist the new avenues to dance. They insist the old ways are best. This is, of course, the full cycle of rebellion: building, producing, perpetuating, and then facing a new rebellion. Without the conviction of a dancer, choreographer, director, or teacher of a once new and vital manifestation of dance, where would the upcoming dance rebels have found their point of view and foundation? The rebels of today become the giants of tomorrow and the classicists of the next day. The only problem is in finding meaningful words to describe the changes—when and if you are able to isolate them.

Modern Dance, Contemporary

In the 1940s dancers like Sybil Shearer, Merle Marsicano, Erick Hawkins, Merce Cunningham, and Katherine Litz began to explore the possibilities for dance development that did not spring from literal or musical domination. They began to examine personal gesture, free-flowing movement, associated movement episodes, contrasts in phrasing and dynamics, kinetic images, improvisations in movement itself, and economies of action, as well as forms out of movement functions and out of principles of surrealism and the assertions of the individuals as well as their movements.

A second generation of modern dancers were at work, and their concerts were met with dismay, shock, and even abhorrence by many, with bravos by a few, and with some members of the audience stalking out in the middle of a dance. It was the same old story: new approaches to choreography, content, accompaniment, costuming, and decor only enhance veneration of the traditional. The old must be better, the new must be bad. And here dancers were really *doing* what they had been saying they were doing since the days of Isadora. They were using movement for itself, not to tell a story. Dance was becoming inventive within its own terms. Cunningham, in his first solo recital in 1944, was the first to mark a complete independence from the first generation "greats" of modern dance. Within an existential framework, movement was freed from the necessity to fit other demands than its own. No longer must dancers accommodate to musical rhythm or story development; they could operate in terms of the laws of action and repose—from dance logic, or, as Alwin Nikolais says, "down to motion as a basis of the art, not emotion."

Modern Jazz

This is yet another variation of jazz dance, a style that uses movement from many dance sources. Some say that ballet training is necessary because it combines this classical dance form with our own native character dance steeped in jazz music. Basic tap dancing is also used, which helps the dancer to move into the floor while using torso and hip movement. An important emphasis is upon isolating particular movements of head, shoulders, arms, rib cage, pelvis, knee, and ankle, all in combination with "jazz" progressions.

To some, this is the American ethnic dance, a return to an old form with all the nuances of a dynamic new world. According to Jack Cole, one of the pioneers in Modern Jazz dance, it is akin to jazz as urban folk music, expressing the society out of which it came. It is available to the untrained, it is "accessible."

Musical Comedy

This encompasses the musical plays that were called operettas, popular in Europe. As in opera, dance has in many instances been incidental to the plot, but since choreographers like George Balanchine, Agnes de Mille, Jerome Robbins, Michael Kidd, Doris Humphrey, and Tamiris, the dance sequences have assumed a major role. The first real dance in a musical was *The Black Crook*, in 1866, and, as with many of the earlier plays, was balletic in style. Soon a freer form of ballet appeared in musical comedy, often called "modern ballet." It was in folk dance, social dance, tap, acrobatic, and other spectacular forms that the real material for this form lay. Agnes de Mille's dances for *Oklahoma,* in

1943, really marked the new era and Jerome Robbins's *Fancy Free* and *On the Town* assured dance a place in this medium.

Pantomime

This is a vast field, a highly specialized form of conventionalized gesture, imitative of nature and natural expression. The movement communicates a story, mood, character, or illusion. The mime is not an imitator, rather he accents, dramatizes, and comments on character. He provides images through which he shows his vision to the world—without words. This is an ancient form of expression and was considered a great art in Greece and Rome. Pantomime has been used extensively in ballet to further the story and develop the action. A few famous pantomimists like Charlie Chaplin, Marcel Marceau, and Etienne Decroux have developed it to performing-art status. Lotte Gosslar has more clearly fused modern dance with her pantomime, excelling in comedy. Many of the great clowns of circus, stage, screen, and television use pantomime.

Preclassic Dance

"Classic" refers to the classical ballet in dance terminology, preclassic to the court dances in the stylized and decorous manner of the early sixteenth century French courts. During the fifteenth century a great dance movement swept across cultural Europe and music was written to serve it. From Provence, in the late Gothic period, the troubadours, according to the precepts of their chivalric code, chose one lady as symbolic of the Virgin, to whom they devoted their service. At first their dances were little more than promenades, but in them was the seed of all the social dances to come.

With political changes in Provence, many troubadours fled to various European courts and took with them their dance and chivalrous style. Their dances were taken indoors and modified to fit the shape of the rooms, resulting in circle and line dance patterns.

The routine for court dances was almost always the same. At one end of the hall the king and queen led the dancing and couples followed according to rank. At the end of the procession couples were lined up along the walls and the dancers who performed at the king's command were at the farthest end. Some of the dances were for small groups or trios, but mostly for couples. The dance position was usually open, or side by side with the gentleman leading the figures.

Members of the court were instructed in social etiquette as well as the dance steps and style. The dancing master made sure that all knew how to greet the king and mingle at court. The costumes of the dancers ranged from fancy powdered wigs to towering hats and jeweled hairpieces; from colorful tight-fitting breeches on the men to voluminous skirts for the ladies, plus pointed-toe shoes, jeweled "stomachers," and fluttering scarves and ribbons. Accompanied by the airs and graces of the aristocracy, these occasions at court became more and more stately and ceremonial. By the time of Louis XIV, considerable refinement of movement and form had taken place and charming conceits had arisen.

Usually dances were repeated many times, often in theme and variation form. They moved from pavanne to galliard to sarabande, the sequence that was later to become the basis for the suite, sonata, and symphony. In these dances there was much advancing and retreating, rising on the toes and down, leg extension and toe pointing, bowing, and dignified promenading.

A sensational manuscript in gold on black paper, *Le Manuscrit des Basses Danses de la Biblioteque de Bourgigne,* in which the theory of the Basse Dance was described, appeared during the first part of the fifteenth century. Another manuscript (*c.* 1490-1500), perhaps the first printed book on social dance, *L'Art et Instruction de Dien Danser* by Thoulouze, repeated much of the "Golden Manuscript." The sixteenth century marked the Italian Renaissance, when all the arts flourished and dancing masters like Domenico of Ferraro, who created the Basse dance, and William the Jew, emphasized style, posture, and display in many dances they composed and exported to France and England. Catherine de Medici, queen of France, fostered her imported Italian dances and blended them into forms suitable for the French court and salon dance. The elegant court dancer became a politically and socially prominent figure. All important people danced, indeed, they learned how to become ladies and gentlemen by studying dance.

The Basse dances were solemn, with slow, grave rhythms. The Haute dances were lively, performed with skipping steps. Of the latter, the lively galliard was a favorite of Queen Elizabeth of Britain and the fast courante was favored by Louis XIV of France. The minuet came to be the leading court dance, changed from the gay folk dance of Poitou to a stately and elegant dance for the formal and precise aristocrats. For over a century and a half the minuet opened every state ball in the civilized world. Some of the more popular preclassic dances included (in chronological order) are:

Carole was an ancient open or closed chain dance.

Basse dance, a descendant of the knightly Middle Ages, had the feet close to the floor in a gliding step, in triple time.

Branle, originally a "follow-the-leader" peasant dance, later developed into a simple two-step, "step-close-step," moving forward, backward, or sideward in direction.

Allemande, in duple meter, beginning on an upbeat, is a slow and sentimental German dance with the dancers' hands joined throughout.

Bouree, in lively duple meter, beginning with an upbeat on the fourth quarter note. It has many crossing and cutting steps.

Chaconne is an early Spanish form in triple meter, usually made up of two lines, with ladies in one, men in the other, performing "couplets."

Courante is in fast triple time, starting on an upbeat. There is much advancing and retreating with runs, small jumps, and glides.

Galliard, in lively triple meter, a gay couple dance with little runs and jumps.

Gavotte, in fast duple time, starting with two eighths on the fourth quarter note. This is usually a circle dance, with the ladies in the center facing in the opposite direction to their men partners; "three steps and ensemble" was a favored step.

Minuet, probably from the Latin *minimus,* was a moderate 3/4 meter dance, completely expressing the artificiality of the French court, made up of stately walks, balances to one's partner, turns, and bows.

Gigue, quickest and liveliest of all, usually in 6/8 meter, similar to the Irish jig.

Pavanne (pavo-peacock), performed in slow duple meter, from the Spanish church ceremony, a proud and formal advance-retreat, glide-turn, elegant, and deep-bowing couple dance, sometimes accompanied by castanets.

Rigaudon, in lively duple meter, starting on the fourth quarter note with two-eighth counts, a light and brittle dance with many runs, hops, turns, and balances.

Sarabande, in triple meter, this is the slowest of all the court dances. Of Spanish origin, it is noble, solemn, beginning definitely on the first beat. A favorite sarabande was performed by taking four slow steps forward, four back, couples walking between the lines formed by other dancers, with many elaborate bows throughout.

Most of what we know of preclassic dances today has been highlighted by the music that was written for it, as well as the forms that came to be the foundation for so much of classical music.

Religious Dance

This is another example of choreographic approach or thematic manipulation, which has often been regarded as a particular kind of dance. Here again, any of the dance forms may be used to relate to religious services. Sometimes this results in acting out the words of a psalm or Biblical verse; it may resemble a procession to the altar or the setting of the mood for spiritual experience. The dance itself is not religious, but the costume, music quality, accompanying narration, and title have religious overtones.

Social or Ballroom Dance

The curious use of "social" to indicate this dance form is only meaningful because we are accustomed to the term.

All kinds of dance are social, in that they are involved with people relating to each other. But in this case it refers to boy-girl, man-woman dancing with each other, as couples—socializing. It may be that the first social dance was a primitive courtship or fertility rite which evolved, through the years, into the socially acceptable male-female relationship we know today.

Langer contends that social dance still evidences "magnetic forces that unit a group, most simply, a couple, of dancers" and that "its normal fate is simply the shift from religious to romantic uses."[7]

The dance we do today has been influenced by earlier dances, dance music, particular bands, social changes, wars, changing attitudes of people, television, films, and a host of personalities who sing, dance, talk, and organize events for young people.

From the beginning, new styles and relationships of dancers occurred as social conditions changed. A marked change from the stately minuets, galliards, and waltzes of the courts to the country dances, quadrilles, and reels of the 1800s, took place in the twentieth century, when ragtime and the blues gave birth to the grizzly bear, the bunny hug, turkey trot, and other animal-named dances. Soon after came the galop, two-step, tango, and foxtrot (the one typically American dance). Irene and Vernon Castle, great American dance innovators, brought grace, poise, and distinction to the social dance scene with their quiet sophistication. One of the young men associated with them was Arthur

Murray, who became one of the great teachers on the American scene. The toddle, shimmy, Charleston and black bottom came in the mid-1920s; the rumba, shag, Suzy Q, and jitterbug in the 1930s; the New Yorker, bebop, mambo, and hokey-pokey in the 1940s; the cha-cha-cha, merengue, and bossa nova in the 1950s; and the twist and rock in the 1960s, with people enjoying each new variation.

With each new name and pattern came a characteristic musical style, orchestration, and performance. Soon the term "ballroom" dancing came to be used interchangeably with "social" dance, because the occasion was still called a "ball" and was held in a "ballroom." Later rock forms were often called "discotheque," or were certainly danced in "discotheques," referring to the French recording disc; and because the dances used less space, they were often done in smaller clubs and coffeehouses. Through improved electronic techniques, increased volume of sound came to mark the whole field of rock music. The youth of the world were entranced.

Before the twist and rock, almost all the dances, each called the current "fad" dance of its time, involved man and woman in closed dance position, the man leading and the woman ready to respond. This leadership role paralleled the commonly accepted roles in society. Perhaps it was the change in woman's view of her place in the world, or a shift in man's sense of responsibility as the ever-present leader, but with the twist and rock dances, contact positions were dropped and males and females stood apart from each other, making their own decisions about the dance patterning. They stayed in one place, no longer progressing counterclockwise around the dance floor. As partners, and aware of the other's presence, they seemed not overly concerned with each other. Perhaps this was an expression of freedom, initiative, women's liberation, or perhaps only a resistance to another traditional form. In addition to the change in dance position, the actual movement of rock dances changed from the sedate and genteel gliding of traditional social dance to a rather nervous emphasis upon individual erotic pelvic actions. What had hitherto been considered fit for the burlesque show only, had now become acceptable for social dancing.

In the early 1970s renewed interest in traditional foxtrots, waltzes, jitterbug, and the Latin forms, as well as the old music forms, reappeared. Young people who had never assumed a contact dance position found this intriguing. The old had again become new!

Spectacular Dance

Essentially performance oriented, this dance form deals with a movement spectacle or extravaganza designed to captivate, entertain, or bedazzle an audience with the dancer's technical virtuosity, the flamboyance of sets and costumes, volume of musical accompaniment, and personality and appeal of the performers. Whether done in a night club, a variety stage show, a circus arena, on a television sound stage, or as a part of a community gathering, the dancer is trying to catch the attention of the spectator and either entertain, delight, amuse, or arouse him.

The movement performed may be adapted from any of the other dance forms, or it may seem little more than a parade of beautiful girls, a display of erotic charms, or a series of precision leg kicks. Sometimes the performer combines singing, jokes, juggling, and narration with the action. The only criteria for what will be included in such a display is the reaction of the audience. The act has been successful if the audience claps and roars its approval.

Some of the popular display forms have included acrobatic dancing, tap dancing, and jazz, with an occasional bit of folk dance, ethnic dance, and social dance mixed in.

Tap Dance

Tap dancing blends the Irish jig and the English clog with the Negro shuffle, coming up with the typically American soft shoe. Sometimes called "song and dance," soft shoe was followed by the syncopated buck and wing, which is the essence of tap dancing. Characteristic of this form is the rhythmic footwork that results from the regular and syncopated tapping or slapping of the ball of the foot, or the heel, on the floor. It is said to have influenced jazz—it is certain to have been influenced by jazz. Two of the greatest tap dancers, Bill Robinson and Fred Astaire, were a part of the vernacular dance that has so influenced what we see today on stage, screen, and television.

Tap dancers use a wide assortment of steps, body movements, rhythms, and combinations of all three. Sometimes there is agreement on names for them, often not. Sometimes the action is limited to movement from the waist down, but more often the whole body is used, even into the air. Some combinations seem balletic in nature. "Jazz" steps consist of body movement like "falling off a log," and "off to

Buffalo." "Flash" steps include acrobatic combinations with large leg and body actions. Step combinations, called "routines," are fitted to music, often starting and finishing with a "time step," which was originally done to set the tempo for musicians in theaters where tap dancers performed. The old timers say that tap dancing has lost its "punch" and has become "move-around dancing" and balletic. More and more it is considered as an adjunct rather than a distinct movement style in itself.

Hindsight

Each of these dance forms came in a blaze of revolt. Some people were shocked, others delighted. But soon each became commonplace, and when the time came, were transformed, disguised, or replaced by a new form. An example of resistance to one of the forms was described in a book published in 1893, written by Rev. W. W. Gardner:

> There is no disguising the fact, that promiscuous dancing, including the Waltz and Round-dances, to which the 'square dances' naturally lead, are *essentially licentious,* and legitimately tend to the violation of the Seventh Commandment. In proof of this fact, 'the chief of Police of New York city in his official Report some years since stated that three fourths (¾) of the abandoned girls of the city were ruined by dancing.'[8]

Looking back, each of the earlier forms were right and plausible because of the nature of the people in that time and place. While some may try to keep, or even return to the old, they are seldom vital unless imbued with the energy of the contemporary world. As period or museum pieces, yes; as manifestations of their time, no.

> Cultural relativity, with its existentialist view of culture, has now destroyed the final prop of fundamentalist tribal man—that inveterate absolutist whose very animal nature it is to embody experiments in value-paradigms. This latest threat to human narcissism seems shattering, for it means that the culture heroes and charismatic ancestors of the sacred past are no longer gods, but only men like ourselves. Still the struggle with each successively dethroned vanity has always heretofore been edifying; and from each discovered limitation we can learn. But it means the scrutiny of a most sacred belief—that our culture is the distilled essence of a cumulative and historic evolution toward an ultimate new Eden of knowledge and truth. . . .[9]

7
Art Is Art Is Art

In art there are no final answers; there are only questions that lead to new ways of understanding.

Katherine Kuh, *critic*

The arts are said to appeal to the idealist, the dreamer, and science to the realist, the pragmatist. But this is another stereotype which has no basis in fact. Many scientists are dreamers and can't balance their checkbooks, while more than a few artists are neat and understand mathematical equations. The differences between artists and scientists are more difficult to discover than the differences in the art of today and of yesterday.

> An art is not responsible for its own reception and quality. The responsibility rests with the state of culture out of which it arises. It is not a separate entity grafted upon a people. It arises from the qualities that characterize the society from which it stems. If the society is a crazy, mixed-up mess, then it is likely that the art will illuminate that fact. If it is tight and moralistic, the art will reflect that. As a matter of fact, this is part of the function of art. It defines the culture of a people. By itself, art cannot change its heritage.[1]

The Esthetic Dilemma

Esthetics is a slippery word that has many overtones and meanings. Yet when the word is used, people nod their heads as if they understood each other. "That is esthetic," says one. Another remarks, "Oh yes, *very* esthetic." And there will be someone with, "Well, it may have some slight esthetic value, but I don't really care for it." How can there be such mixed response? Is this thing called "esthetic" a characteristic possessed *by* something, or is it a quality conferred *upon* something by the perceiver? Obviously it is the object that stimulates a response from the observer. It would be helpful to examine the bases for such appraisals made by different people, but the more we attempt to unclutter the problem the more complicated it becomes. The very word "esthetic," and its underlying concepts, seem to encompass any number of reactions, ranging from the sensually pleasing and morally suitable, to the traditionally acceptable. Often the word is used as if the mere statement in itself were sufficient, as if in the uttering of "esthetic" an obvious ultimate is either present or lacking. Clive Bell remarked, "about no subject has so little been said that is at all to the purpose."[2]

Is "esthetic" a universally recognized state, or is it a changing and variable phenomenon? Could it be a fleeting and intangible "something" that is impossible to qualify? Almost universally the term is associated with art, but esthetic perception is not limited to art products. It may occur as delight and approval of nature, personal attributes, games, food, arguments, daydreams, companionship, or even the exhilaration of being in a crowd. It appears that there are relatively few controversies about esthetic judgments in anything except art, probably because it is pointless to criticize clouds, shells, or sunsets. But there are great conflicts in the field of art, as well as its varying standards of excellence.

Widespread use of the word "esthetic" characterizes an experience or a product that is beautiful, harmonious, pleasurable, valued, or even truthful—certainly acceptable in some way. But there is little agreement about the particular nature of such an experience that would differentiate it from one that is nonesthetic. Some of the conditions ascribed to the esthetic experience include significance, perfection, clarity, coherence, form, and unified vitality. These, like all of the other elusive and subtle qualities, are identified and evaluated according to the taste and appreciation of the participant-beholder who is prejudiced and guided by his own intent and experience. Spinoza once said: "We desire nothing because it is good, it is good only because we desire it."

From the Greek word *aisthetikos*, meaning perception-feeling, the philosopher Baumgarten coined the word "aesthetics" to identify "the science of sensuous knowledge." Generally accepted as that branch of philosophy dealing with values in expression-perception, esthetics has been called the "philosophy of art," the "science of beauty," "the theory of taste," and "the analysis and interpretation of formulated experience." Santayana called it "the theory of perception or susceptibility"; to Langer it was "the sensuous presentation given in any experience," and always affected by imagination. Dewey said it was "the heightened awareness of experience"; to Kant, "the judgment of beauty in art and nature"; and to Hegel, "beauty in art alone." To Clive Bell, "the esthetic experience always arises from the personal experience of a *peculiar* emotion." Dewey wrote:

> An object is peculiarly and dominantly esthetic, yielding the enjoyment characteristic of esthetic perception, when the factors that determine anything which can be called *an* experience are lifted high above the threshold of perception and are made manifest for their own sake.[3]

The apparent agreement among many about beauty as the key aspect of the esthetic is only helpful at first glance. This does not clarify anything, for there is even less agreement about the nature of beauty. Variously it is that which agrees with some predetermined criteria, perpetuates some technique form, or simply that which delights the observer. To some, beauty is the vivid expression of reality, regardless of unpleasant attributes; to others, beauty must be uplifting, "ideal." Santayana wrote that "esthetics is concerned with the perception of values," and continued, "beauty is a species of value."[4]

What is the esthetic experience? Sometimes identified with moralistic, sometimes intellectual, and often hedonistic (self-pleasure) reactions, it evokes positive and satisfying response with little conscious reasoning. Intuition seems sharp and clear. There is a state of alert and poised awareness, an interaction and being-at-one with the experience that *does something to us*. Such a phrase as, "that is an esthetic experience, the other is not," implies the presence or absence of constituent characteristics. Another usage, "This is *more* esthetic than that," implies a relative scale of attributes.

But is it possible to dissect out and agree on some of the essentials? Is there an international esthetic, something that is the same among all men, regardless of time and place? Are esthetic concepts of inland New Guinea the same as urban New York? Were they the same in prewar as in postwar Japan? Were first century Greek values different from those of Athens in 1974? And what of the values in colonial Virginia as compared to those of contemporary Hollywood?

Concepts of the esthetic readily change according to the time, place, and all of the things that affect man. But some values seem to go on forever; for example, there are many today who still agree with the ancient and ultimate tenet of Golden Age Greece: the Parthenon manifests an order and harmonious form that represents the valued standards of truth, beauty, and the moral—all according to an established formula. And standards such as these revolutionized the Western world. Indeed, there are few of us today who do not still cherish some of these standards. How do you stand on such an esthetic ultimate?

With new perspectives, increased concern for the individual, churning social changes, fantastic scientific and technological discoveries, changing value systems, and old as well as newly-acquired prejudices, the artist of today seeks new significances beyond the readily observable reality, beyond the nicely packaged rules of Greek unity-coherence-symmetry. He, with Shahn, considers form as the shape of content, and, with McLuhan, the medium its own message. And he is often considered untrained (because he forsakes the old forms), uncontrolled (because he develops new methods), and an anathema to acceptable taste in art (because he finds a new condition for the esthetic). He has forsaken the traditional pattern of excellence. Could it be that the artist of today has found another pattern?

The principles of classical Greece are no more or less esthetic than those of the contemporary world—they are simply different. Different because this is a different world and it is a different time. Many people in this world have accepted some of the changed values, others resist with a dogged and morbid tenacity. Perhaps as communications and interaction among people improve, so will concepts of their esthetic experiences have more in common. But people and times will continue to change, and as they change so too will their values and taste.

It has been said that people make evaluative judgments on the basis of relative merit. Some of the criteria for appraisal are moral or intellectual, some are religious or economic, and some of them are esthetic. It is difficult to distinguish the esthetic criteria from all the rest because there are no clear characteristics or associated emotions. This may account for some of the confusion we face in attempting to isolate such factors. The avowed esthetic response may well be intellectual or erotic, for there is bound to be considerable interaction among all of them. Clearly it is the whole person who is reacting, with all of his experiences, biases, interacting values, and habitual responses. That he can identify bits and pieces of criteria upon which he bases his appraisal is remarkable. To sift out all of the "esthetic criteria" is impossible.

Perhaps we are asking the wrong question. We may be attempting to define something that can't be defined. We may be trying to isolate how many of certain properties of something there are, when there really are no such properties. Can we identify "esthetic" as a closed concept? Or is it a relative and open one? We may need fewer confusing inquiries about elements of the esthetics and more descriptions of the conditions under which we use the term. How then can we understand and describe the functioning of the concept?

Each man's connotations of his perceptions are his own, and so too are his values for judging his perceptions. There seem to be few unchanging and identifiable things which all people agree are common to the esthetic experience, rather it is a complicated construct made up of innumerable interacting elements.

What anyone considers esthetic is affected by his perceptual acuity, emotional state, imagination, freedom, taste, experience, breadth of appreciation and, more particularly, his idea of beauty, truth, pleasure, and reality. Some of the inevitable forces that act upon him, as he proposes his value estimates, are cherished value systems; the security of the readily and traditionally acceptable, moral, and religious principles; political and social propaganda; and even some barely hidden elements of magic.

Esthetics is concerned with philosophic theory and offers no objective formulae or proofs; it simply deals with the value aspect of perception. The term functions to assess values that depend upon group and/or individually held standards, intangible as they may be.

Esthetics and Movement

Human movement is man's most pervasive and characteristic attribute, and he values movement for many reasons. There is the private manifestation of movement, that is, *my* movement, and the public form, which is *your* movement. The first is a matter of my own participation, under my control; the other is the observed performance of someone else. The purpose the movement serves will necessarily affect the performer's or the observer's judgment of it.

Movement serving functional objectives is not only desirable but necessary for every human being. The more man's movement serves his function, the better it is for him, and this he values. It is especially good when needs are met with maximum efficiency and minimum effort—with apparent ease, control, and with no unnecessary action. It is the controlled tension that results in the qualities of "grace," "poise," and "beauty"—sometimes called "esthetic."

Certainly the exhilaration and feeling of personal power of *my* movement fulfilling its purpose is recognized by anyone who has excelled in movement. Watching others move with power, range, and coordination—serving their purpose with equal skill—is a positive experience with potential value for the observer.

In most games, sports, and play activities, the element of competition is paramount, though efficiency and ease of performance are surely important to such success. In other activities such as skating, gymnastics, and diving it is not just the correct execution and accomplishment of the act that is important but "the way it is done," the quality and style—the "breath"—the spirit of the performance that is stressed. Here premium is placed not on the immediate win-or-lose of the action but upon the formed performance in itself, initiated and completed by the performer.

And so we not only value movement for its potential to easily fulfill functional needs, but we appreciate the quality and style of its performance. In games and sports we place great premium upon its use to outmaneuver, overpower, outlast an opponent.

And what's more, we have the tribal stereotypes, the shape and action clichés which insidiously affect our concepts of "the acceptable." At one extreme is the bulging muscleman who evidences the conformation of the "virile male," who moves with relentless strength, endurance, and precision. The stereotyped "woman" is long-limbed, lithe, measuring 36-22-36, moving with "cat-like grace and poise." Among any group of people, for a variety of reasons, the favored shape and action will influence their evaluation of the worth of the attributes.

Our concepts of acceptable and unacceptable posture and movement patterns derive from many other sources, some social, racial, and

Shizuko Iwamatsu

even national. For example, we praise the baby who pats the top of his head, "smart baby," we say. But when he waggles his thumb on the end of his nose, we snatch at his hand and shout "no no no." In one of our classes an exchange student from rural, central Africa disliked standing opposite students practicing an overhead basketball shot—it was too much like the action of throwing a spear. One of our graduate students resented the gesture of a right arm raised diagonally upward. He had been in the Dutch underground during the Hitler terror. To the kindergarten teacher the arm raised simply means "May I go to the bathroom," but that, too, is not considered "esthetic."

"Little girls," says grandmama, "do not stand with their feet spread wide apart"; "Big boys do *not* skip," growls Uncle Jonathan. "Stand up when the band plays *Dixie*"; "Salute when you pass an officer"; "Bow to your elders." Certain movements are good—right—appropriate, and beautiful; others are bad—wrong—in poor taste, and ugly. And you may be sure that these directives, and the memory of these directives, will affect our future choice of movement as well as our appraisal of the movement of others.

A teacher of a social-recreational dance class in our department was distressed because one of the physical education students seemed incapable of performing a polka step. The teacher had explained, demonstrated, and cajoled, but the student still could not distinguish a walk from a hop. And this student was one of the great javelin throwers of the track team. On the field, in appropriate shorts, jacket, and shoes he performed a walk, a hop, a run, and a step-close-step-hop with exquisite skill and conviction. In one situation the disguised action of a polka was valued and meaningful, in the other it was irrelevant, confusing, and impossible to perform. He found different meanings in each situation, and certainly valued the significance of one more than the other.

Some people consider golf a great and challenging movement experience, to others it is a witless walk after a little ball, another swat, and another pursit of the ball. Some people love to swim, others resent the temperatures, texture, and questionable support of the water; they would rather ski. Nonskiers dislike the slippery surface, the biting wind, the chapped lips, the aching knees. Some play tennis, not because they enjoy the game but because they meet the right people at the tennis club; one girl I know rides a horse through the park every dawn because the most eligible bachelor in town has done this for years.

Some people enjoy watching soccer, others prefer football; and then some like bird watching. To many the spectacle of the ballet is a delight; others favor bullfights.

Even greater discrepancy of detail is possible about the likes and dislikes of movement. Some people enjoy slow, smooth, and sweeping movement; others like it jerky, jabbing, and accented. Some like motion high into the air; others love to crawl about on the floor. To some, small and contained movement is best; but to others the broad, open, and striking gesture is better. Why do people vary so in their attitudes to movement? Well, probably because there are so many variables involved, so much potential for variation and, most important, because people have variable experiences, preferences, and responses. This is further substantiated by the fact that even those living within a relatively tight group show equal evidence of individual taste, attitude, and sense of value.

The extent to which our movement habits and preferences are related to personality, or vice versa, makes for interesting speculation. Among psychologically disturbed patients there are quite characteristic gestures and actions to be observed. And the very essence of dramatic characterization by the actor or the dancer calls for conscious adaptation, use, and exaggeration of identifiable posture and movement patterns.

But we are not interested in the facts or verifications *of* movement but rather in the interpretation, appraisal, or value judgments *about* movement. Values, unlike facts, are often imaginary, usually private, and mostly peculiar. While facts have uniform character for many observers, values are intangible and depend upon subjective preferences.

"Every Little Movement Has a Meaning of Its Own," went the old song. But it is even more complicated than that; every little movement has several meanings of its own, and it is usually different in different kinds of situations, in the presence of different people. And then, too, the same movement may mean different things to different people at different times of the day and the year.

It is rather amazing that movement, which is so easily executed and often so thoughtlessly performed or observed, can have so *many* different connotations. But, of course, it is this property of symbolization—of finding significances and relating them to other experiences—that is characteristic of man.

The following seem to be some of the conditions under which *I* favor *my own* movement:

1. It fulfills a personal need, serves a function.
2. I can do it with minimum effort and maximum results.
3. It makes me feel good, perhaps relieves tension, increases circulation, reestablishes equilibrium, etc.

4. It reminds me of a positive situation, person, event.
5. It fits within my value system, agrees with my taste, augments what I hold to be "right," "good," "true," and "worthy."
6. It increases my personal status, power, ego, acceptance.
7. It celebrates or fulfills some habit, cherished ceremonial, or social rite.
8. It projects and communicates as a performing art.
9. It fulfills its point as entertainment or spectacle.

And the following are conditions under which I favor the movement of others.

1. The performers have excellent technical skill.
2. There is projection of power, ease, and control.
3. The action is devoid of strain, can be seen for its own sake and not for its effort.
4. There is personal involvement with the performer or the action.
5. It reminds me of a pleasant occasion, person, event.
6. The performance proceeds according to my estimate (I win the bet).
7. Augments my taste and values, is not counter to my standards.
8. Presents a moving and surprising formulation of movement, one which adds to my perceptual experience.
9. Has erotic or entertainment appeal.
10. Fulfills racial, social, or nationalistic needs.
11. Perpetuates a traditional form that I cherish.
12. Has dramatic, emotional appeal that moves me.
13. Communicates as a performing art.

Seldom does anyone stop to analyze a movement event, rather they react with satisfaction or discouragement with their own action and praise or rejection of the action of others. To the extent that these reactions are judgments of value they are in the range of the concept "esthetics." Esthetic appraisals encompass the broad spectrum of human behavior and experience, and philosophers, called "estheticians," have long been probing this area and have proposed many theories and written voluminously about it.

What Is Art?

Everyone wants to understand art. Why not try to understand the songs of a bird?

Pablo Picasso, painter

The question "What is Art?" is actually several questions in the guise of one apparently simple one. There is no chance of coming up with a universally acceptable answer. In a society where such a premium is put upon numbers and verification, art is a stranger. It is easy enough to classify the number of pictures painted, determine the ratio of color to line, compare tonal and rhythmic structures in music, or count the number of dancers within a particular stage area, but these are all mechanics, not the art form.

Complexity only increases, because art is concerned not with just the product but with the process of creativity as well. The art product is the completed work, the public display, the presentation, or representation. It is the painting, sculpture, building, poem, novel, or the performed music, dance, drama, or whatever. Entangled within this is the intention of the maker and the response of the observer. There is even controversy as to whether it is an art product when no one perceives it; some say it is just therapy for the artist! Is the product perceived? Is it understood? Is it appreciated? Is it criticized? What makes for good or bad art?

The art process is fundamentally the creative action involving skill, formulation, personal conviction, and perseverance. There is no magic formula, and no one is quite sure when the process ends—sometimes the artist simply stops. There seems to be a continual battle as to whether form or content is most important, as if one could exist without the other.

The bases for perception, judgment, and evaluation are as diverse as the people who perceive, judge, and evaluate. The degree to which a critic does whatever a critic *should* do only outlines the cycle of the merry-go-round. Around and around we go, following the same path but not really getting anywhere. We continue to ask the singular question, "What is Art?"

As with esthetics, many people here suggested that we reject the hopeless task of determining *the* nature of art and, rather, investigate the conditions under which we use the term, and apply it to art products. From a mass of available literature on all aspects of art, the anthology edited by Melvin Rader is an example of the mind-boggling array of diverse opinion. In his *A Modern Book of Esthetics*,[5] art is considered, among other things, as: illusion, play, beauty, imitation of nature, expression of emotion, catharsis, intuition, imagination, wish fulfillment, will to power, pleasure, craft, and significant form. In W. E. Kerrick's *Art and Philosophy*,[6] another example of an impressive collection of points of view about the nature of art, problems of interpretation, and criticism are presented. Susanne Langer's *Reflections on Art*[7] includes views by artists, critics, and philosophers from widely scattered publications of the past sixty years, collected and assembled by one of the great philosophers of this era. Each of these is significant in its contribution to art theory.

Few of us ponder at great length the nature of art. Rather we assume what is called art is art. Or if it is beautiful, it is art; or if it pleases us, it is art; or if it is in a gallery, performance hall, or museum, it is art. "I don't know anything about art, but I know what I like" is the classic remark; or, there is the pleasant assumption that "if you say it's art, it's art."

There is a widespread though mistaken tendency to equate art with painting, an artist with a painter, artistic as referring to some aspect of a painted picture, studying art with learning to paint, and an art exhibit with a showing of paintings. But there are other arts. Painting is concerned with visually experienced line, color, and design, manifest within two-dimensional space. Music, on the other hand, involves audio perception of tone, rhythm, and pattern of sound as it proceeds in time. Poetry depends upon metaphor and simile in the manipulation of words and language. Sculptors form three-dimensional figures in stone or clay to be seen or touched. Dramatists write words in a play for actors to perform in a theater. Dancers move through space, in time, and with dynamic control of their kinetic energy. While art forms differ in medium, form, and perception, they share the common attributes of art.

The use of terms like "fine arts," "industrial arts," "domestic arts," "black arts," "useful arts," "martial arts," and "popular arts" probably grew out of the association of the word "art," first among the Greeks, with skill or craft. Fine arts has usually included painting, sculpture, music, literature, drama, architecture, and dance, though even this has varied throughout the years. The widespread use of art to qualify anything done expertly may lend prestige to that activity, but it only dilutes the meaning of art. We hear of "the art of making a cake, scrubbing a floor, or jumping rope," and it is obvious that the reference is to performance skill only.

To many, in our pragmatic world, art is a luxury, a special kind of activity far removed from everyday living, to be enjoyed on vacations, rainy weekends, or after retirement. Sometimes the excuse is: "I don't know anything about art, it's wasted on me," or "Someday I'll have time to learn more about art, then I can go to a gallery or concert and know what's going on." To others, art is a part of everyday life, a thing of joy, a basis for fulfillment. One's point of view will be determined by whether art is considered some unchanging and particular manifestation which is either "art" or "not-art"; or as an open concept of formed experience with a variety of techniques and manifestations.

The question "Is it art?" has become almost irrelevant because concepts of art change so rapidly. Distinction between painting and sculpture, as separate mediums, is less obvious. Between plastic arts and theater is the "happening," which raises questions about traditional assumptions. A new interaction between art and life seems to affirm that new relationships are possible. The question "Is it art?", with its assumption of absolute and identifiable standards, seems less and less possible in a world where everything else is relative.

Origins of Art

Early man must have improvised with sound, movement, scratching on stone and sand, molding, and using signs, either haphazardly, out of anxiety, for amusement, or as a magical evocation. When he developed his mystical ceremonies and rites is not known, but that he did practice them is sure, and he continues to do so. If anything could be considered the seed of art to come it would be these communal ceremonies. Collingwood has suggested that magic is a part of the process of arousing emotion either to consolidate effective forces for collective morale or to generate in others the emotions that are detrimental to them. In short, the function of magic is to raise or damage morale. "Magical activity is a kind of dynamo supplying the mechanism of practical life with the emotional current that drives it."[8]

Rites have changed immeasurably since prehistoric times, but man still struggles to come to terms with the unknown whether "hunting the mammoth or the moon." According to Susanne Langer, "The forms of expressive acts—speech and gesture, song and sacrifice—are the symbolic transformations which minds of certain species, at certain stages of their development . . . produce."[9] The strange red symbols on the walls at Altamira have been surmised to be sacred, magical symbols, known only to the initiated. They probably were abstractions of the original magical meanings as well as simplification and concentration of natural forms. According to many artists, this is the essential element in all art: the transformation of material to a planned and vital illusion.

The roots of art, as his religion, reach back to the start of man's behavior, mythology, specialized rites, ceremonial rituals, and growing awareness of his human potential. Early attempts at self-adornment, simple inventions, and passionate need to express his wants, hopes, fears, and ideas ranged free and were unhampered by tradition or rule. He was not concerned with pleasing, only in evoking. Koestler wrote that, "Art originates in sympathetic magic"[10] and that our contemporary theater is directly reflected in such rites, the actors and characters being identified with the masked dancers.

Theories of the origin of art range from the worship of the dead or fertility spirits to the mythological accounts of supernatural visitations by great heroes, teachers, or leaders, bringing incentive and/or methodology for art to mankind. According to John Dewey, "Art is the extension of the power of rites and ceremonies to unite men, through a shared celebration, to all incidents and scenes of life."[11]

The art of early people was an exercise in the elemental senses of love, hate, and fear, made more vital by skilled and sensitive members of the group. Art began when function ceased, yet it remained communal because it expressed ideas close to the practical rites.

> When magical art reaches a high aesthetic level, this is because the society . . . demands of it an aesthetic excellence quite other than the very modest degree of competence which would enable it to fulfill its magical function.[12]

The following definitions, descriptions, and remarks by a cross section of concerned artists, critics, dancers, philosophers, writers, teachers, psychiatrists, and estheticians indicate something of the range and complexity of considered points of view.

What They Say

Alexander Eliot suggested a basic reason for the confusion:

> The maps to art fall under certain categories of seeing. For example, the maps of the experts are based on scholarly, authoritative seeing. The critics' maps are based on judgments—critical seeing. The materialists' maps are based solely on what the physical eyes can see. The aestheticians' maps are based on a cool, theoretical sort of seeing. All these are useful. But a better way to the treasure lies through personal, imaginative vision. And for this new maps are needed.[13]

There is nothing new about a bold and startling definition of, or statement about, art. Sometimes it doesn't really tell you anything but simply announces something about the process or product that seems important to the person speaking.

> Art is the extension of the power of rites and ceremonies to unite men, through a shared celebration, to all incidents and scenes of life.
> *John Dewey*, philosopher

> No one can say with assurance what a work of art is—or, more important, what is not a work of art.
> *Harold Rosenberg*, critic

> Altamira, too, is really a place of worship. These beasts come stampeding through the cave of one's own ribs. Possibly they did have magical or even documentary purposes; no matter: their main purpose was and is to awaken the spirit and enlighten the human soul. And this is true of all the greatest art forever.
> *Alexander Eliot*, critic

> The artist depends on nobody but himself. To the centuries to come he offers nothing but his own works; he only commits his own responsibility.
> *Charles Baudelaire*, writer

> Art seeks the point in space where the obvious and the remote coincide.
> *Jean Helion*, painter

> It is the chief function of art to overcome tragic consequences of man's voracious but untutored aesthetic taste. The tendencies that pseudo-art merely confirms, real art trains and transforms.
> *Iredell Jenkins*, esthetician

> A work of art is born of the artist in a mysterious and secret way. Detached from him it acquires autonomous life, becomes an entity. Nor is its existence casual and inconsequent; it has a definite and purposeful strength, alike in its material and spiritual life. It exists and has power to create spiritual atmosphere.
> *Wassily Kandinsky*, painter

> A great work of art is like a dream; for all its apparent obviousness it does not explain itself and is never unequivocal.
> *Carl Jung*, psychologist

> The business of art is to reveal the relation between man and his circumambient universe, at the living moment. As mankind is always struggling in the toils of old relationships, art is always ahead of the 'times' which themselves are always far in the rear of the living moment.
> *D. H. Lawrence*, writer

Art is the great means of making life possible, the great seducer to life, the great stimulus of life.

Friedrich Nietzsche, philosopher

Art disputes reality, but does not hide from it . . . it tries to give its form to an illusive value which the future perpetually promises, but of which the artist has a presentiment and wishes to snatch from the grasp of history.

Albert Camus, writer

Art is for the common man, but he will always be its enemy. He believes only what he sees, he sees only what he can put his hands on.

Frank Lloyd Wright, architect

. . . art is like a hall of mirrors or a whispering gallery. Each form conjures up a thousand memories and after images.

Lancelot Law Whyte, philosopher

A work of art is the affirmation of individuality against the hostility of the environment.

Matta Echaurren, painter

. . . cultures containing art have outlived and replaced those that have not, because art adapts the psyche to the environment, and is therefore one of the conditions of the development of society.

Christopher Caudwell, writer

Art is organization, discipline, restraint, no less than abandonment to the sweep of passion; art is the vital check as well as the vital urge; art has its asceticism, its puritanism, no less strict than those of the religious and the moralist.

Albert L. Guerard, writer

Experiment is not art; discovery and invention are that and no more; newness is irrelevant to art, in which there is change rather than progress. Purity can be a vice. Much great art is impure; the impurities, like trace elements in the soil, strengthen it.

George Rickey, painter

A work of art can be seen as an ineffable function of unreality. Always darting back and forth, the imagination often comes close to reality in the work of art but then veers off, faithful to its function of unreality.

Dore Ashton, critic

In 1896 Leo Tolstoy assembled definitions of art from major estheticians from the early eighteenth century in his book *What Is Art.*

"Art is beauty" was the popular conviction of the day. After many years of controversy and art activity, this remains the common denominator for many responses to art.

> . . . that which in general and necessarily without reasonings and without practical advantage, pleases.
> *Immanuel Kant,* philosopher

> Beauty is pleasure regarded as the quality of a thing. Art is objectification of esthetic pleasure.
> *George Santayana,* philosopher

> The Fine Arts aim at producing, by the object they make, joy or delight in the mind through the intuition of the senses.
> *Jacques Maritain,* philosopher

> In works of art men and women have embodied their experience of value, and these experiences are communicable to those who perceive the molded medium. Art is the language for the communication of values.
> *Charles W. Morris,* philosopher

> Art cannot be known but only experienced, and art belongs to man. When great art is so deeply felt and understood, it ceases to be a collection of beautiful objects and becomes instead a succession of gateways. And whenever this happens art reveals the path of beauty.
> *Alexander Eliot,* critic

> Art has nothing to do with beauty. If you find it marvelous and complete, it becomes beautiful.
> *David Hare,* painter

Art as intuition, a vision or even an outburst of imagination are commonly held views of art, as evidenced by the following.

> . . . he trusts his work to intuitions.
> *William DeKooning,* painter

> Art is always visionary. Art always disturbs present realities, however satisfactory they may seem to the rest of the world.
> *Ben Shahn,* painter

> . . . art is *vision* or *intuition.* The artist produces an image. . . . The person who enjoys art turns his eyes in the direction which the artist has pointed out to him, peers through the hole which has been opened for him, and reproduces in himself the artist's image.
> *Benedetto Croce,* philosopher

> . . . art is not an imitation . . . of external reality nor the inner reality of the unconscious. It is always a vision, an attempt to express visibly what a particular age . . . society . . . person has viewed as the true nature and essence of reality. . . .
> *Bruno Bettelheim*, psychologist

> 1. To us, art is an adventure into an unknown world, which can be explored only by those willing to take the risks.
> 2. This world of the imagination is fancy-free and violently opposed to common sense.
> 3. It is our function as artists to make the spectator see the world our way, not his way.
> *Adolph Gottlieb* and *Mark Rothko*, painters

> Art, then, is an expression and a stimulus of the imaginative life, which is separated from actual life by the absence of responsive action.
> *Roger Fry*, critic

Perhaps "art is expression" is the most universal response to the question. Often a qualifying "self" is added to make it "self-expression." But expression of what? Is it of the artist's state of being, or his personal life? Is it an expression of emotion, of feelings, or personality?

> Art expresses emotional meanings in the organized patterns of a medium. It is that event in which the heart and mind *really* see what they are looking at.
> *Allen Leepa*, critic

> The function of the *modern* artist is by definition the felt expression of modern reality. This implies that reality changes. . . .
> *Robert Motherwell*, painter

> Art is creation of forms symbolic of human feeling. The effect exists as a whole, not an assemblage of its elements, just as a living creature is more than the assemblage of constituent molecules. Probably *call* it emotion, but it's *more than* commonly named emotion.
> *Susanne K. Langer*, philosopher

> . . . art expresses artist's felt conception of reality—his feelings, ideas, fantasies, anxieties are fabric of his impassioned creations.
> *Allen Leepa*, critic

> Art is self-illumination, gestured toward a public reality.
> *Jasper Johns*, painter

> The artist aims not at beauty but objective self-expression.
> *Curt John Ducasse*, philosopher

A true work of art acts as a bridge between two worlds of feeling and perception, giving definition to feeling and form to perception. . . . Art is an affirmation, not of reality, but man's ability to create something beyond reality.

Herbert Read, philosopher

Every work of art must express something. This means, first of all, that the content of the work must go beyond the presentation of the individual objects of which it consists.

Rudolf Arnheim, psychologist

. . . art is the manifestation of emotion, obtaining external interpretation, now by expressive arrangements of line or color, now by a series of gestures, sounds, or words governed by particular rhythmical cadence.

Eugene Veron, esthetician

It [art] is an act that gives form to the most subtle, fugitive and inner forces that exist; it is a more concrete and positive type of self-revelation than appreciation; there is an assumption of responsibility for the revealing of not only the obvious but something that is difficult to reveal; the forces of which the world is made up, and deep, meaningful experience.

Allen Leepa, critic

The starting point for all systems of aesthetics must be the personal experience of a particular emotion. The objects that provoke this emotion we call works of art.

Clive Bell, philosopher

The work of art . . . is an organized complex of sensuous and expressive elements, and its organization is its form.

Melvin Rader, philosopher

Art is intuition which serves to reveal nature to us.

Henri Bergson, philosopher

. . . art may be defined in its result as the adequate translation of emotional experience into some external form. It is the expression of the feeling within by means of line, or color, or sound, or movement so that others may share the feeling.

Margaret H'Doubler, teacher

In art there is . . . an affective quality which . . . is not a mere recognition of order and interrelation; every part, as well as the whole, becomes suffused with an emotional tone. . . . It may be that art really calls up, as it were, the residual traces left on the spirit by the different emotions of life, without however recalling the actual experiences, so that we get an echo of the emotion without the limitation and particular direction which it had in experience.

Roger Fry, critic

The work of art is at once form and content, an affirmation and a deception, play and revelation, natural and artificial, purposeful and purposeless, within history and outside of history, personal and superpersonal. . . . A work of art must express its own novel and particular view.

Arnold Hauser, esthetician

Art being the expression of the intrinsic, the great work of art is a revelation sudden and indescribable because impenetrable.

Nicolas Calas, artist

Art . . . may be defined as the practice of creating perceptible forms expressive of human feelings.

Susanne K. Langer, philosopher

Every work of art . . . is an organic complex, presented in a sensuous medium, which complex is composed of elements, their expressive characteristics and the relation obtaining among them.

Morris Weitz, philosopher

I paint not the things I see but the feelings they arouse in me.

Franz Kline, painter

Because a work of art does not aim at reproducing natural appearances, it is not, therefore, an escape from life . . . not a sedative or drug, not just the exercise of good taste, the provision of pleasant shapes and colours in a pleasing combination, not a decoration to life but an expression of the significance of life, a stimulation to greater effort in living.

Henry Moore, sculptor

Art is a human activity consisting in this, that one man consciously by means of certain external signs, hands on to others feelings he has lived through, and that others are infected *by* these feelings and also experience them.

Leo Tolstoy, writer

A work of art is neither the faithful nor distorted representation, it is the immediate, unadorned record of an authentic intellecto-emotional REACTION of the artist in space.

John Graham, painter

. . . to use art as a means to the emotions of life is to use a telescope for reading the news.

Clive Bell, philosopher

One of the oldest concepts of art was that held by the Greeks: "Art is imitation of nature." The present-day comment "but it doesn't *look* like a tree," reflects that very concept.

> An art object is an imitation of nature.
> *Plato*, philosopher

> Art is a fragment of nature seen through a temperament.
> *Emile Zola*, writer

> Art is man added to nature.
> *Francis Bacon*, writer

> The artist must imitate that which is within the thing, that which is active through form and figure and discourse to us by symbols.
> *Samuel Taylor Coleridge*, writer

> A true looking glass included in a work of an artist who does not believe in imitation offers the beholder an excellent opportunity to reflect upon the meaning of reflections.
> *Robert Rauschenberg*, painter

The art object is an image; sometimes an image of the known, sometimes an unknown.

> All art is image-making and all image-making is rooted in the creation of substitutes.
> *E. H. Gombrich*, philosopher

> Art consists, not in calling a thing by the right name, and not in calling it by the wrong name, but in evoking that which has no name.
> *Albert L. Guerard*, writer

> Art does not reflect the visible but makes visible.
> *Paul Klee*, painter

> ... if the art work did not *magically act* upon the spectator, I would not waste my time with sculpting.
> *Jacques Lipchitz*, sculptor

> The artist creates out of the world that has made him in order to remake it according to the image of his inner world.
> *Walter Sorell*, critic

> Art does not deal with unknowns. Art strives to create an image of that which was unknown, making it thus known. ...
> *Naum Gabo*, painter

The creation of a work of art . . . must of necessity . . . be accompanied by distortion of the natural form. For, therein is nature reborn.

Paul Klee, painter

Art forms do not give directly; we get their meanings indirectly from the imagery of the creator who embodies the experience. The real . . . value of a work of art . . . lies not so much in what we actually see . . . as in how we react to all that we perceive.

Margaret H'Doubler, teacher

Art is a way of knowing an image that bridges rationality and impulse, free of instrumental 'knowing.'

Jerome Bruner, teacher

Art is a language of images, independent of the language of signs; and this language of images may be used to communicate what we loosely call feelings . . . [and] intuitions of the unknown.

Herbert Read, philosopher

Emphasis upon art as a means of communication was expressed in the following examples.

Art is communication spoken by man for humanity in a language raised above the everyday happening. What would be the sense of an art that robs itself of its communication and arrogantly believes that it can turn away from man?

Mary Wigman, dancer

The artist is like Sunday's child—he alone sees the spirits. But after he has told of their appearing to him, everybody sees them.

Wolfgang Goethe, writer

Art is a kind of language that says more, and with greater intensity than does ordinary conversation.

Allen Leepa, critic

The greatest art enlightens the conscious mind. . . .

Jacques Lipchitz, sculptor

Art is the giving by each man of his evidence to the world.

Robert Henri, painter

Art is a form of communication that insinuates. We *expect* the artist to have more to say than what he communicated, and to *suspect* that what he said was a subterfuge for hiding something.

Nicolas Calas, artist

The imposition of form, the finding of form, or the disciplined act of finding a way to formulate material is important to all artists. These are some who felt strongly about order.

> Art is the result of the creative consciousness of the order of existence.
> *John Sloan,* painter

> Art is not the application of a canon of beauty, but what instinct and intellect can conceive independently of the canon.
> *Pablo Picasso,* painter

> Art is not ornamentation or distraction but a means of giving form and sense to life . . . to express emotional meaning in organized patterns of a medium.
> *Allen Leepa,* critic

> Art is form imposed by taste, upon playful imagination.
> *Konrad Lange,* esthetician

> Sculpture is the conversion of any mass of matter without formal meaning into a mass that has been given formal meaning as the result of human will.
> *R. H. Wilenski,* critic

> Art is a natural discipline. Its rules are the proportions and rhythms inherent in our universe; and the instinctive observation of these rules which came about in the creative industry of the arts, brings the individual . . . into sympathetic harmony with his environment.
> *Herbert Read,* philosopher

> Art is the result of the creative consciousness of the order of existence . . . the evidence of man's understanding, the evidence of civilization.
> *John Sloan,* painter

> Art has no consequences. It gives form to something that is simply there, as the intuitive organizing functions of sense give form to objects and spaces, color and sound. It gives what Bertrand Russell calls 'knowledge by acquaintance' of effective experience, below the level of belief, on the deeper level of insight.
> *Suzanne K. Langer,* philosopher

> Art is an escape from chaos. It is movement ordained in numbers; it is mass confined in measure; it is the in-determination of matter seeking the rhythm of life.
> *Herbert Read,* philosopher

> Anything which is art is an instance of significant form; and anything which is not art has no such form. Art . . . has no set of necessary and

sufficient properties, hence a theory of it is logically impossible and not merely factually difficult.

Morris Weitz, philosopher

Art has its language of symbols whilst science has a language of signs. The creative imagination has a logic no less strict than the logic of scientific reasoning. They [works of art] are constructions, concretely physical. What is verifiable is a perceptible form which communicates a notion of being, a man-made piece of reality.

Herbert Read, philosopher

The artist does what no camera, no mere imitation, no mere document can do, namely, selects aspects for emphasis and gives significant order; that is, his work is a creation. The artist must open our eyes to what unaided we could not see.

Albert C. Barnes, historian

The esthetic act is to take possession of a segment of reality—to establish its dimensions—define its form. What we articulate is communicable only in virtue of its esthetic form.

Herbert Read, philosopher

To some, especially the psychiatrists and psychologists, art is a kind of therapy, a catharsis, a means of wish-fulfillment.

Art is phantasy making—an unconscious wish fulfillment.

Sigmund Freud, psychiatrist

Art fulfills the will to power.

Friedrich Nietzsche, philosopher

Art relieves pressures.

Yrjo Hirn, philosopher

A true artist . . . understands how to elaborate his daydreams, so that they lose that personal note . . . he possesses the mysterious ability to mold his particular material until it expresses his phantasy faithfully.

Sigmund Freud, psychiatrist

Art as Experience is the title of John Dewey's book on art, and he is the foremost proponent of the view. He is, of course, using the term in a specialized way, not to imply that *any* experience is art.

Art is experience organized more vividly and coherently than real life permits.

A work of art . . . is actually . . . a work of art only when it lives in some individualized experience.
John Dewey, philosopher

Art is involuntary dramatisation of subjective experience. In other words, the crystallisation of a state of mind in images.
Ananda K. Coomaraswamy, philosopher

No one can deny that the artist somehow manipulates his medium in order to transform or change it from what it was, to what it now is.

I have not sought to reproduce nature; I have represented it.
Paul Cezanne, painter

Art is the evocation of man's inner nature. Through art, which finds its roots in man's unconscious race-memory—is the history and psyche of race brought into focus. Great art never ignores human values. Therein lie its roots. This is why forms change.
Martha Graham, dancer

Art transports us from the world of man's activity to a world of aesthetic exaltation. For a moment we are shut off from human interests; our anticipations and memories are arrested; we are lifted above the stream of life.
Clive Bell, philosopher

We all know that art is not truth. Art is a lie that makes us realize the truth.
Pablo Picasso, painter

Art grows out of the basic cause of existence. From there it draws its creative and constructive forces. From there it receives strength to renew, rejuvenate, transform itself. And there only is it imperishable, eternal.
Mary Wigman, dancer

. . . the work of art is primarily creation, it is never experienced as a mere product. Art is always seeking . . . [it is a] state in which abstract forms can become meaningful, or else pure symbols as constant as numbers and letters. Art does not reflect the visible but *makes* visible.
Paul Klee, painter

Real art can never be escape from life. The world of illusion which the audience expects from the artist is, in fact, the world of their real selves, the image of their own world, the transformation of their hopes and fears, their joys and sufferings into the magic of the stage.
Charles Weidman, dancer

> Art is born from one's belief, by the pressure of over-abundance. It starts to live when it no longer suffices for the expression of life.
>
> *Andre Gide,* writer

> The work of art is an artificial object which permits the creator to place the spectator in the state he wishes.
>
> *Le Corbusier* (Charles-Edouard Jenneret) architect and *Amadie Ozenfant,* painter.

To think of art as a language and, further, as a symbolic language seems to be relevant to many. Susanne K. Langer, considered "the dancer's philosopher," is one among others who represent this point of view.

> A work of art presents feeling . . . for our contemplation, making it visible or audible or in some way perceivable through a symbol, not inferable from a symptom.
>
> A work of art expresses a conception of life, emotion, inward reality. But it is neither a confessional nor a frozen tantrum; it is a developed metaphor, a non-discursive symbol that articulates what is verbally ineffable—the logic of consciousness itself.
>
> *Susanne K. Langer,* philosopher

> All art originates in the human mind, in our reactions to the world rather than in the visible world itself, and it is precisely because all art is 'conceptual' that all representations are recognizable by their style.
>
> *E. H. Gombrich,* philosopher

> Art is symbolic language.
>
> *Ernst Cassirer,* philosopher

There are few artists who do not use the process of abstraction, but to some it is the entire focus of their art.

> I could never employ forms by proceeding from logical processes, only those born within me by an inner necessity. The form of a horse becomes more magical the further I depart from an actual horse.
>
> *Wassily Kandinsky,* painter

> Low art is just telling things; as There is the night. High art gives the feel of the night. The latter is nearer reality although the former is a copy. A painter should be interested not in the incident but in the essence of his subject.
>
> *Robert Henri,* painter

Perhaps R. G. Collingwood is the most vocal of those holding convictions that art objects are simply stimuli, and that the art phenomena rest entirely in the eye of the beholder.

> The work of art proper is something not seen or heard, but something imagined . . . a world wholly self-contained, a complete universe which has nothing outside it.
> The music to which we listen is not heard sound, but that sound as amended in various ways by the listener's imagination, and so with the other arts.
> *R. G. Collingwood*, esthetician

> All architecture is what you do to it when you look upon it. (Did you think it was in the whole or gray stone, or the lines of the arches and cornices?)
> All music is what awakens you when you are reminded by the instruments.
> It is not the violins and the cornets, it is not the oboe, nor the beating drums, nor the score of the baritone singing his sweet romanza, nor that of the men's chorus, nor that of the women's chorus. It is nearer and farther than they.
> *Walt Whitman*, poet

The cryptic remark, "Art is whatever the artist says is art," hardly offers any clue to differentiation or hope for more than a personal symptom. Nevertheless, this is becoming a common response.

> Anything that an artist presents as having experiential significance is considered art.
> *Michael Kirby*, sculptor

> I'm interested in making things as machine-like as possible.
> *George Rickey*, artist

> I want to make things that are fun to look at.
> *Alexander Calder*, sculptor

More and more, as Weitz has written, many are realizing that concepts of art change as art forms change, and vice versa, that what our fathers or grandfathers considered art does not necessarily remain unchanged. It is possible that art may be considered subject to new views and interpretations.

> Art, itself, is an open concept. New conditions (cases) have constantly arisen and will undoubtedly arise; new art forms, new movements will merge . . . which will demand decisions on the part of those interested,

usually professional critics, as to whether the concept should be extended or not. With 'art' its conditions of application can never be exhaustively enumerated since new cases can always be envisaged or created by artists, or even nature, which would call for a decision . . . to extend or to close the old or to invent a new concept. (For example, 'it's not a sculpture, it's a mobile.')

Morris Weitz, philosopher

Whether influenced by existentialism, phenomonology or current events, many people are both proposing and believing that art is whatever it is, not what it should be.

The art-object represents a world whose being is prior to every form of judgment, and therefore immune to every judgment . . . a *presentation*, rather than a *re*-presentation. It is an original—a *first* presentation of a possibility truly felt and imagined. It can remind us, really, only of itself.

Arturo B. Fallico, philosopher

The one thing to say about art is its breathlessness, lifelessness, deathlessness, contentlessness, formlessness, spacelessness, and timelessness. This is always the end of art.

Ad Reinhardt, painter

To explain a poem is impossible, every poem is its own explanation. A poem should not mean but be.

Archibald MacLeish, poet

Reprise

There is general agreement among most artists, critics, and estheticians that art is a man-made product which has been formed according to the intent of the artist. Even though experimentation and chance may have had major influence, he, nevertheless, decided which chance bit to use. What results is necessarily affected by the artist's personality, experience, skill, and sensitivity, within his time and place, as well as the medium and materials at his disposal.

There is less agreement about the work approach of the artist, of how he manipulates his reality, his content, his intent. Some of the expressed ways include:

1. Duplication of reality (represent or recreate what is there).
2. Expression of reality (choose from what is there on the basis of discrimination and held values).
3. Impression of reality (extended or fuzzy view of what is there).

4. Comment on reality (artist's view of truth, beauty, morality, or state of what is there; opportunity for propaganda).
5. Abstraction of reality (essence or skeleton of what is there).
6. Projected vision (images from imagination and fantasy).
7. Gratification of senses (soothing, entertaining, arousing, intensifying).
8. Educational (enrich perception and understanding, foster imagination, find significance).
9. Explore sensuous material with direct or chance discrimination.
10. Express personality or emotions of the artist (exhibitionism, therapy).
11. Present an image or significant form (hoping to evoke response).

There is even less agreement about the bases for the process of forming the product. Some of the expressed ways include:

1. Seeking significant form according to:
   a. An agreed system of signs with common usage. These, like language, have commonly accepted meanings.
   b. Symbols or evocative images, abstractions, or distortions of reality as we know it.
   c. Inclination of the materials or selection from improvisation.
2. Impose form on the materials according to:
   a. Preconceived formula, "the" way, classical rule, or traditional pattern.
   b. The skills, experience, or security of the artist or performer.
   c. Judgment of the artist, as part of the creative act (selecting details according to intent, design, expression, function or esthetic discrimination).
   d. Relevance of the evolving form (derived from medium, process, or intent).

Criteria for perception/evaluation of the art product are even more difficult to pin down—agreement seldom occurs. Some of the expressed bases for evaluation of the art product include:

3. "I enjoyed the beauty" (security of perfection, grace, pretty, good; legibility of the reality we hope for—absolute Utopia).
4. "Excellent technique" (the lines were all straight, the finish was smooth, they had good balance, etc.; intrigue with the personal power and virtuosity of the artist).

5. Provided impetus for immersion in the materials of the product (springboard for the imagination; to find fresh relationships and implications).
6. All in accord with my esthetic and artistic views (agrees with values held, equal to expectations, did not upset the system).
7. Enriched my perceptual field, widened my view of experience (provided a fresh and vivid look).

It is not always easy to identify our own criteria for judging art. From the extreme of "there is so little that is good in art today," to "everything is interesting," it is difficult to maintain any middle ground. In the former there is reverence for the past and what time has proven great; in the latter there is the tendency to accept anything and thereby reject any critical faculty.

Perhaps we might consider the "degree of becoming." Much of what we see is experimental, a kind of a game in trial and error. While these excursions may become art, they are not necessarily so in the process. Though we value experience, it is not necessarily all art. Art is not an accident, not a random happening but a controlled structuring of a medium in order to communicate a vivid image of experience. There must be focus, organizing intelligence, and an artist's eye to find significance in chaos.

What we need is an esthetic with room for the irrational, the magical, the fluctuating, the unique, as well as the traditional and known. More important than mere arrangement of things is the "intersecting fields of energy" which form a dialogue between the forming artist and a sensitive and alert audience.

The following are suggestions for your consideration.

1. The art product is a man-made formulation that means whatever it *is*. Recognizing that the materials may have been used to reveal more than is immediately apparent, it is, in this event, necessary to look beyond the materials used. If the material is used for its own sake, then look for the wonder and delight of what is available. Don't wish for something else, enjoy what is there.
2. The art product that exists precludes any imperative of truth or beauty. It is a simple and direct presentation with no necessity for fitting standards or prejudgments.
3. The art work is composed and independent, it is an original, resulting from the artist's "felt possibility."
4. It reminds us only of itself. We may remind ourselves of some-

thing extraneous to it, but the art product "opens our eyes to it" with an innocence, a naiveté, a first look.

5. The art product exists in our presence, it is the "present-felt image," nonexistent until it is a presence.

6 We may not like the art work, we may disagree with the form, intent, execution, or any of a dozen more aspects of it. Or we may like some of it. But if we lose ourselves in it, if we become one with it, nothing else matters. This is the ultimate art experience.

8
The Artist and His Tools

> ... the artist acts like a
> mediumistic being who, from
> the labyrinth beyond time
> and space, seeks his way out to
> a clearing.
> Marcel Duchamp, *painter*

The Artist

Because of the difficulty in describing the art product and process, there is equal confusion in identifying the artist and his work. Resorting to circular generalities, we usually come up with something like: "Artists, through a process of creative forming, produce art." Among the other generalities about artists there are a number of strange stereotypes, like characters from a dreary melodrama. The artist is a lonely, brooding man with unkempt beard and halting speech; he is a pale, tubercular phantom who seldom sleeps or eats; he is a nervous and frustrated wretch who ridicules the world for not appreciating him. And a favorite, old gag reminds us that "artists don't have to be crazy, but it helps."

We don't hear much of those artists who are happy family members, or even housewives who manage to live fairly normal lives and still produce art. Artists are people, just people, with the ordinary assets and liabilities. But this picture doesn't fit the "poster blowup icon" of the celebrity. We seem to like the cliché of compulsive and self-destructive behavior attributed to artistic genius. When poets die young, when scandal or suicide occurs, the public image is enflamed, and the hero becomes the stuff of myth and mystery. This is probably the reason why so many artists search for seclusion and solitude so that they may work in peace, away from a curious crowd.

Allen Leepa said,

> . . . the artist is a member of society like any other person. He is . . . influenced by the same forces, tensions, and anxieties. He is subject to the same perceptions of the meaning of life . . . what he does is synthesize the feelings and ideas we know, drawing on the sensed meaning of these forces and perceptions.[1]

The work of the artist seldom occurs in public or on call. Creativity cannot be turned on like a light switch. "An artist . . . is one who is not only gifted in powers of execution but in unusual sensitivity to the qualities of things. This sensitivity also directs his doing and makings."[2] With varying degrees of intensity the artist is searching for a point of transcendence where his personal vision blends with the public reality. "The artist," wrote Collingwood, "must prophesy not in the sense that he foretells things to come but in the sense that he tells his audience, at risk of their displeasure, the secrets of their own hearts."[3] Calling all art idealization, Edman wrote, "It is one of the chief functions of the artist to render experience arresting by rendering it alive."[4]

According to Read, "The artist must be ready to delve below the level of normal consciousness, the crust of conventional thought and behavior, into his own unconscious, and into the collective unconscious of his group. . . ."[5] And Langer said, "An artist . . . formulates that elusive aspect of reality that is commonly taken to be amorphous and chaotic; that is, he objectifies the subjective realm."[6] She went on to insist that the artist is not expressing his own feelings, rather drawing from what he knows of human feelings.

As suggested by André Gide, nature supplies the materials and the artist shapes and transforms them. The shaping process, the forming of the product, and the work done by the artist are all affected by the time, place, environment, point of view, materials, medium, personality, and intent of the artist. Gombrich, in Art and Illusion,[7] asked if artists are more successful because they see more or because their skill in presentation of ideas is better. The secret probably lies midway between, for one without the other is useless.

After Kaelin differentiated the artist as inventing forms, from the artisan as copying forms, he warned, "The business of the artist . . . is not to display his immediate selfhood. Style he must have, but his style is only a means to the end of communication . . . not an end in itself."[8]

"The major problem confronting the artist," said Oskar Kokoschka, "is whether or not he is gifted enough to apprehend the real, and communicate it directly, in a manner articulate enough to convey his vision to others."[9]

According to John Dewey, "An artist, in comparison with his fellows, is one who is not only especially gifted in powers of execution but in unusual sensitivity to the qualities of things. This sensitivity also directs his doings and makings."[10]

In his famous simile Paul Klee explained that:

> . . . the artist . . . is like a tree. He has coped with the bewildering world—reasonably well. He knows how to find his way in it. This orientation . . . [is] like the root part of our tree. From there the artist—who is the trunk of the tree—receives the sap that flows through him and through his eye. Under the pressure of this mighty flow, he transmits what he has seen to his work. His work, then, is like the crown of the tree, spreading in time and space for all to see.[11]

In speaking of his own painting, Kandinsky declared that he could never employ forms proceeding from logical processes, only those born by an inner necessity. "That is beautiful which is produced by internal necessity, which springs from the soul."[12]

In writing of art as the renewal of spontaneity, Fallico suggested that the artist "is impelled more strongly than others by the sense of radical incompleteness of his existence and by the submerged memory of what it is like *really to be*."[13] Alexander Eliot, who called all artists "children of light," wrote that "Artists come into the world not to fill their own bellies but to bring new nourishment to mankind."[14]

David Smith concluded:

> From the artist there is no conscious effort to find universal truth or beauty, no effort to analyze other men's minds in order to speak for them. His act in art is an act of personal conviction and identity. If there is truth in art, it is his own truth. If beauty is involved, it is only the metaphor of imagination.[15]

And in his *Essays*, Collingwood said, "To be an artist is to create for oneself a world of imaginary objects whose function is to express to oneself one's own mind."[16]

Allen Leepa wrote:

> One of the fundamental problems of the artist is that of discovering the roots of his own emotional expression and creative experience. Part of the solution to this problem is found in the relationship between the outward appearance of the world and man's inner vision.[17]

According to Marcel Duchamp:

> In the creative act, the artist goes from intention to realization through a chain of totally subjective reactions.[18]

And John Dewey wrote:

> Until the artist is satisfied in perception with what he is doing, he continues shaping and reshaping. The making comes to an end when its result is experienced as good....[19]

There have been many investigations attempting to quantify the views and actions of artists, but the activity of creativity is illusive and intangible, not susceptible to objective scrutiny. What we can observe is the concentration and devotion of the artist, the selfless yet extremely selfish conviction that his is *the* way. But is this so bad? At best we agree and welcome the result, and at worst we simply reject it and turn away.

There is a mystery and excitement about the work of many artists. The painter Miró said, "It is difficult for me to talk about my painting, for it is always born in a state of hallucination provoked by some shock, objective or subjective, for which I am entirely irresponsible."[20] Kandinsky is said to have been convinced that his paintings were endowed with magical power. Miró explains that "It is as if the artist were amusing himself behind the mask. In actuality though, he is escaping, eluding the world in which he lives, and amid those myths that for him are the reflection and the reverse of that world, himself becomes Myth."[21]

Creativity

Creativity is an elusive phenomenon, hard to describe but probably present, to a greater or lesser degree, in all human beings. Certainly the greatest limitation is in the point of view that persists in seeing only the commonplace or cliché in the familiar. Often we are blinded by our own conservatism as we continue to seek what we are looking for, and we lose contact with what might be there. The truly creative person "serves as the eyes of a society blinded by reality."

The painter Marcel Duchamp contended, "In the creative act, the artist goes from intention to realization through a chain of totally subjective reactions . . . a series of efforts, pains, satisfactions, refusals, decisions, which . . . must not be fully self-conscious, at least on the esthetic plane."[22]

Creativity occurs in art, but not only in art. The inventor, historian, scientist, explorer, indeed all of those who reach out, who seek and search for new horizons, relationships, and things, are creative. Some are more creative than others. The following are characteristic responses to the question: "What do you mean by creativity?"

1. It is the generation or development of an objective product.
2. It is a single act of personal discovery.
3. Anything fresh or new.
4. Rearrangement of the old.
5. Development or variation.
6. Solution to any problem.
7. Identification of something worth bothering about.
8. Process of search resulting in a product.
9. A part of living.
10. Pointing out new relationships.

Obviously the responses to such a question reflect different points of view and frames of reference. It may be impossible to find any universally acceptable criteria for all concepts of creativity.

Whether one can identify creativity as a process or a product is immaterial. The fact that a product may result from the process is obvious. We somehow expect a painter, poet, or choreographer to produce a painting, poem, or dance. Certainly one aspect of creativity results in an art product. The process is the selection and organization of the materials, the formulation and presentation of the completed work.

Shizuko Iwamatsu and Ted Courtenay with choreography class.

Amy Lowell compared the start of creativity to "The idea dropped into the subconscious, like a letter into a mailbox." Rollo May wrote of creativity as "encounter of the intensively conscious human being with his world." Jerome Bruner called it "effective surprise." Eric Fromm said it was the "ability to see and respond." Arthur Koestler called it both a conscious and an unconscious process of "emotionally charged participation and discovery." In almost all discussions of creativity it is considered more than reshaping, rather the drawing into its new existence. Generally it is agreed to entail a great outpouring, rigidly controlled by a highly critical mind. As Carl Rogers put it, it is "the emergence in action of a novel relational product."

The origin of the creative process is not the sensation itself but in the response of the imagination to sense perceptions. The psychologist Guilford maintained the key to the creative personality as the ability to be sensitive to one's surroundings. "Every creative act," said Harold Rugg, "is an autonomous forming, patterned process below the threshold of awareness. The imagined conception is the key to all creative acts."[23] Vincent Thomas suggested that "creative activity in art . . is activity subject to critical control by the artist, although not by virtue of the fact that he foresees the final result of the activity."[24]

This is a function of openness and drive, a product of rich experience, self-confidence, sensitivity, and willingness to be as well as to become. According to Leepa, the crux of the creative act, "lies in complete freedom from superimposed idea and convention." Conformity is antithetical to creativity because it restricts, orders, and controls. Creativity fosters freedom, experimentation, expression, and facility along with vitality and energy of the imagination. Central to the creative process is the ability to shatter rules and regulation, to dismiss traditional ways, for the sake of the way, and to dare to follow the dictates of the imagination.

Characteristics of Creative People

Such people are sensitive to their environment and world, and in this relationship they are willing to take a stand. They are responsive to sensory stimuli, though responsive *in their own way*. They are observant, aware, curious, and usually prejudiced. Their likes and dislikes are marked. They can usually see more than others, and are open to those things that interest them. They usually have a vivid imagination and are sensitive according to their interests. So interested are they in things that they tend to become obsessed by their own projects. Aware of themselves as individuals, they have great self-confidence. They are capable of extremes of concentration and enjoy working endlessly on whatever challenges them. They work alone, both figuratively and physically.

Susanne Langer's illuminating differentiation between creation and other productive work is helpful. She wrote:

> . . . an ordinary object, say a shoe, is made by putting pieces of leather together; the pieces were there before. The shoe is a construction of leather. It has a special shape and use and name, but it is still an article of leather, and is thought of as such. A picture is made by deploying pigments on a piece of canvas, but the picture is not a pigment-and-canvas structure. The picture that emerges from the process is a structure of space, and the space itself is an emergent whole of shapes, visible colored volumes. Neither the space nor the things in it were in the room before. Pigments and canvas are not in the pictorial space; they are in the space of the room, as they were before, though we no longer find them there by sight without a great effort of attention. For touch they are still there. But for touch there is no pictorial space. The picture, in short, is an apparition. . . . The whole picture is a piece of purely visual space. It is nothing but a vision.[25]

Creative people are original and eager to try new things, especially uncommon things that contact fantasy. Free in observation, thought, and action, they revel in a new way. Sometimes they seem to be very destructive in their haste to be constructive. Discarding the old, they tend to be indifferent to cultural stereotypes. With the naiveté of a child they often see relationships with striking clarity. Creative people are necessarily fluent but often with a narrow range of expression. An ability to analyze and synthesize, in their own medium, is probably responsible for any equilibrium and form that is found in their work.

Some of the common blocks to creativity are often found in schools where a premium is placed upon quiet, clean, and orderly classrooms. Administrators, teachers, and parents who demand conformity will stifle some creativity, except for those who will create in spite of them. Because of a lingering stereotype of romanticism and tenderness often associated with the creative person, especially in the arts, there is often a fear of loss of masculinity. Certainly many people may not care to be different from the rest of the crowd. They may turn to standardized goals, means, and ends rather than face the insecurity of finding their own solutions and way. And parents are not sure of permissiveness and freedom. Real creativity is a frightening thing because it involves personal responsibility, self-direction, and courage.

Healthy creativity occurs in a fusion of unconscious and conscious processes. To live both with fantasy and then to fulfill a personal goal is not easy. As Maslow says, "If you can be comfortable in both worlds, o.k.; otherwise, being in only one is madness." The following represent some of the things that interfere with creativity.

1. Overabundant fantasy, continual "emotional crop-dusting."
2. Lack of skill, inability to find form and method.

3. Submitting to routinized operations, fitting to what *should* come out.
4. Meaningless materials, of no real concern to individual.
5. Undue concern for security and safety.
6. Unrealistic and undisciplined work habits.
7. Undue concern for other people's opinions.
8. Complete disregard for opinions of others.

For creativity to occur there needs to be:

1. Personal involvement, with a greater concern for this thing to be done than the potential liabilities.
2. Sensitivity, which includes a sense of relevance and relationship, curiosity, and an open mind, at least at the start.
3. Fluency and originality which is shown by a wide perceptual range and interest in uncommon things or aspects of the common. To be unsatisfied with the cliché and eager for clarity of expression is great, but more important is ability to use the tools of the craft with a wide range of expression.

The following profile of a creative person may serve as a resume of fairly well-documented evidence of the behavior of many creative people.

1. High perceptive acuity.
2. Sustained curiosity.
3. Independent and assertive.
4. Dedicated and involved.
5. Bold and courageous.
6. Spontaneous and enthusiastic.
7. Adventurous and original.
8. Adaptable and resourceful.
9. Honest and persistent.
10. Egocentric as well as introspective.
11. Emotionally responsive and excitable.
12. Dominant and domineering.
13. Irritable and stubborn.
14. Anxious and complex.
15. Skeptical, critical, and precise.

The creative person is usually highly tolerant of:

1. Ambiguity.
2. Disorder.
3. Emotional instability.

4. New experiences.
5. Puzzles and strange ideas.
6. Intellectual pursuits.

And he has little regard for:

1. Job security and routine.
2. People and their opinion or trivia.
3. Traditional judgment.
4. Order for the sake of orderliness.
5. Logic, as such.
6. Conventional morality.
7. Clubs, lodges, and social societies.
8. Many close friends.
9. Time and schedules.

Form and Content

One of the most persistent controversies in art is of the relative importance of form and content. Generally form refers to *how* the materials are used and how relationships among elements are achieved. Content is concerned with what theme or idea is being formed. In representational art the subject or thing denoted exists as a recognizable symbol. This is the association which is presumed necessary by the observer who remarks, "I don't understand what it is about." But content is more than the thing denoted, it is all that is in the work, all of the relationships which have been formed. It is "about" what is there to be perceived in the work. Melvin Rader wrote: "The work of art . . . is an organized complex of sensuous and expressive elements, and its organization is its form." "Content," said Lou Harrison, "is elements in relation. Form is relation among elements."

Different views of form and content have resulted in the many "schools" or approaches to art, from the most traditional and classical to the most modern and avant-garde.

Form, according to the dictionary, is not just one thing, rather it is the aspect under which a thing appears, the shape, mold, style, method of arranging details, official document, state of health, etiquette, or even device to assume a position. Needless to say the term may be used within many contexts. When it refers to the outer appearance of things, as the shape of a rose, form is determined by forces within the object itself. Lancelot L. Whyte reminds us that along with the tendency toward form in external nature there is a similar urge in human perception and thought. We observe complexity and our brain selects and forms what interests us and makes it appear simple as distracting elements are ruled out.

In art, form is imposed upon the material by the artist, giving existence to a new being. But many artists contend that they sometimes lose control and the materials of their medium take over. The painter Miró remarked, "I start painting, and as I paint, the picture begins to assert itself, or suggest itself under my brush." In discussing the process of choreography, Gay Cheney reported:

> One was in motion; one was in the mind; one was subjectively feeling; one was objectively thinking. One went from whole to part and part to whole, from allowing to willing, from waiting to taking hold, from choice to chance, and from there back again. The matter of inconsistency and necessity for alteration of activities was finally accepted.[26]

We think of pattern, structure, and configuration and we speak of unity of spatials and/or temporal and dynamic form. And we mean by this, what goes where, when and how; the relationship of all the parts and the way it becomes what it will be. The form may be intrinsic or extrinsic to the idea or intent. When the idea is fitted to a form, whether free or ruled, it is the classical approach. Disregard of preexistent forms and development of a form functional to the content allows for free growth of the form with no need to fit a mold.

In a catalog for a New York exhibition in 1960, Edgard Varése declared form to be the result of a process, not a pattern to be followed. "Ultimately," he wrote, "the work of art . . . discovers its own form." Gombrich, in *Art and Illusion,* asks if the artist can really differentiate the *will to form* from the *will to conform.* This concept is of serious concern to the artist. The tendency to fit materials to an existing form is not always easy to recognize. The artist may say, and really believe, the form is growing out of the medium, but some preexisting and esthetically pleasant form may insinuate itself below the level of awareness.

Of course the artist may have planned fitting to some form, in which case there is no problem. But there is increasing concern for that form which is distinctly unique to the particular work, "organic," and, as Ben Shahn has written, "the shape of the content." There are times when the artist may wish to resort to chance, or noninterference, but, as George Riley said: "Abdicating authority in favor of chance, he can choose not to choose."

Music is more than a sum of tones, rather it has sequence, order, and place among the sounds. It may be a sonata form or an unknown pattern of relationships but it is the way it is because some composer decided it would be that way. Painting may be in a variety of media, on a number of surfaces, but even though developed by chance, consciously or unconsciously, the ultimate decisions were made by the painter. Dance may employ improvisation and endless variation but it is a dance rather than movement and perspiration because some choreographer decided what action was to occur within the time frame and the space available. It is not a random happening but proceeds according to plan. Susanne Langer, in *Problems of Art*, described form as "structure, articulation, a whole resulting from the relation of mutually dependent factors."

John B. Flannagan wrote movingly of "The Image in the Rock," and Henry Moore spoke of his stones as having an inner life that dictated form; but nonetheless, it was the artist who found and manipulated these tendencies. Hans Hofmann spoke of the "constant struggle" of the artist as to whether he controls or gives in to his materials.

The term "significant form" has been used by many and refers to that order essential to, equated with, and inevitable to the content, emotion, and intent of the work. It is that intangible without which the object is something else! Clive Bell called it, "the right form for the right emotion," or that which "communicates the ecstasy of the event." Etienne Gilson wrote that "Form is that on account of which a certain thing is the very thing that it is."

According to Langer, "'significant form' or 'expressive form,' is not an abstracted structure, but an apparition; and the vital processes of sense and emotion that a good work of art expresses seem to the beholder to be directly contained in it, not symbolized but really presented. The congruence is so striking that symbol and meaning appear as one reality."[27] In her book *Unknown Shore*, Dore Ashton wrote that the artist can "bring us to the brink of chaos and at a critical moment express its opposite: FORM."

In "On Problems of Artistic Form," Paul Stern observed artistic form to be attained when all aspects of the image are in tune with the vitality of the whole, "when . . . the clarity of the image coincides with the clarity of the inner content." Ben Shahn, in *The Shape of Content*, proposed form as the only possible shape of a certain content. This refers not only to the *intent*, but the embodiment of the content.

Dewitt H. Parker, in "The Problem of Esthetic Form," called for consideration of:

1. Organic unity in which each distinct element is necessary to the value of the whole.
2. A dominant characteristic as theme.
3. Balance of contrasting elements.
4. Points of hierarchy of greater or lesser importance.
5. Elaboration or variation of the theme.
6. Evolution or development of the major idea.[28]

According to Picasso:

> When you begin a picture, you often make some pretty discoveries. You must guard against these. Destroy the thing, do it over several times. In each destroying of a beautiful discovery, the artist does not really suppress it, but rather transforms it, condenses it, makes it more substantial. What comes out in the end is the result of discarded finds. Otherwise you become your own connoisseur.[29]

In his classic "Meditations on a Hobby Horse," Gombrich suggested that as a child might substitute a wooden stick (hobbyhorse) for a pony, so the artist can develop a functional substitute as his ideational form. Kandinsky, who painted many horses, maintained that his horse became even more magical as he departed from the realistic form, and finally would become pure energy with only the emotive form of the original. Critic Katherine Kuh observed that it is a characteristic of modern art that the subject is transcended by breaking up the form, color, content, and space of its being. She was, of course, speaking of painting, but it is equally true in other art forms. Schoenberg in music, Cunningham in dance, Joyce in literature, and Lipchitz in sculpture have all accomplished this in their own ways.

Jean Dubuffet maintained that "The artist must be harnessed to chance . . . but with flexibility applies himself to making the best of every accident as it occurs. . . ."

There is increasing unanimity among artists, critics, and philosophers that distinction between form and content in a work of art is not possible. The content is conceived to be the expressive element organized and complete. The form is concerned with the unification of the expressive constituents. If true, then form and content are inseparable, made up of coordinating elements in relations. So, when we speak of art as significant form, we also mean significant content.

One Style or Another

There is an ever-increasing literature dealing with "schools" of painting and with various views and methods of painters. With each exhibit, new labels appear, some similar to others, some quite different. Whether painters and their critics really talk and write more, or whether their views are simply more available, cannot be said. It is certain that the most complete picture of changes in style are recorded in the literature dealing with painting. There is considerable written about music, literature, sculpture, theater, poetry, and architecture, though the vocabularies and points of view are often at odds both with the painters and each other. Since the advent of modern dance there has been more reference to esthetic principles in this performing art than before. Stories of the ballets and the lives of the dancers made up much of the previous dance literature. From the more general field of esthetics there is some reference to fundamental concepts about changing emphases in the arts.

The classical view of art as technique and craft treated the product much as a functional artifact. The carved fetish had magical powers, a great temple served to honor the gods or glorify a community. Statues in Greece perpetuated man's memory, and in Egypt assured immortality. An epic poem like the *Kalevala* preserved a people's tradition and a totem pole enhanced the dignity of a clan. Each form was a means to something else of value. Up to the time of the Renaissance the artist was considered a workman and his work either magico-social or utilitarian. Then came the rise of fine arts.

Among primitives there were simple, naturalistic forms, or simple transformations into things of magic. The Egyptians represented not only what they saw but what they knew and believed. The Greeks sought to breathe perfection and life into their images. Medieval art tried to project a sacred story, and Oriental art to further contemplation. With the Renaissance, the whole concept of humanism and humanistic man turned attention to the artist as a special kind of a person.

Modern esthetics began in the eighteenth century when a German, Baumgarten, suggested that esthetic pleasure derived from mere apprehension of an art work. It was assumed that beauty resided within the work of art, deriving its character from whatever it depicted. In a time when indulgence in art needed justification, it was innocent pleasure, beneficial relaxation, exercise of mental faculties, and the cultivation of higher intellectual and moral impulses that were considered valuable.

In the mid-1800s, the Romantic period began. Words like creative imagination, genius, originality, expression, emotion, communication, symbolism, and sentiment came to be associated with the artist. Suddenly he no longer was ruled by church, court, or state, he was on his own, "expressing himself." Clive Bell was emphasizing feeling above reason and writing about "significant form." He suggested that beauty, rather than in the object, was in the emotional response of the observer. Kant was speaking of esthetic experience as a direct emotional awareness, unique from other kinds of judgments. Repudiating intellectualism as the basis, he proposed that beauty, as such, has no set properties but depends upon a subjective judgment based on taste. No longer was art considered a mirror through which one could glimpse reality, but, rather, a means for contacting the creative mind of the artist. The artist was the inspired and imaginative genius who could communicate substance beyond ordinary experience.

By the end of the nineteenth century artists were more and more stirred by forms that did not resemble or symbolize any known subject matter. Painters like Albert Gleizes were insisting that painting was its own reason for being and did not need to resemble anything. At the world-famous Bauhaus school in Weimar, Germany, a number of artists including Kandinsky, Klee, Albers, and Moholy-Nagy were exploring materials, tools, and techniques as well as expressive ideas as new springboards for painters and other artists. Art and concepts of art from the Greek ideals of realism, colored by the European Renaissance, were changing. Fantasy and invention were replacing imitation.

With the twentieth century there were again many shifts in viewpoint about esthetics, values, and approaches to art. To look at a Byzantine icon today is to see it as a work of art, not necessarily as a Christian symbol; and a carved African fetish can be viewed as an esthetically beautiful form rather than a passport to the supernatural.

This has been a time of emancipation from naturalism and instrumentalism which so long dominated the Western world. No longer is art bound to the literal story, but has become meaningful and complete in itself. There are a number of terms and titles used to differentiate offshoots of different methodologies, points of view, periods, and media for the producing of art works. The basic views, however, probably fall within the broader areas of "realism," "expressionism," and "super-realism" or "cubism."

Realism refers to the artist who is striving to imitate nature, to conform to reality by subordinating everything to the object. Sometimes exact duplication, or "mirror-image" is sought. The standard of excellence for such a painting is, "It looks like it, you can be sure of what you are looking at." A dance resembles some piece of reality, a sculptured steel resembles its model. This is the oldest and most generally held criterion for art—that it be a true and clear likeness of something in real experience. The artist aims to produce convincing facsimiles.

The degree and means of handling reality have varied. In some cases it has served only as a base from which the artist has abstracted, distorted, or in other ways deviated his materials, still intent upon the original reality of his image.

Expressionism, as an approach to the art work, refers directly to the involved projection of the artist's views, personal convictions, emotions, and ideas, all consciously used as the basis for forming the work. The personality and skill of the individual is important in any approach used, but in expressionism the artist relies solely on his "sensuous hold of the subject," *how he* perceives or feels about it. Actually it becomes a caricature of the artist. The remark, "a work of art is an expression of the artist," reflects this view.

Super-Realism is when the artist is involved with spiritual or immaterial values, experiences, and concepts beyond or above the realities of the world. The artist finds greatest interest in images, symbolisms, dreamlike visions, strange and unreal fantasies, and relationships. Projections of the future, memories of the past, illusions of the present, and reactions of the subconscious roam free. There is concern for the unreal.

Cubism refers to any preoccupation with forms and qualities inherent in materials, ideas, or objects. It reflects a concern with the existing function or being of the subject, as imagined or experienced by intuition. Things are not necessarily real or unreal but rather constructions of possibilities. Because the observer must necessarily participate in a fresh look, with an unprejudiced eye, and a "letting it be what it is" attitude, there is often popular rejection of this style. The necessity for adjusting preconceived ideas of the importance of reality to art is obvious. The great Dutch painter Piet Mondrian wrote of the need for, "a liberation, a freeing of the human spirit from the oppression of the subject."

Modern art, as a general term, encompasses meanings and motivations rather than dates and techniques. From nineteenth century impressionism, expressionism, cubism, to futurism, surrealism, and abtract expressionism there was increasing disregard for traditional forms. From principles of abstraction, distortion, and nonobjectivity to what Katherine Kuh has identified as "break-up," the term "modern art" has been used to describe the gamut of forms from misty impressionisms to gaunt avant-garde structures.

According to Katherine Kuh, it is necessary to relate any art to the life and society it comes from. She looked at contemporary life and discovered the "basic symptoms reflecting unrest and change" that also occurred in the arts. Of painting and sculpture, she described "shattered surfaces, broken color, segmented composition, dissolving forms, and shredded images." All of these she called "break-ups" and analogous to social life. As war shattered society, as science smashed the atom, artists shattered traditional forms of perception by breaking up constituent elements of art.[30]

One of the great sculptors of this period expressed a view held by many of his fellow artists:

> The violent quarrel between the abstractionists and the surrealists seems to me quite unnecessary. All good art has contained both abstract and surrealist elements, just as it has contained both classical and romantic elements—order and surprise, intellect and imagination, conscious and unconscious. Both sides of the artist's personality must play their part. And I think the first inception of a painting or a sculpture may begin from either end. As far as my own experience is concerned, I sometimes begin a drawing with no preconceived problem to solve, with only the desire to use pencil on paper, and make lines, tones, and shapes with no conscious aim; but as my mind takes in what is so produced, a point arrives where some idea becomes conscious and crystallizes, and then a control and ordering begin to take place.[31]

9
Dance as a Performing Art

The dancer, or dancers, must transform the stage for the audience as well as for themselves into an autonomous, complete, virtual realm, and all motions into a play of visible forces in unbroken, virtual time. . . . Both space and time, as perceptible factors, disappear almost entirely in the dance illusion.

Susanne K. Langer,
philosopher

*F*rom the magic ritual of early man to the latest avant-garde concert today, dance has been a part of the life and culture of its time. In the beginning there was only one kind of dance, but today, among the many different forms, it is dance as a performing art that presents the most confusion. Indeed it is within this area that great controversies rage. Just as in the other arts, dance faces many preconceived ideas and prejudices, not only in terms of what is or what is not art, but with what fulfills the elusive and intangible criteria for best, good, poor, or unacceptable art. This is particularly difficult for the critic who is expected to have vast knowledge of these criteria, as well as an ability to report favorably in terms of all their variations. An impossible task!

Edwin Denby, one of the great dance critics, wrote:

> It is difficult to see the great dance effects as they happen, to see them accurately, catch them fast in memory. It is even more difficult to verbalize them for critical discussion. The particular essence of a performance, its human sweep of articulate rhythm in space and in time has no specific terminology to describe it by.[1]

Many people insist that the dance form they favor is "an art," and their favorite dancer, high stepper or stripper, "is an artist in her own right." Such statements verify their taste, judgment, or even their ignorance of the nature of art. Usual criteria are in terms of skilled movement, dazzling personality, or exciting display. While it may be difficult to identify *the* criteria of art, we can be sure that these are *not*.

Dance is unique in the arts because it is equally concerned with the control of spatial, temporal, and dynamic elements. The dancer must know *where* he is going and be ever alert to design, level, direction, size, relation to other dancers, and the audience, to the spaces where he has been as well as where he now is. He must understand space as few mortals do. A dancer must know *when*—exactly when— he is to move, stop, change, and interrelate with other dancers, accompaniment, and intent of the dance. Without dynamic or energy control he would stumble, bump, collapse, or fall off his performance area. And a dancer needs far more than minimum control of his movement skill; he needs maximum energy, and ability to direct his energy, with exact control of intensity, accent, and quality.

Of course it is impossible for humans to operate without contending with all of these, but only in dance does the artist need to have full control of them all, all the time. In painting, the artist is manipulating line, color, shade, design, and relationships in space. These are his tools. Time and energy are secondary to his initial focus. The musician works with rhythms, tempi, and all kinds of relationships of sounds in time. Dynamics are important in producing certain kinds of sounds, but the energy concerned is not as violent as that of a dancer's.

Because of all this, the dancer has many problems and needs. Aware of space, as a painter, sculptor, or architect, it is in a more personal way that he affects it. His nerves, muscles, and attention must be as sensitive as a musician's to time spans, rhythmic patterning, and actually coping with these in action. No athlete, acrobat, or anatomist has greater regard or awareness of his body's potential for movement than a well-trained dancer. He knows exactly where he is in space and time and how to move in unbelievable leaps and subtle tremors. He is one with his body, in time, and space. According to Martha Graham, "It takes ten years, usually, to make a dancer. It takes ten years of handling this instrument, handling the material with which you are dealing, for you to know it completely."[2]

In addition to the controls that a dancer must have, he must learn to use his techniques to project the intent of the choreographer. While his phenomenal skills are necessary tools, they are not enough. From a being of great movement virtuosity he must become the performing artist, the interpreter, agent, or connector between the choreographer and the audience. It is in this role that the dancer may become great, one who literally affects his audience by his moving performance of a fine choreography.

And then there are the discrepancies between dance as a performing art for the professional dancer and dance as a performing art for the student in school. While the materials are the same in each case, the performer is essentially concerned with the final product; the teacher and student with the creative and self-actualizing process. Differences in objective as well as point of view about these two quite different emphases are at the root of much of the controversy about "where should dance be housed in the schools?" The crux of the problem concerns dance as an art form, not the more obvious, yet highly relevant social, recreational, and theatrical forms. The superficial assumption that dance as a performing art should be in the School of Art or theater, because "they deal with art" and not in the Department of Physical Education, for example, because "they are unconcerned with art," hardly solves any problem. It is better not to be misled by titles but to consider where the philosophy and objectives can best operate.

In attempting to identify dance as a performing art we will draw upon a wide range of points of view and synthesize, as well as simplify, an increasingly complicated aspect of performing art.

Student concert

The Nature of Performing Art

There are many common elements among the arts, but there is one profound difference between the plastic and performing arts. Painting, sculpture, and architecture are available to the observer in finished form, the result of the creative, forming process. There they are, with no variables save in the actual place in which they are put, light and shadow on them and the personal differences in the observer's perceptions. The finished art work changes little in itself. But dance, drama, and music are available only in performance and are "of the instant." Santayana wrote:

> The beauties of nature and of the plastic arts are not consumed by being enjoyed; they retain all of the efficacy to impress a second beholder. But this circumstance is accidental, and those aesthetic objects which depend upon change and are exhausted in time, as are all performances, are things the enjoyment of which is an object of rivalry and is coveted as much as any other pleasure.[3]

While all performance arts have been designed previous to their showing, it is only in the performance that they attain their being. Before that they are either musical or dance notation or words written on a page. While the form is set, the directions clear, and the timing sure, performances are never twice the same, for these are live presentations and the performers are human beings with all of their idiosyncrasies. The presentation is a cooperative affair involving production crew, light, costume and set designers, rehearsal schedules, piano tuners, theater managers, and innumerable interacting production agencies, all of whom are important to the final production.

Cinema, television, and new technologies tend to confuse the issue, for, while they are concerned with performing arts, it is a matter of the transmitting of performance. Once taped or filmed and edited, it remains intact with no chance for performance changes unless the entire process is repeated.

There are two aspects to consider in art. One is in *making* something, like a painting, sculpture, story, musical composition, poem, or dance. But having made a music composition or a dance, the composer has not finished as has the painter, sculptor, or poet. The music or dance notation must be performed to be perceived. It is this *doing* that is the mark of a performing art. The thing planned must be embodied, and this happens in the act of *doing*. The musical score, the notated dance, and the words of the drama are only blueprints or directions for the important event.

The doing is a concentrated effort on one particular occasion, with the audience limited to those present at the occasion, unless it is transmitted by film or tape. When you *make* something you can work quietly and perfect it alone. In performing arts the action is done before this audience once, and then is finished. The audience and the performers must have personal contact. And while the performers may hope to duplicate or improve on another occasion, for now, that's it. You can enjoy a Henry Moore sculpture in New York even though he is in the English countryside. But you can only enjoy Merce Cunningham when he himself performs in your presence.

Dance: A Performing Art

"If you are looking for something to be brave about," said Robert Frost, "consider the arts. Neither sport nor war, but art is the deepest channel for aggressive interests, for will to power, and art's laurels last."[4] And if you seek, beyond bravery, to a sheer lunatic demand for complication, consider many in the performing art of dance who, as choreographers, first design the dance; then find performers with skill, time,

Student rehearsal

perseverance, and sensitivity; train and rehearse them; execute or direct the design of accompaniment, costuming, staging, lighting, publicity, and find rehearsal and performance space and time; manipulate and oversee all aspects of production and, sometimes, even dance the lead role.

As an art form, as a performing art, dance serves a purpose beyond the immediacy of entertainment or spectacular display, recreation or therapy, celebration of national festival, or projection of personal virtuosity. The artistic act of the performed dance is a conscious resolution of the choreographer's comment on his world, through the craft and projection of sensitive dancers. When imagination, emotion, thought, and skill are converted into this perceptible form—this dynamic image—the work of dance art is made available for public viewing. Until performed the dance does not exist, and after the performance it remains only as clues in the choreographer's head, notation on paper, or in the kinetic memory of the dancers.

Individual movements have no significance in themselves; they are not signs which denote things, nor are they signals calling for a particular response. Rather they are materials for evoking, awakening, or stimulating the viewer in an essentially nonverbal way. It is the formulation, the interaction, dynamics, and rhythm of the movement which results in a symbolic image that is presented for the viewer's perception. What you see is the interaction of many actions within a space, with a resulting design of dynamic and temporal elements. Where the dancers are, when they get there, and how they use their power are the important variables. The patterning, sequence, and relationships among these elements are determined by the choreographer. Seldom is the viewer aware of all of these happenings, for only a few outstanding features can be grasped in the rapidly changing picture. Another dance critic, Walter Sorell, remarked:

> No dance work can fully exist at the very moment of its being nor survive this moment in our memory, if it does not have some mystery which lives in the secret of its elusiveness, in the magic of what we see, or think we see. . . .[5]

The painted canvas, the written poem, or the performed dance are each a means chosen by the artist to express his intent. Each is a language for converting the artist's comment into images appropriate to his medium. Dance is a special kind of body language, and while there are no literal words or messages in the language of dance, it may enhance a literal idea or even a story. But it is not a means for factual information, nor is it propaganda, though it can reinforce either. All these things are incidental to the purpose because, in dance as art, one advances beyond journalistic reporting into a realm of metaphysical illusions and images that "tell" more than is there, and "tell it" in movements of the body, designs in space, and rhythmic sequences, all of which demand a response beyond the casual seeing or literal understanding. The sensitive viewer will enter the kinesthetic experience with the performers and will empathize and feel these images.

The great painter, Marcel Duchamp contended:

> . . . the creative act is not performed by the artist alone; the spectator brings the work in contact with the external world by . . . interpreting its inner qualifications and thus adds his contribution to the creative act.[6]

These words of dance are movement phrases designed by the choreographer, but none of it is possible if the dancers are not technically able and psychologically and emotionally concerned with the whole plan. A wide range of approaches are used by choreographers and directors. In some cases the movement is choreographed for particular dancers; in others the dancers must acquire the necessary skills to perform the choreography. With some, the choreographer chooses the action from the dancer's improvisation, or may even ask for their own formulation of certain phrases. In any event the choreographer must respect and rely on his dancers, and vice versa.

Who is the artist in dance, the choreographer or the dancer? Who is the artist in music, the composer or the performer? Each is mutually dependent upon the other, one being impossible without the other, unless the composer and the performer are the same person, in which case he is wearing two hats. There are two distinct sets of tasks, objectives, and procedures, and each must be completed and fulfilled.

The Dance Artist: Choreographer

The choreographer is the one who designs, directs, and stands responsible for the dance. He decides how the rest of the production elements interact and, while he may have assistance, makes the final decision as to how the dance will be produced. The ideal characteristics of a choreographer are:

1. Experience in dance productions, both as performer and viewer.
2. Interest in dance as an art and a desire to choreograph.
3. Sensitivity, imagination, and a broad range of perceptual acuity.
4. Ability to cope with the assets and limitations of dancers, performance and rehearsal places, and production procedures.
5. Educational background, knowledge of people, places and periods.
6. Adequate financial backing, rehearsal and performance space.
7. Plenty of time, courage, and strength.
8. Assistance with design, construction, and details of production and the problems of publicity and business.
9. The ability to benefit from friendly and objective criticism.
10. The empathy to work with cooperative, skilled, and able dancers.

Erick Hawkins, one of the more literate of the contemporary choreographers, wrote:

> When the choreographer presents movement in and for its own sake, he is not communicating. He is then not using the movement as a language. He is not 'saying' something. The movement just 'is.' This difficult innocence of the pure fact of movement just 'being' in and for itself, before it communicates, yields that strange, holy center that is

the only thing we know about being alive. Such movement has its own significant purpose of filling the audience with wonder and delight. . . .
When uncommunicating, be wondrous.
When communicating, communicate.[7]

The Dance Artist: Performer

The time is long past when the dancer is just a well-trained machine, for technical virtuosity is simply the required craft which frees the individual to become the artist. It always helps if he is young, attractive, and conscientious. Some of the ideal characteristics of a performer are:

1. Experience and skill in a number of dance forms, especially the one represented by the choreographer.
2. Interest in the arts and a great desire to dance.
3. Strong, healthy body, with a practical regard for joint action.
4. Broad perceptual field and an open mind.
5. Lots of energy, courage, patience, and strength.
6. The ability to cooperate and get along with others.
7. To take criticism and suggestions easily.
8. To move with conviction and projection.
9. To have time and energy for rehearsals, and a willingness to work.
10. The ability to move with urgency and passion.

Isadora Duncan, first of the moderns, wrote:

There are likewise three kinds of dancers: first, those who consider dancing as a sort of gymnastic drill, made up of impersonal and graceful arabesques; second, those who, by concentrating their minds, lead the body into the rhythm of a desired emotion, expressing a remembered feeling or experience. And finally, there are those who convert the body into a luminous fluidity, surrendering it to the inspiration of the soul.[8]

The Dance

The reality of the dance is the sum of the elements which compose it. First, the dancer—moving through a space, exerting degrees of energy within a time frame—costumed, accompanied, lighted, and staged. Second, the perceptions of the viewer. The painter André Masson, in speaking of his own work said, "But what it expresses is necessarily something *unreal*. And we might add that the artist, whatever pretext he may have for his work, always makes his appeal to the imagination of other people." And as Picasso said of painting, so it is true of dance: ". . . it lives only through the man who is looking at it."

Dance is not the particular turn, leap, or fall but the relationships among all the acts of movement which finally resolve into the completed and whole form. Dance is not the gesture of despair or joy; it is not the personality of the dancer nor is it the breathless encompassing of a space by a virtuoso performer. Rather it is the transitory, space-time image that emerges because of careful choreographic design and meticulous and sensitive performance.

The final work of art is an illusion. To paraphrase R. G. Collingwood,[9] the dance is not what is seen but what is transferred from the choreographer's act. What is done by the dancers is not the dance at all, it is only the means by which an audience, if they are sensitive, can reconstruct for themselves the imaginary dance that previously existed in the choreographer's head. There is more to the dance than the sight and sound of the dancers moving. The viewer must construct in his own perception, by his own efforts, something inaccessible to the person who cannot or will not see beyond the stark reality of the man in action. This must have been what William Blake meant when he said, "See through, not with the eye."

> What dancers create is a dance; and a dance is an apparition of active powers, a *dynamic image*. Everything a dancer actually does serves to create what we really see; but what we really see is a virtual entity. The physical realities are given; place, gravity, body, muscular strength, muscular control and secondary assets such as light, sound or things. All these are actual. But in the dance, they disappear; the more perfect the dance, the less we see the actualities.[10]

According to the intent of the choreographer, and the concept of art held, it is possible that any form of movement may be material for dance as an art. But just because it is well performed, or even in a serious vein, it is not necessarily art. On the other hand, we must not rule out those forms that do not agree with a narrow concept of art.

Dance as an art may be comic as well as solemn, literal as well as abstract, objective as well as nonobjective, simple as well as complex, dramatic as well as natural, spectacular as well as reserved. It can be made up of any style or quality of movement or position. Movement may be used in order to project or augment a literal story, particular mood, design, or ideational content. But then movement may also be used as an end in itself, with no purpose other than an action purpose complete in itself. With so vast a potential one sometimes wonders why so many choreographers limit themselves to only one possibility.

It is at this point that many dancers, choreographers, critics, and members of the audience disagree, so I have called this the "open-and-closed dichotomy." The traditional and closed view holds that dance as an art uses bodily movement as its means of expression and seeks to communicate a sense of beauty, truth, and significance. The beauty and truth are, I suppose, dependent upon the more commonly accepted criteria of beauty and truth, usually "my" truth and "my" beauty. Certainly neither are as universal as usually assumed. The significance or meaning is usually quite literal and must be communicated to the audience in order that the dance be successful. Here movement is organized in order to evoke images that literally tell a story.

In spite of their common practice, most choreographers insist that they are concerned with independent, original, and composed movement to project their intent—"Movement comes first, nothing else is as important," they say. But they are the ones who then say, "Before I start I must find some music," or, "What shall I dance *about*?" And a classic response of an observer is, "His dance tells the story of these two people fighting over . . . ," or "It was a strange dance, I never found out what was going on."

The implication for the choreographer is that he must manipulate recognizable clues within his movement phrase so that meaning will be clear. The alternative is a set of responses like:

"What does it mean?"

"Why didn't he clarify his meaning with program notes?"

"Even his title was misleading."

"I see absolutely no meaning in just standing around, or walking up and down carrying that two-by-four."

The open view presumes dance to be a performance precluding any imperative of truth, beauty, or specific meaning. It simply *is*, as a direct presentation, with no injunction attached. There is no pretense for what *ought* to be. It presents itself into the world of existence free of any intent to fit some esthetic or standard. Here is an independent, original formulation. It is a presentation, not a representation, of a "sincerely felt possibility." This dance reminds us only of itself, though we may, while perceiving it, remind ourselves of things extraneous yet related to it. The dance opens our eyes to itself, innocently, "as if for the first time."

This dance presents nothing that exists, has ever existed, or ever will exist. This is all there is to it—it is the "present felt-image." Before the presentation there was only a plan, and after it is over it is done, it no longer exists. Here is a man-made formulation of man in motion. It means what it is!

As with everything else in the world, neither one answer nor the other is sufficient. It is not so much that we have an open or a closed view, as that we recognize the influence of open and closed concepts on our views. The more we can accept any movement as a potentially significant experience in itself, the more open our view. The more we insist upon mimetic gesture and traditional form, the more closed it is. That is not to say that dance as a performing art cannot include both, and the choreographer who can operate at both ends and the middle has a remarkably broad scope. Usually the choreographer operates in ways that are in accord with his experience, blended with his prejudices and suited to his intent.

In a kind of brainwashing procedure, young dancers are often led to believe that only modern dance or classical ballet is the avenue to art dance. And what then of ethnic dance which uses a rigid code of movement, in highly stylized form with unchanging traditional content, and presented as a moving theatrical event? Is this less an art than classical ballet with its rigid code of movement, in highly stylized form, with practically unchanging traditional content, and presented as a moving theatrical event? What is it that determines art-status?

When or by whom the dance was choreographed, the movement used, or the content or implication are irrelevant as bases for being or not being art. Petipa's *Swan Lake,* Doris Humphrey's *Shakers,* Ted Shawn's *Kinetic Malpai,* Agnes de Mille's *Rodeo,* Shan Kar's *Indra,* Jerome Robbins's dances for *West Side Story,* Deborah Hays's *26 Variations of 8 Activities for 13 People,* Martha Graham's *Appalachian Spring,* Antony Tudor's *Dark Elegies,* Merce Cunningham's *Rain Forest,* or George Balanchine's *Four Temperaments* are no less art because they represent different times, movement codes, form, content, and points of view. Just as paintings of Leonardo da Vinci differ from those of Paul Klee, so do the verses of Walt Whitman differ from T. S. Eliot; but no one questions their place as painting or poetry.

Dance as an art is a theatrical experience that culminates and affirms both the choreographer's and performer's ability to create in movement some comment on the experience they know and cherish. Dance art creates and projects movement images which, if they are effective for the audience, enrich its perceptual powers and even increase its sensitivity to many kinds of reality. Rather than a fleeting exposure to dance virtuosity, something remains of a fresh, moving, and vital experience after the performance is over.

What They Say Dance Is

Dance is the most perishable of the arts. Ballets are forgotten, ballerinas retire, choreographers die—and what remains of that glorious production which so excited us a decade ago, a year ago, or even last night?

Jack Anderson, critic

... the dance is a language with which man is born, the ecstatic manifestation of his existence.

Mary Wigman, dancer

The dance ... speaks of potentialities and aspects of man that are antecedent to words, antecedent even to the spheres of personal recollection, and constitute the primary heritage of the embodied human spirit.

Jean Erdman, dancer

Of all the arts, it is surely the dance ... that should be the first to receive attention, for it is first intrinsically in the nature of man. It is the art out of which all others grow, and it touches the issues of life itself as none of them is equipped to do. Its philosophical implications are profound and practical, for it reveals the vision of the wholeness of man and provides a simple means for making that vision real.

John Martin, critic

... inheritors took the life-giving substance from their [Duncan and St. Denis] hands, molded it in ever expanding ways and made of it the contemporary art dance. This new form was born in the theater, was designed to be a communication on a spiritual level, and still bears only fleeting traces of other values, such as spectacle, entertainment, folk or ritual influences.

Doris Humphrey, dancer

Man must speak, then sing, then dance. The speaking is the brain, the thinking man. The singing is the emotion. The dancing is the Dionysian ecstasy which carries away all.

Isadora Duncan, dancer

The dance exists exclusively in terms of the movement of the body, not only in the obvious sense that the dancer moves, but also in the less apparent sense that its response in the spectator is likewise a matter of body movement.

John Martin, critic

Dancing is a very living art. It is essentially of the moment, although a very old art. A dancer's art is lived while he is dancing. Nothing is left of his art except the pictures and the memories—when his dancing days are over. What he has to contribute to the sum total of human experience must be done through the dance. It cannot be transmitted at any other time, in any other way.

Martha Graham, dancer

Rhythmic movement having as its aim the creation of visual designs by a series of poses and tracing of patterns through space in the course of measured units of time, the two components, static and kinetic, receiving varying emphasis (as in ballet, natya and modern dance) and being executed by different parts of the body in accordance with temperament, artistic precept and purpose: the art of dancing.

Attributed to *Louis Horst*, musician

Dance is an art, because it demands vocation, knowledge and ability. It is a fine art, because it aims towards an ideal, not only of plastic beauty, but also of lyric and dramatic expressiveness.

August Bournoville, ballet master

Basic dance—and I should qualify the word basic—is primarily concerned with motion. So immediately you will say but the basketball player is concerned with motion. That is so—but he is not concerned with it *primarily*. His action is a means towards an end beyond motion. In basic dance the motion is its own end—that is, it is concerned with nothing beyond itself.

Alwin Nikolais, choreographer

A dance, like any other work of art, is a perceptible form that expresses the nature of human feeling—the rhythms and connections, crises and breaks, the complexity and richness of what is sometimes called man's 'inner life. . . .'

Susanne K. Langer, philosopher

The dance, just as the performance of the actor, is kinesthetic art, art of the muscle sense. The awareness of tension and relaxation within his own body, the sense of balance that distinguishes the proud stability of the vertical from the risky adventures of thrusting and falling—these are the tools of the dancer.

Rudolf Arnheim, psychologist

What They Say about Dance

For young artists to follow in the footsteps of titans is not a particularly happy lot. . . . The titans had made the break with the past, evolved new principles, battled convention, won the rebellion. What was left to be done? . . . A few had the good sense to learn all they could from the titans, to be influenced but not intimidated. . . .

Walter Terry, critic

Ballet is an art which depends for its existence on patrons, either private or public. Consequently its organizers must always cater to the Establishment. . . .

Clive Barnes, critic

No other art offers such a challenge. In a society desperately in need of all its art and artists, the art of the dance offers a rare opportunity for those with the vision of its ancient grandeur to speak of it anew.

Jose Limon, dancer

No art suffers more misunderstanding, sentimental judgment, and mystical interpretation than the art of dancing.

Susanne K. Langer, philosopher

One's cultural heritage serves to flavor one's work, and the groups that are segregated socially, politically, and economically from the body of society tend to keep their cultural identity strongly intact, most often giving the national culture its mark of uniqueness—witness the music, dance, and crafts of the Yemenite Jew in Israel; the song and dance of the gypsy in Spain; the tremendous contribution of the Negro to American music. One cannot help but be moved by these forces, no matter what one's birthright, and they become national and international treasures, for art knows no boundaries.

Donald McKayle, dancer

The modern dance is a point of view, an attitude toward the function of art in the contemporary world. As that world changes, the modern dance will change, for the symbols will again—as they become acceptable—lose their power to evoke the hidden realities. They will again have to be recharged, revitalized; even demolished and re-created anew in order to serve their function. Unless this happens, the modern dance is not modern—it is dead.

Selma Jeanne Cohen, critic

. . . the dance can only maintain its vitality there [in the theater] by continuing its experimentations, by developing its techniques, by giving performers opportunities to develop their talents. By this I mean enlarging the field of independent dance, dance on its own terms and not only in its collaborative role in the theater.

Helen Tamiris, dancer

Again and again in the history of art, the scene repeats itself. The 'old' revolutionary entrenched in the esthetic structure which he has raised in the name of his ideals stands facing the 'new' revolutionary. On both sides there is antagonism—the established artist seeking to conserve the stronghold of his accomplishment, the newcomer demanding 'lebensraum' for his own esthetic creed. Behind each is the public he has drawn unto himself. Such a scene is taking place at present between the traditionalists and the avant-gardists in the modern dance.

Ernestine Stodelle, critic

No artist is ahead of his time. He *is* his time: it is just that others are behind the time.

Martha Graham, dancer

In the strictest sense of the word I do not believe there is any such thing as contemporary or modern art. What is really meant by those words is the contemporary aspect or vista of art. We would hardly say there is a contemporary moon or contemporary stars. Yet we might describe the moon as we see it today—that is, from the vantage point of a contemporary time.

Alwin Nikolais, choreographer

What is modern about modern dance is its resistance to the past, its response to the present, its constant redefining of the *idea* of dance.

Marcia B. Siegel, critic

. . . nothing is more revealing than movement. What you are finds expression in what you do. The dance reveals the spirit of the country in which it takes root. No sooner does it fail to do this than the dance begins to lose its indispensable integrity and significance.

Martha Graham, dancer

My dance creates me as all men and it creates me as myself. It creates in me the meaning of human beingness. I can dance like an animal, a marionette, or a god, but only *like*. These dances remind me that my consciousness and incarnation are human, and my only possible movement is mine.

Sondra Horton Fraleigh, dancer

Now for a simple recipe for the enjoyment of modern dancing. When entering the theatre it is well first of all to leave as much of the intellect as possible in the check room with the hat. Do not bring in any preconceived idea of what the dancer is to do, such as interpret the music or enact pantomimes or play charades. When the performance begins, abandon all effort to figure out what it means; it will not mean anything unless you do this. Merely relax and let the muscles do the thinking. If it is not easy at first, persistence will have its effect in due time.

John Martin, critic

Because both personal experience and artistic restraint are necessary to expression, it is clear that, no matter what the source of a dancer's initial impulse, it is the richness of experience and the sensitivity of the selecting personality which control and color the material, and which make of movement—a dance.

Margaret H'Doubler, teacher

Few people would deny that classic ballet and the established 'schools' of modern dance technique are ways of moving which dancers and audiences continue to find beautiful and expressive; therefore they continue to be worth doing. But they are not the only ways of moving. Rudy Perez says, 'Too many people are slaves to the academic technique in which they've been trained. Any kind of movement using space can be dance. There's no reason why dance should be only what you learn in class.' Judith Dunn points out: 'Obviously it's not a matter of *anything goes*. I don't think I'm dancing when I walk down the street carrying groceries.'

Jack Anderson, critic

The 'war' between the 'classicists' and the 'moderns' is always with us. The first are conservative, accepting the wisdom and the working principles of the past as they have been evolved from period to period, building squarely upon them and abandoning only what by common consent has become too obsolete or outmoded to have any further present usefulness. The others are more radical. Impatient with what they feel are the outworn traditions and restrictions of the past, they seek to create wholly new and spontaneous forms, drawn from the direct, first-hand and personal experiences of the individual creators themselves.

Ruth Page, dancer

What is the most beautiful dance? . . . Dance that knows the most beautiful and true movement starts in the pelvis and spine and flows into the tassel-like legs, arms and head. . . . Dance that uses technique that is an organic whole, not a grab-bag or eclecticism. . . . Dance that senses itself instant-by-instant. . . . Dance that knows that the art is more than the personality of the dancer. . . . Dance that knows dance can be, should be, and is a way of saying now.

Erick Hawkins, dancer

I want my movements to ignite the space about me. Within the duration of a dance, it is possible to evoke changing aspects of space and to play with their identities. The air around me seems to have the capacity to solidify or melt. It can be heavy, then rarified, or agitated and then becalmed. Sometimes I have to force my way through it, and at other times I am driven by it.

Merle Marsicano, dancer

Nothing so clearly and inevitably reveals the inner man than movement and gesture. It is quite possible, if one chooses, to conceal and dissimulate behind words or paintings or statues or other forms of human expression, but the moment you move you stand revealed, for good or ill, for what you are.

Doris Humphrey, dancer

Movement is an intrinsic part of the 'total theatre' concept. The logic of one event coming as responsive to another seems inadequate now. We look at and listen to several at once. For dance it was all those words about meaning that got in the way. Right now they are broken up: they do not quite fit, we have to shuffle and deal them out again.

Merce Cunningham, dancer

The dance for two thousand years has been an art imprisoned. All my life I have been trying to break its chains, to open the gates and give it back its freedom. Once liberated the dance will be the great inspirational force among the arts. . . . Before I danced, all dancers were imprisoned in tight clothes, repeating year after year some mechanical gestures; since I began thousands of people have begun dancing, in all countries of the world, clothed only in light tunics, and knowing for the first time the free rhythm of the human body, and its accordance with the harmonious movements of nature. . . .

Isadora Duncan, dancer

Dance today is clearly in an unsettled state. Old forms and traditions are being given up. New ones are arising to take their place. A time of change presents a confused picture. That there is this change is proof that dance is organically vital—and much more so than it has ever before been in this country. As in all times of transition, some will be set adrift, others will see clearly where they are going, and leaders will continue to arise, who, it is predictable, will become authoritative and dogmatic.

Margaret H'Doubler, teacher

Unquestionably the members of the avant-garde have made a significant contribution to the art of dance. They have tremendously broadened the range of the dance vocabulary and revealed its wealth of connotative power. They have explored new relationships between movement and sound, movement and light and color. They have stimulated a fresh awareness of the uniqueness of the medium of dance. If they have not demonstrated that dance must do away with content and narrative or emotional continuity, they have shown that dances can be formed without them.

Selma Jeanne Cohen, critic

The real dance is the complete dance experience which the artist made, first for himself and then for others, and this consummated dance event is the true object of critical attention and evaluation; hence the critic's primary responsibility to make that experience fully come to be in himself, so that he may sound, exhaust and bound it. But this takes time and goes way beyond the first personal responses, even at their most accurate.

George Beiswanger, critic

... dance is the only art that employs the same instrument for both the life and the art experience. The body as a housing for both the pedestrian action and the sensitized motion has to be trained to make this distinction. And so the dancer does train to extend this physical range. ...

Murray Louis, choreographer

Dance is a transient mode of expression, performed in a given form and style by the human body moving in space. Dance occurs through purposefully selected and controlled rhythmic movements; the resulting phenomenon is recognized as dance both by the performer and the observing members of a given group.

Joann Kealiinohomoku, anthropologist

Dance is concerned with the single instant as it comes along.

Merce Cunningham, dancer

If our art, imperfect as it is, seduce and captivate the spectator: if dancing stripped of the charm of expression sometimes occasion us trouble and emotion, and throw our thoughts into a pleasing disorder; what power and domination might it not achieve over us if its movements were directed by brains and its pictures painted with feeling? There is no doubt that ballets will rival painting in attraction when the executants display less of the automaton and the composers are better trained.

Jean Georges Noverre, ballet master

Dance, one of the oldest forms of artistic expression, requires only the human body for its realization. Since there are two types of human bodies, male and female, dance can find its mode of expression through one or the other. In the beginning of the dance on stage the man was the only interpreter. In time woman joined him behind the footlights. Eventually the fusion of masculine and feminine dance, incorporating theatrical elements, created a new art form—the ballet.

Igor Youskevitch, dancer

What They Say about Dancers

If one had to define one essential gift with which a dancer needs to be endowed, there might be a rush of answers. A beautiful body, grace of line, graciousness of spirit, joy in the work, ability to please, unswerving integrity, relentless ambition towards some abstract perfection. Certainly all these factors determine a dancer's character, and every element exists in some combination within the performing artist's presence.

Lincoln Kirstein, critic

So many dancers rely on some sort of magic happening on the stage. They never, for various reasons, work full out in rehearsal. That's very uncreative. They don't discover the kinds of things that add up to a remarkable performance.

Benjamin Harkarvy, ballet master

I would like to tell all dancers to forget themselves and the desire for self display. They must become completely absorbed in the dance. Even in a classical variation there should never be any thought of a dancer *doing* a variation—he should become identified with it.

Antony Tudor, dancer

I will make an average man into an average dancer, provided he be passably well made. I will teach him how to move his arms and legs, to turn his head. I will give him steadiness, brilliancy and speed; but I cannot endow him with that fire and intelligence, those graces and that expression of feeling which is the soul of true pantomime. Nature was always superior to art, it is not for her to perform miracles.

Jean Georges Noverre, ballet master

When you watch ballet dancers dancing you are observing a young woman or a young man in fancy dress, and you like it if they look attractive, if they are well built and have what seems to be an open face. You notice the youthful spring in starting, the grace of carriage, the strength in stopping. You like it if they know what to do and where to go, if they can throw in a surprising trick or two, if they seem to be enjoying their part and are pleasantly sociable as performers. All this is proper juvenile charm, and it often gives a very sharp pleasure in watching dancers. But you are ready too for other qualities besides charm.

Edwin Denby, critic

The dancer learns a language, a form, that expresses an idea and once that form is achieved it begins to communicate. Within the form you will find there is plenty of room for you to live. When there is a living being in the form it is recognized by the public. There is a truth in it. You have to live within this form. If you do not live in it, it can't become real; it is only a masquerade.

Erik Bruhn, dancer

The special thing about Miss Graham is not that she is a modernist. Almost no one nowadays is anything else. . . . I keep being struck in all her work by its intellectual seriousness, its inventiveness and its exact workmanship; and these are qualities I can't think of as heretical or contrary.

Edwin Denby, critic

Fokine freed movement; he made the dancer move like a human being on stage. Tudor went further. He made the dancer become a human being on stage.

Nora Kaye, dancer

He [Tudor] departs in almost every respect from the romanticism, the ethnological interest, the tendency toward dramatic generalization, which were so typical of Fokine. His dramatic direction is mainly toward the specific and the psychological, toward believable tensions instead of generic ones.

John Martin, critic

Tudor had a great influence on my early work and a great influence on all of contemporary ballet. Tremendous respect is due him for this.

Jerome Robbins, choreographer

It was Anna Pavlova, and no one else, who opened the world to ballet. It was she who did the back-breaking work of pioneering. It was Pavlova who found and cultivated audiences for contemporary ballet companies. Her service to ballet is priceless. No other single human being did more for ballet than she. To all the millions of people for whom she danced she brought a little of herself . . . what remains of Pavlova today is not a movement in the art, not a tendency, not even a series of dances. It is something far less concrete, but possibly more valuable: inspiration.

Hilda Dutsova, dancer

The dancer does not act upon the world, he behaves in it. And his behavior has meaning only when performed for others. Creative vanity molds the appearance of the self into an image of the world.

Rudolf Arnheim, psychologist

What is expressive in a dance is not the dancer's opinions, psychological, political or moral. It isn't even what she thinks about episodes in her private life. What is expressive in dancing is the way she moves about the stage, the way she exhibits her body in motion.

Edwin Denby, critic

What They Say about Technique

I think there will always be a basic, technical distinction between modern dance and ballet, because the modern conception of training is different. But in dance works there should be no idioms. It is not technique that makes a dance modern; you can have a modern dance on pointes. It is not subject matter either. Tudor's *Pillar of Fire* has a romantic story like *Giselle*, but it doesn't reflect the conventional concept of romance. It's a difference in point of view. The modern attitude does not eliminate fantasy or romantic and poetic ideas. But we don't handle them the way the nineteenth century did. We are not representational; we are imaginative.

Anna Sokolow, dancer

. . . through the Cecchetti method the dancer, having definite rules and theories to guide him, acquires a control of his technique that enables him eventually to lose himself in a wider vista of expression.

Enrico Cecchetti, ballet master

Most dancers think they have achieved the peak of their technique when they feel comfortable in the execution of their movements. It is too often, however, a state of 'not wishing to be disturbed.' But there is another stage of comfort in which the dancer has acquired so much ability that he no longer [has] to think of his technique, it has become second nature to him.

George Balanchine, choreographer

Technique transforms experience into the form of its expression.

Margaret H'Doubler, teacher

Dancing should be interpretive. It should not degenerate into mere gymnastics. Ballet must have a complete unity of expression, a unity which is made up of a harmonious blending of the three elements—music, painting and plastic art.

Michel Fokine, dancer

Children of Terpsichore, renounce *cabrioles, entrechats* and over-complicated steps; renounce grimaces to study sentiments, artless graces and expression; study how to make your gestures noble, never forget that it is the life-blood of dancing; put judgment and sense into your *pas de deux;* let willpower order their course and good taste preside over all situations; away with those lifeless masks but feeble copies of nature. . . .

Jean Georges Noverre, ballet master

Discipline is, or should be, a voluntary course of regulated and regular actions where efforts bring about desired results. Too often it becomes something else. I am not so interested in how high a person can extend his leg or how high he jumps into the air, but rather what he looks like while he is doing these things.

Judith Dunn, dancer

All dance has expression. If there is no expression, I prefer the circus. The performers do more dangerous, more difficult technical things than we do. But we are dancers. We have to express and we have to project.

Luis Fuente, dancer

I have always cared about the classic discipline, and, now it seems that I am increasingly pulled toward the classic ballet. It seems that the more modern my thinking becomes, the more traditional and classical my expression becomes. I believe that clear movement is a sign of clear thinking, and we live in a time for thinking very clearly—and feeling very deeply.

Maurice Bejart, dancer

As I have watched the development of dance, in all areas, in all styles, I have seen that there is a greater and greater emphasis on technique, but less and less thought given to artistry. I do not mean to imply that technique is not important—it is ever and ever more important, to give the dancer mastery and control. But the most important thing about technique is to have the ability to hide the technical facility, to perform with so much ease that none of the technical difficulties are obvious.

Pauline Koner, dancer

No, I don't teach technique as such, but the great old variations help them secure their technique, to prepare themselves for other roles. I teach them how to hold a pose, just in case there is applause at performance. At the end of a class, they are required to bow, but it is not to me—it is to the mirror behind where I am sitting, it is to the audience they may one day meet.

Alicia Markova, dancer

What I like is the line and technical range that classical ballet gives to the body. But I still want to project to the audience the expressiveness that only modern dance offers, especially for the inner kind of things.

Alvin Ailey, dancer

An art process is not essentially a natural process; it is an invented one. It can take actions of organization from the way nature functions, but essentially man invents the process. And from or for that process he derives a discipline to make and keep the process functioning. That discipline too is not a natural process. The daily discipline, the continued keeping of the elasticity of the muscles, the continued control of the mind over the body's actions, the constant hoped-for flow of the spirit into physical movement, both new and renewed, is not a natural way. It is unnatural in its demands on all the sources of energy. But the final synthesis can be a natural one, natural in the sense that the mind, body and spirit function as one.

Merce Cunningham, dancer

A feat expresses friction, struggle. But a spectacular leap becomes dance when it says, 'I move in effortless harmony with the forces of nature.' First through my own dancing and later through my teaching, I have spent most of my life trying to solve problems of transforming the feat into the dance.

Mia Slavenska, dancer

What They Say about Choreography

The dance itself should be long dreamed over, the instinctive movement invited, glimpses and visions welcomed to entrap the imagination. The strict technical considerations, one may hope, are operating subconsciously to save the choreographer from the worst mistakes; but on the surface all is rapt excitement, the discovery of a new country.

Doris Humphrey, dancer

While some choreographers assert that their works should not 'mean' but 'be,' others feel that their dances do contain meanings. In Alwin Nikolais' words, they 'let the movement speak for itself.'

Selma Jeanne Cohen, critic

I look upon this polygamy of motion, shape, color and sound as the basic art of the theatre. To me, the art of drama is one thing; the art of theatre is another. In the latter, a magical panorama of things, sounds, colors, shapes, lights, illusions, and events happen before your eyes and ears. I find my needs cannot be wholly satisfied by one art. I like to mix my magics.

Alwin Nikolais, choreographer

Despite the catch-as-catch-can type of training that is certainly more the rule than the exception here, I think that our best dancers possess a vitality, a directness, and an honesty that are unique. Since I feel that it is the choreographer who is at the center of his art, these qualities in the best American dancers, along with a wonderful lack of pretentiousness, strike me as ideal for a dancer, the medium through which choreographic invention is displayed.

Benjamin Harkarvy, choreographer

. . . the intellectualizing process . . . is not my way of doing. I prefer to drop a simple, single idea into my brain and let it rummage around for several months, with no particular efforts toward consciousness on my part. Then, two or three weeks before I begin to choreograph, I attempt to cast up the results of the Rorschach process. Then I like to choreograph swiftly and within a short span of time. I feel that in this outpouring I keep the channels of my subject open.

Alwin Nikolais, choreographer

Avant-garde dancers have developed what has come to be known as the choreography of discontinuity. The old verities of the development of theme, unity, contrast, climax, the beginning-middle-end syndrome, fixed time and formal structures give way to chance composition, aleatory techniques, repetition, ambiguity, lack of climax, open-ended construction, an a-logical, anarchistic form with the parts quite independent of each other.

Gertrude Lippincott, dancer

In my choreographic creations I have always been dependent on music. I feel a choreographer can't invent rhythms, he only reflects them in movement. The body is his sole medium and, unaided, the body will improvise for a short breath. But the organizing of rhythm on a grand scale is a sustained process. It is a function of the musical mind. Planning rhythm is like planning a house, it needs a structural operation.

George Balanchine, choreographer

The dance-maker is the first person to exercise the critical function with respect to his own work because there is no way for him to engage in making dances, on however spontaneous a plane, without taking note of what he is doing and appraising what is getting done. He has to be assured that what he is turning out amounts to something in the performing, and this requires that he view what he is doing in order to shape the doing by what the viewing shows it to be in the doing.

George Beiswanger, critic

With every new ballet that I produce I seek to empty myself of some plastic obsession and every ballet I do is, for me, the solving of a balletic problem.

Frederick Ashton, dancer

I dance images in my head—no, I have no idea how they come—they just do. Some dancers prefer to work with a mirror. I don't like to work that way—except in involved places. Rather, I like to get an image in my head of something—just about anything—the slow gait of a five-gaited horse, a giraffe running over a plain, a rubber band being stretched—and I let the image work through the rest of my body.

Tommy Tune, dancer

The choreographer cannot deliberately make a ballet to appeal to an audience, he has to start from personal inspirations. He has to trust the ballet, to let it stand on its own strengths or fall on its weaknesses. If it reaches the audience, then he is lucky that round!

Gerald Arpino, choreographer

I deplore the artist who makes of his art a withdrawal from the travail of his time; who sterilizes and dehumanizes it into empty formalism; who renounces the vision of man as perfectable, a 'golden impossibility,' and makes him into a shabby scarecrow of the beatniks; who forgets that the artist's function is perpetually to be the voice and conscience of his time. It was Doris Humphrey who first taught me that man is the fittest subject for choreography. And Martha Graham continues, triumphantly to prove that his passions, grandeurs, and vices are the ingredients of great dance, great theatre, and great art.

Jose Limon, dancer

So many dances leave one untouched, unmoved. A dancer should be able to raise an arm and make someone cry—in the way Isadora Duncan did. It is a necessity for any art to move you.

Pauline Koner, dancer

No doubt, it is useful for an artist to know all the forms of art which have preceded or which accompany his. That is a sign of strength if it is a question of looking for stimulus or recognizing mistakes he must avoid. But he must be very careful not to look for models. As soon as one artist takes another as model, he is lost. There is no other model, or rather no other point of departure than reality.

Pablo Picasso, painter

These, then, are some of the reminders which have been learned by painful experience and which should help the choreographer to avoid some of the commonest mistakes:

> Symmetry is lifeless
> Two-dimensional design is lifeless
> The eye is faster than the ear
> Movement looks slower and weaker on the stage
> All dances are too long
> A good ending is forty percent of the dance
> Monotony is fatal; look for contrasts
> Don't be a slave to, or a mutilator of, the music
> Listen to qualified advice; don't be arrogant
> Don't intellectualize; motivate movement
> Don't leave the ending to the end

Doris Humphrey, dancer

When Dancers Speak

My dancing is just dancing. It is not an attempt to interpret life in a literary sense. It is the affirmation of life through movement. Its only aim is to impart the sensation of living, to energize the spectator into keener awareness, of the vigor, of the mystery, the humor, the variety and the wonder of life; to send the spectator away with a fuller sense of his own potentialities and the power of realizing them, whatever the medium of his activity.

Martha Graham, dancer

. . . I came to see that movement is one of the great laws of life. It is the primary medium of our aliveness, the flow of energy going on in us like a river all the time, awake or asleep, twenty-four hours a day. Our movement is our behavior; there is a direct connection between what we are like and how we move. . . . As people begin to move in their own way, they are faced with feelings of surprise and delight and often of anxiety and embarrassment. Judgments, corrections and explanations are of no use. It is *their* movement, and it happened just that way.

Mary Whitehouse, dance therapist

The artist must not run away from himself, from his 'center of being.' He is the bearer of a message, and it is his responsibility to tell it—in whatever medium it may be—intelligibly, forcefully and with his utmost artistic ability. He may sometimes fail in the delivery of his message, but he must not fail in his purpose.

Charles Weidman, dancer

The performer is responsible to his conscience, to his colleagues, and, if you like, to his audience.

Erik Bruhn, dancer

The exponent of modern dancing has to fight two things. One is the belief that it simply means self-expression and the other that no technic is required.

Martha Graham, dancer

There is a difference between acting a movement and actually doing it. In the final analysis it is meaningless to count the amount of jumps you can do, because one small gesture which is right and proves the oneness of purpose in what is being done will far outweigh everything else.

Hanya Holm, dancer

I wanted to dance in modern works, to stretch myself. It is part of the dance of our time, part of the dancer's world. But I also wanted to show that a ballet dancer is not limited, that no dancer is limited, if he will learn . . . if he is willing to learn. Dance is in many and various dimensions: we are free to move in all of them. I think that what I have done, too, is made a freedom for other dancers, with the public, who sees me as a danseur in the ballet and also as a dancer in modern works.

Rudolf Nureyev, dancer

I would like to make it clear from the start that these dances are primarily meant to be a kind of food for the eye. If they evoke dramatic images and riddles, the key to their solution lies not so much in the brain, but in the senses and the eye of the spectator. It was not my intention to present literary messages, although certain dances here have as their focal point a common subject with certain writings.

Paul Taylor, dancer

I spent long days and nights in the studio seeking that dance which might be the divine expression of the human spirit through the medium of the body's movement. For hours I would stand quite still, my two

hands folded between my breasts, covering the solar plexus. . . . I was seeking and finally discovered the central spring of all movement, the crater of motor power, the unity from which all diversities of movement are born, the mirror of vision for the creation of the dance.
Isadora Duncan, dancer

I do everything I know how in a dance.
Twyla Tharp, dancer

I'm very excited about dance and love it with a deep passion. I also struggle, tire and become discouraged. But what has always revived me . . . has been the rebirth of energy each time the creative process is awakened and artistic activity begins to unfold even in some infinitesimal measure.
Ann Halprin, dancer

Doris Humphrey said to me, 'Pauline, we must never forget what dance really means to us, what we are trying to say. We must never forget we are human beings—and what could be more important?' She feared this concept would not be fought for after she was gone, but everything great and important is timeless.
Pauline Koner, dancer

Standing still before a mirror, I found that first the body began to sway. Then, letting myself go, three things happened. I began to fall, the speed increasing as I went down. The body in an involuntary effort to resist the fall, made a design. The accent came at the conclusion, when I hit the floor. Out of the substance of this movement evolved an idea. So, starting with movement suggested drama. Later I learned to start with a dramatic idea and devise movements to express it.
Doris Humphrey, dancer

The technique of the classical pas de deux is based on the assistance a male gives his female partner in the execution of the dance steps that they customarily perform together. This, in a way, is an over-statement of life situations where a man always helps a woman and is a gallant gentleman, voluntarily enduring certain hardships for her comfort and well-being. The entire structure of their dance together, starting with the male's place onstage behind the female, is based on the stronger sex patronizing the weaker. Besides, a natural feeling between the sexes is like a spark that gives to the execution of dance steps at least an emotional overtone, often even a definite love theme.
Igor Youskevitch, dancer

One of the more disappointing phenomena in the dance scene here is that, although many American ballet companies have embraced modern dance choreographers, they do not seem to feel that it is important to do the same with their techniques.
Benjamin Harkarvy, choreographer

A dancer on the stage should be in command of all things physical. His work will become more clear and precise as his body becomes more certain and flexible. His performance should have an exact logic. The difference between the artist and the non-artist is not a greater capacity for feeling. The secret is that the artist can objectify, can make apparent the feelings we all have.

Martha Graham, dancer

To dance is to challenge the body which is also the self. To generate an action which has a force of its own and allow the movement *to penetrate the inner sensibilities,* or to calculate the action and try to tune out—this is difficult, perhaps impossible.

Katherine Litz, dancer

Dancing should look easy; like an optical illusion. It should seem effortless. When you do a difficult variation, the audience is aware that it is demanding and that you have the power and strength to do it. But in the end, when you take your bow, you should look as if you were saying, 'Oh, it was nothing. I could do it again.'

Helgi Tomasson, dancer

One word comes to mind over and over again and I guess that word is 'weight.' That's the quality I find in so many of the male dancers I think exciting; they have a special relationship to the ground. Rudolf Nureyev has it tremendously. There's a kind of a cat-like clawing of the ground before he goes up in the air; it's as if he grabs the ground with his feet before he goes up.

Bruce Marks, dancer

I have a big feeling about muscle—to have a muscle, to feel a muscle, to have a muscle warmed up and toned and ready to do something—it's a marvelous, sensual feeling. Then to feel and sense the quality of a movement, to have it inside, absolutely in the middle of your muscles, so that it can emanate and move and come out. Then preparing the role. There is a certain instinct involved. Your background and experience begin to emerge; the idea falls out of you into your hands where you can feel it and examine it. You can taste it with your mouth and decide whether you like it or not; you can spit it out or swallow and digest it.

Edward Villella, dancer

A dancer is involved in learning to execute a dance movement precisely in shape and time. A dancer is occupied with placement, stage spacing, the quality of a leap, the softness of a foot—whether the movement goes out to the audience or spirals inward upon itself. These are some of the things a dancer is concerned with, but actually what we see is more than a foot or a curved back. We see an individual, and we see what an individual is. All this exact training and dance stylization cannot abstract a body into a nonentity. A person is going to be revealed.

Paul Taylor, dancer

I believe we must do more than build or service technical instruments. We must be not only trainers, but teachers as well. For technique is not only to be achieved—it is to be used. We must believe, first and last, that the stage is not a place where one proselytizes about movement technique but rather the place where the dancer becomes the worthy instrument of an idea.

Cary Rick, dancer

The artist who attempts to escape the present, either by delving into the past or the future, is running away from his center of being. But it is not enough for the artist alone to assume his responsibilities as mentor and preceptor. His audience also must do so, especially in the case of an artistic form which concerns the theatre.

Charles Weidman, dancer

The dancer of today is more intelligent, more 'with it,' than the dancer of ten years ago.

Gerald Arpino, choreographer

Dancer's faces are curious. They have more bones than most people, and on the days when you work very hard you are sure that you have somehow accumulated more bones than you started with. Dancer's faces are full of bones. I looked at Markova the other day. There is that face, the bones. I looked at Nora Kaye. Same bones. I looked at some of the men. Same bones. Why? Because the constancy of the exercise makes your flesh lay back against your frame.

Martha Graham, dancer

As a dancer, if you're lucky, powerful people have been molding you. But then, eventually, in teaching, something materializes in front of you, that isn't any more somebody else's reflection and so must be you.

Lucas Hoving, dancer

Some say my style is a cross between ballet and modern. But I never try to make my dancers look like ballet dancers. I just use basic movements of the body, that do relate to ballet, too.

I think the one thing we always start with is the dancer in the studio, moving or standing still. When I work on different pieces, they seem to grow, rather than start from any preconceived ideas. And they seem to end up in their finished state because they make their own logic. I try to work them out that way, and a lot of it is in experiment, working with the dancer in the studio.

Paul Taylor, dancer

Don't get hung up on verbalizing what the feeling is. Time and space cannot be defined independently of one another, that is, independently of motion.

I would like to allow each dancer to appear in his own way as a dancer, and that implies a good deal of trust between us—all of us.

Merce Cunningham, dancer

I am not a choreographer; I am a masterscorer. I create the process for the score, and everyone participates in its creation—I'm like a project director. . . . Dance needs a broader societal value system. Dance has been a Western, white, WASP thing, not reflecting the other life styles and value systems of the nation. We have to listen to minority input. Revolution for me is learning to listen to minorities. I don't get along with the melting pot idea. Like someone said we either listen like brothers or die like fools.

Ann Halprin, dancer

The novelty of our work derives therefore from our having moved away from simply private human concerns towards the world of nature and society of which all of us are a part. Our intention is to affirm this life, not to bring order out of chaos nor to suggest improvements in creation, but simply to wake up to the very life we're living which is so excellent once one gets one's mind and one's desires out of the way and lets it act of its own accord.

John Cage, musician

One is born to be a great dancer. No teacher can work miracles, nor will years of training make a good dancer of an untalented pupil. One may be able to acquire a certain technical facility, but no one can ever 'acquire an exceptional talent.' I have never prided myself on having an unusually gifted pupil. A Pavlova is no one's pupil but God's.

George Balanchine, choreographer

10
Selected Readings

The reading of all good books is . . . like a conversation with the noblest men . . . who were the authors of them . . . in which they reveal to us none but the best of their thoughts.
　　Rene Descartes, *philosopher*

*I*n order that this chapter does not become top-heavy with the listing of all the best books in all of the fields concerned, an effort was made to limit the number in each category. Seldom has this writer had a more harrowing task, for there are many excellent sources—in one way or another—so it was hard to make a final selection. The only way to reconcile such a problem is to plead with the reader not to miss the *other* splendid books available. If you are really interested, take advantage of the catalogs in your library and browse through bookstores, giving special attention to the increasing number of paperback reprints.

This listing is the result of arbitrary choice, personally biased, but based on some forty years of attempting to stimulate young people, dancers, and students to read and think about all aspects of dance, esthetics, and art. Brief annotations are provided so that the reader may know more about the book than its author, title, publisher, and date.

ESTHETICS

Kennick, W. E., ed. *Art and Philosophy*. New York: St. Martin's Press, 1964.
    Kennick, as editor, has collected some forty essays and articles ranging from the nature, esthetics, range, expression, interpretation, and criticism of art. Contributors are varied, from Plato to Freud, Tolstoy to Santayana, Langer to Weitz.

Langer, Susanne K., ed. *Reflections On Art*. New York: Oxford University Press. (Galaxy Paperback GB60), 1961.
    This is a source book of significant writings by artists, critics, and philosophers of the first six decades of this century. Mrs. Langer selected these on the basis of real contribution to art, either as new theory or clarification of a confused one.

Philipson, Morris. *Aesthetics Today*. New York: World Publishing Co. (Meridian Book M112), 1961.
    Twenty essays or chapters are concerned with: relations among the arts, general cultural purposes, form-content-style, interpretation and relations between art and other aspects of human behavior and knowing. Historians, critics, philosophers, artists, and social scientists are well represented.

Rader, Melvin, ed. *A Modern Book of Esthetics*. New York: Holt, Rinehart & Winston. 3d ed., 1962.
    An excellent collection of conflicting views covering the entire field of esthetics of art as it developed. Definitions, works of art, and criticism are discussed in great detail. The preliminary writings of Rader before each section are especially helpful.

ART

Collingwood, R. G. *The Principles of Art.* New York: Oxford University Press (Galaxy Book GB11), fourth printing, 1963.

First published in 1938, this has become one of the classics in the field and, while it doesn't read like a best seller, is, nevertheless, an excellent source for understanding basic concepts of art. "The Work of Art as an Imaginary Object" explains one of the more characteristic views of this philosopher.

Eliot, Alexander. *Sight and Insight.* New York: E. P. Dutton (Dutton Everyman Paperback D65), 1960.

To see art with the inner eye of the imagination as well as the outer eye is the recommendation of Eliot, well-known art critic and writer. The clear and often poetic prose makes this little book a delight to read as well as an inspiration to further understanding.

Fallico, Arturo B. *Art and Existentialism.* Englewood Cliffs, N.J.: Prentice-Hall, 1962.

This is the first readable existentialist theory of art in English. It proposes art as an essential factor of human expression, the mainspring of human spontaneity, freedom, and emotional fulfillment. Fallico, both artist and philosopher, has given us a broad view of art with relevant bits from Sartre, Heidegger, and Camus.

Kuh, Katherine. *Break-up: The Core of Modern Art.* Greenwich, Conn.: New York Graphic Society, 1965.

Katherine Kuh proposed not to write another history of art but ". . . to uncover meanings and motivations." She relates art happenings to life in its time and place. The term "break-up" refers to the shattering of the dogma of color, space, texture, form, content, etc. Easy to read, with illustrations, this book refers mainly to the art of painting but is easily referred to dance practice.

Langer, Susanne K. *Feeling and Form, A Theory of Art.* New York: Charles Scribner's Sons, 1953.

An original structure of ideas dealing with major philosophies of art, with emphasis upon those of the makers and performers themselves. While it is not a ponderous book, it does demand close attention of the reader; it is well worth the effort.

———. *Problems of Art.* New York: Charles Scribner's Sons, 1957.

One of the easiest of all Langer's works, this book is made up of ten lectures, each of which is valuable for the dancer. This is probably one of the works that has been responsible for Langer to be termed "the dancer's philosopher." The first lecture, entitled "Some Philosophical Reflections on Dance," should be required reading. Here is no dull philosophical diatribe, but a moving and fascinating clarification of many of the confusing issues about dance as art.

Read, Herbert. *The Grass Roots of Art.* New York: World Book Publishing Co. (Meridian Book M108), 1961.

These are lectures on the social aspects of art in an industrial age. Such titles as "Roots of the Artist," "Society and Culture," and "The Irrelevance of Realism" are some of them that are included. Herbert Read is one of the most prolific of all writers about art and any of his works are well-worth reading. Some six to eight of them are available as paperbacks.

REFERENCE

Beaumont, Cyril, W. *Bibliography of Dancing.* New York: Benjamin Blom, 1963.

This is a reprint of an original work that has been an invaluable source for locating information about particular dances.

Chujoy, Anatole, and Manchester, P. W., eds. *The Dance Encyclopedia.* New York: Simon and Schuster, 1967.

A revised and enlarged edition of an earlier one by Chujoy, this is a thorough one-volume guide to technical and artistic bases of dance, with photographs.

Magriel, Paul David, ed. *A Bibliography of Dancing.* New York: Benjamin Blom, 1966.

This is a reprint of the original 1936 edition. It is a comprehensive listing of reference to all aspects of dance, arranged by subject category. There are fourteen facsimiles of title pages of important works on dance.

Raffe, W. G. *Dictionary of the Dance.* New York: A. S. Barnes, 1964.

This is a series of short articles from around the world about dance and dancers.

HISTORY

Backman, E. Louis. *Religious Dances.* London: George Allen and Unwin, 1952.

This is an account of the origins and history of religious dances and their significance in the Christian Church. There is particular attention paid to the dancing epidemics of the Middle Ages and the role of dance in the history of medicine and the healing of sickness.

Clarke, Mary and Crisp, Clement. *Ballet: An Illustrated History.* New York: Universal Books, 1973.

A well-organized, interesting, profusely illustrated, and valuable source.

De Mille, Agnes. *The Book of the Dance.* New York: Golden Press, 1963.

This is a lavishly illustrated and fascinating survey of all phases of dance from prehistory to present day. It is an extravagant, colorful overview of dance.

Emery, Lynne F. *Black Dance in the United States from 1619-1970.* Palo Alto, Calif.: National Press, 1972.

An authentic, well-documented, and thoroughly readable story and source book for the history, development, and nature of black dance in the United States.

Kraus, Richard. *History of the Dance.* Englewood Cliffs, N. J.: Prentice-Hall, 1969.

This is a well-organized and comprehensive history of dance, including materials on the early development and current practice of dance in education. There is an interesting chapter on "Dance Education: The Years Ahead."

Lawler, Lillian B. *The Dance in Ancient Greece.* Middletown, Conn.: Wesleyan University Press, 1964.
> Lawler has given us a marvelous account of many kinds of dance in ancient Greece: shrine and festival, animal, dance-drama, orgiastic, religious, popular, and a section on pantomime leading to the Roman transition. This is one of the classics in dance history.

Magriel, Paul. *Chronicles of the American Dance.* New York: Henry Holt, 1948.
> This is a book about historical aspects of early American dance from Shaker ritual to "The Black Crook" and "The White Fawn." Mary Ann Lee, first American Giselle; Augusta Maywood and George Washington Smith are also discussed. The innovators (Duncan, Loie Fuller, Maud Allen, and Graham) are also included.

Martin, John. *John Martin's Book of the Dance: The Background and Development of the Dance in all Forms and Periods.* New York: Tudor, 1963.
> Since 1946, when Martin's *The Dance* was first published, there have been many unforseen changes, and Martin has been watching all of them. This book sums up his views and reactions, and, of course, is of great value to any dancer. His format is the same as the earlier book: *Basic Dance, Dance for the Sake of the Dancer, Dance as a Spectacle, Dance as a Means of Communication.* This is a must for any dancer's library. There are some 365 photographs.

Sachs, Curt. *A World History of the Dance.* New York: Norton, 1937 (Norton Library, 1963).
> This is one of the most comprehensive of all dance histories and ranges from prehistory to the twentieth century. From magic and the dance of primitives through a wealth of descriptive materials representing the ages of man, this is an important asset to any dancer's library. Beyond the wealth of information is a sense of exhilaration and power that gives some of the essence of dance.

Sorell, Walter. *The Dance Through the Ages.* New York: Grosset and Dunlap, 1967.
> This is another interesting and vividly illustrated chronicle of dance from ancient to avant-garde. It includes Oriental, folk, early ballet, romantic ballet, Diaghilev days, new beginnings of modern, after Diaghilev, mass media dance, jazz dance, and what he calls "afternote." The illustrations are both in black and white and color.

BALLET

Guest, Ivor. *The Dancer's Heritage.* New York: Macmillan, 1961.
> Written as a text for the Royal Ballet School, this is a brief but very complete view of the beginning and growth of the classical ballet.

Haskell, Arnold L. *Ballet Retrospect.* New York: Viking Press, 1965.
> This is a survey of the ballet tradition from 1581 to its postwar transformation. Personal reminiscences, illustrations, great dancers, and succinct chronologies are all included.

Maynard, Olga. *The American Ballet.* Philadelphia: Macrae Smith, 1960.
> From the early commedia dell-arte ventures, "The Black Crook," Isadora and modern influences, to the pioneer classicists: Catherine Littlefield

and Ruth Page, to the Christensens, the exiles: Bolm, Fokine, Mordkin, Massine up to Balanchine, Maynard has given us a vast picture of American happenings in ballet.

Noverre, Jean Georges. *Letters on Dancing and Ballets.* Translated by Cyril Beaumont. New York: Dance Horizons (reprint), 1966.

This early nineteenth-century classic marked a transition in the classical ballet. Noverre proposed great reforms which even today seem important. No equal in the literature of ballet. Originally published in 1803.

Terry, Walter. *The Ballet Companion: A Popular Guide for The Ballet-Goer.* New York: Dodd, Mead (Apollo edition A292), 1968.

This book covers ballet as a technique, as a company of dancers, and as a production. The author tells the history, development, problems of choreography, music, costumes, and decor of the art. There is an interesting section on how to choose a teacher.

Verwer, Hans. *Guide to the Ballet.* New York: Barnes and Noble (no. 282), 1963.

This is a neat and concise history of ballet, with descriptions of selected, major ballets. It is an excellent source for a brief overview of the art of ballet. Illustrated.

MODERN

McDonagh, Don. *The Rise and Fall and Rise of Modern Dance.* New York: New American Library (Mentor Book MY 1117), 1970.

From Isadora Duncan to Martha Graham, from Merce Cunningham to Twyla Tharp and Meredith Monk, with a brief history of what has happened. Points of view of many of the artists are given. Any modern dancer, indeed, any dancer, should read this book.

Martin, John. *Introduction To The Dance.* New York: Barnes, 1933. Also available as Dance Horizons reprint.

This is a classic of the early days and still very relevant today. A philosophy, critique, and thoroughly readable account of the early modern dance and its leaders; it presents a history of dance from the primitive.

———. *America Dancing.* New York: Dodge Publishing Co., 1936.

It is in this book that the famous "Layman's Guide," "How to," and "How not to look at dance" are presented. There is an excellent account of the theory and development of modern dance. Also available as a Dance Horizons reprint.

ABOUT DANCE

H'Doubler, Margaret. *Dance a Creative Art Experience.* Madison, Wis.: University of Wisconsin Press. 2d ed., 1959.

H'Doubler, pioneer in educational dance, has provided us with the classical work on the role of dance in education. She presents a philosophy and approach to teaching that is invaluable.

Hawkins, Alma. *Creating Through Dance.* Englewood Cliffs, N. J.: Prentice-Hall, 1964.

Dr. Hawkins writes of dance as a creative experience and suggests ways to develop creativity and to increase esthetic awareness. This book is particularly valuable for the choreographer.

Sheets, Maxine. *The Phenomenology of Dance.* Madison, Wis.: University of Wisconsin Press, 1966.
> Of particular importance to those concerned with dance in education, this book analyzes the experience of dance as a lived experience and presents a philosophy of this art that is in accord with the tenets of phenomonolgy.

ABOUT SOME DANCERS

Armitage, Merle. *Martha Graham.* New York: Dance Horizons, 1966.
> This is a republication of an original edition of one thousand copies published in 1937. The contributors include John Martin, Lincoln Kirstein, Louis Danz, Wallingford Reigger, and others. Perhaps more valuable is the section of "affirmations" by Graham from 1926 on.

Clarke, Mary. *Six Great Dancers: Taglioni, Pavlova, Nijinsky, Karsavina, Ulanova,* and *Fonteyn.* London: H. Hamilton, 1957.
> This book is made up of short biographical sketches of the six dancers listed.

Cohen, Selma Jean. *The Modern Dance: Seven Statements of Belief.* Middletown, Conn.: Wesleyan University Press, 1966.
> This is a fascinating book which clarifies many views of dance, including Cohen's. Perhaps most interesting are the illuminating solutions to a choreographic problem posed by the author. In answering the question we learn much of the philosophy of each of the seven dancers: Limon, Sokolow, Hawkins, McKayle, Nikolais, Koner, and Taylor.

———. *Doris Humphrey: An Artist First.* Middletown, Conn.: Wesleyan Press, 1972.
> Part autobiography and part biography, her life and legend are presented. As artist, teacher, friend, we learn more about this charming lady and her choreographic achievements. The book ends with her epitaph, "May her own words praise her at the gates."

De Valois, Ninette. *Invitation to the Ballet.* London: John Lane, The Bodley Head, 1953.
> These are reflections of a master of the ballet and theater, its history, point of view, and process.

Dolin, Anton. *Alicia Markova, Her Life and Art.* New York: Hermitage House, 1953.
> This is a chronicle of one of the world's greatest classical ballerinas, written by her former partner and friend. Twenty-four pages of photographs trace her career from childhood to the peak of her work.

Duncan, Isadora. *The Art of the Dance.* Edited by Sheldon Cheney. New York: Theatre Arts, 1928.
> With an introduction by Cheney and forewords by famous friends, these essays of Isadora's provide some primary information about her views and approach to her art. Drawings and photographs enhance the text.

Laban, Rudolf. *The Mastery of Movement.* 2d ed., revised by Lisa Ullman. London: MacDonald and Evans, 1961.
> This revision presents a broad view of the work of Laban who developed a useful method for analyzing and notating human movement. The first publication was under the title *The Mastery of Movement on the Stage.*

McDonagh, Don. *Martha Graham: A Biography.* New York: Praeger, 1973.

An extensive biography from Graham's childhood, early performances with Denishawn to her development as a mature artist in her own right. There have been questions raised by several critics about the materials and the photographs, but it does represent one of the latest views of this great dancer and choreographer.

Maynard, Olga. *American Modern Dancers.* New York: Atlantic Monthly Press, 1965.

A history of modern dance told through the lives and work of its pioneers: Delsarte, Dalcroze, Wigman, Duncan, Denishawn, Humphrey, Graham, Weidman, Holm, and Tamaris.

Migel, Parmenia. *The Ballerinas from the Court of Louis XIV to Pavlova.* New York: Macmillan, 1972.

Here is the story of the lives, loves, and careers of the great ballet dancers from Mlle. de la Fontaine in the 1681 version of *Le Triomphe de l'Amour* as "the first of the great women dancers" to Pavlova in the rebirth of the ballet in the twentieth century.

Money, Keith. *Fonteyn: The Making of a Legend.* New York: Morrow, 1974.

This is a remarkable memoir, one of the most interesting available about any dancer, on and off stage. There are some 800 photographs, some never seen before.

Moore, Lillian. *Artists of the Dance.* New York: Benjamin Blom, 1968. Also available as a Dance Horizons reprint, 1969.

The author has chosen to write about those dancers she considers to have materially affected the course of dance development, or whose careers have some particularly interesting aspects. Divided into those from the early classic ballet, the romantic ballet, the Russian ballet, the Spanish dance, and the modern dance up to Graham.

Siegal, Marcia, ed. "Nik: A Documentary," *Dance Perspectives* 48 (winter 1971).

A delightful panoramic view of Alwin Nikolais as choreographer, musician, producer, teacher, and person.

Sorell, Walter, ed. *The Dance Has Many Faces.* 2d ed. New York: Columbia University Press, 1966.

This book is made up of sketches and essays on performance, point of view, choreography, and status of dance by notable dancers.

Taper, Bernard. *Balanchine.* New York: Harper & Row, 1963.

This is the story of Balanchine from his birth in Russia (1904) to the establishment of the New York City Ballet. There is full discussion of his work, lists of his ballets and an interesting overview of his role in the dance world.

Terry, Walter. *Miss Ruth.* New York: Dodd, Mead, 1969.

This is the biography of the great Ruth St. Denis. Being the "more living life" from infancy to "Rhada," her life and work with Ted Shawn, and the development of Denishawn House.

Wigman, Mary. *The Language of Dance.* Translated by Walter Sorell. Middletown, Conn.: Wesleyan University Press, 1966.

From one of the greatest of the pioneers in modern dance this book tells of her process of creativity in dance; indeed, it reveals her growth and development as one of the greatest dancers of the century.

CHOREOGRAPHY

Cunningham, Merce. *Changes: Notes on Choreography.* New York: Something Else Press, 1968.

This is actually a look into the working notebooks of Merce Cunningham, with in-progress notes indicating method, speculations, and definitions of the problems. Cunningham approaches dance in terms of its primary elements, movement in space and time, and their source—stillness.

De Mille, Agnes. *Lizzie Borden: A Dance of Death.* Boston: Atlantic-Little, Brown, 1968.

In this book Miss de Mille has outlined the beginning and development of the ballet, "The Fall River Legend." It includes a view of the background, development, actual choreography, performance, and response.

Ellfeldt, Lois. *A Primer for Choreographers.* Palo Alto, Calif.: National Press, 1967.

This is a simple and basic view of the choreographic process, especially geared to the novice.

Ellfeldt, Lois, and Carnes, Edwin. *Dance Production Handbook or Later Is Too Late.* Palo Alto, Calif.: National Press, 1971.

This is a handbook on every conceivable aspect of dance production, organized into sections dealing with before rehearsals begin, as you move into performance area, before performance, performance, and after performance. All aspects of staging, costuming, music, etc.

Horst, Louis, and Russell, Carroll. *Modern Dance Forms.* San Francisco: Impulse Publications, 1961. Also available as a Dance Horizons reprint.

In his inimitable manner, Horst gives us his views of dance in relation to the other arts. This is valuable in terms of source, viewpoint, and actual approach to choreography.

Lynes, George Platt, ed. *The Notebooks of Martha Graham.* New York: Harcourt Brace, 1973.

Martha Graham, the great dramatist, reveals her preparations for over thirty of her works, including source for ideas, short quotes, questions she asked herself, and some musings and actual instructions she developed for her dances.

Turner, Margery J. *New Dance, Approaches to Nonliteral Choreography.* Pittsburgh: University of Pittsburgh Press, 1971.

Geared to teachers and students, this book presents a view of leaders and their ideas in nonliteral dance. She suggests some ways of starting such choreography. There is a chapter on music for dance and lighting.

Van Praagh, Peggy, and Brinson, Peter. *The Choreographic Art.* New York: Alfred A. Knopf, 1963.

Here is a comprehensive book about the whole of ballet as an important art. Practical problems of the choreographic craft, as well as relationships to other aspects of production, are given.

Walker, Katherine S. *Dance and Its Creators. Choreographers at Work.* New York: John Day Co., 1972.

This is a story of the choreographic process, mainly in ballet. Included are discussions of the works of Ashton, Balanchine, Cranko, Fokine, Massine, Petipa, Tudor, and many others.

CRITICISM

American Federation of Arts. *The Critic and the Visual Arts.* Papers delivered at the 52d. convention, Boston, 1965. New York: October House, 1965.
> While these views are all directed to painting and the plastic visual arts, the views are most appropriate for dancers to read. The critics include Katherine Kuh, Rudolf Arnheim, Max Kozloff, among others.

Denby, Edwin. *Looking at the Dance.* New York: Horizon Press, 1968.
> From one of the most respected of all dance critics comes his views on some of the major dance achievements of our time. He discusses meaning, dancers, elements of production, books, and a variety of forms. A classic in dance criticism.

Siegel, Marcia. *At the Vanishing Point. A Critic Looks at Dance.* New York: Saturday Review Press, 1972.
> A collection of reviews of ballet, pop, modern, black, and experimental dance. In addition it is a thoroughly readable illustrated volume.

Kinds of Dance

PRIMITIVE

Angas, G. F. *Australian Life and Scenes in Australia and New Zealand,* London: Smith, Elder, 1847.
> A marvelous source for some of the authentic ritual dances of this part of the world.

Boas, Franziska, ed. *The Function of Dance in Human Society,* N. Y.: Dance Horizons Reprint, 1973.
> These are papers read at a seminar on primitive dance, including dance of Kwakuitl Indians, African forms, Haitian, and Balinese,.

Bowra, C. M. *Primitive Song.* New York: New American Library (Mentor MT499), 1962.
> This is a fascinating book about the development from meaningless sound to elaborate constructions in music. Early dance songs and other discussions enhance our understanding of this period. A must for those interested in primitive dance.

Campbell, Joseph. *The Masks of God: Primitive Mythology.* New York: Viking Press, 1959.
> Here is a treasury of myth and practice with many references to dance and ritual.

———. *The Masks of God: Oriental Mythology.* New York: Viking Press, 1962.
> From creation to Egypt *c.* 2900 B.C., Crete and Indus *c.* 2600 B.C., China *c.* 1600 B.C., and America within the next thousand years.

Gorer, Geoffery. *Africa Dances.* New York: W. W. Norton, 1962.
> First published in 1935 as an account of a trip through West Africa, it was probably accurate at that time. Book 4, entitled "Africans Dance," is the nucleus of the dance descriptions.

Grimal, Pierre, ed. *Larousse World Mythology.* New York: Hamlyn, 1973.
  Some twenty-three authors survey the major myths of the world's principal societies. Form and function are examined, variations and similarities noted, and recurrent themes are pointed out. From the cave-bound rites of prehistoric man to the gods of classical Greece and Rome.

Hambly, W. D. *Tribal Dancing and Social Development.* London: H. F. and G. Witherby, 1926.
  This is one of the classical anthropological accounts of dance as a phase of social life. Among others there are interesting accounts of the war and death dances of many people.

Harrison, Jane Ellen. *Ancient Art and Ritual.* New York: Greenwood Press, 1951.
  Showing the connection between art and ritual, there are many fascinating accounts of dance to be found in this book.

Marshack, Alexander. *The Roots of Civilization.* New York: McGraw-Hill, 1972.
  This remarkable book changes ideas, dates, and sequence of events of prehistory, as well as its implications for today. It marks a major breakthrough in the interpretation of Upper Paleolithic art. It illuminates new evidence about early man's intellectual capacity and level of symbolic development. There is verification given of masked dancers in cave art.

Oesterly, W. O. E. *The Sacred Dance: A Study in Comparative Folklore.* New York: Dance Horizons Reprint.
  Originally published in 1923, it is particularly gratifying that Dance Horizons has made this available to more people. The information about dance origins and practices among early people is invaluable.

ETHNIC

Bowers, Faubion. *Theatre in the East.* New York: Nelson, 1956.
  Theatre in the East is a comprehensive survey of Asian dance and drama from India to Japan. Bowers has also written *Japanese Theatre,* and *Dance in India,* both of which have become standard references.

De Zoete, Beryl. *Dance and Magic Drama in Ceylon.* London: Faber and Faber, 1958.
  Stories of island life and many of the ancient and colorful dance rituals which live on in the heritage of Ceylon are described. Almost in the form of a diary, this is a highly personal record of events. There are illustrations and photographs. De Zoete has also written *The Other Mind,* a study of dance in south India, *The Thunder and the Freshness,* with a fine description of Kathakali dance, and, with Walter Spies, *Dance and Drama in Bali.*

Hughes, Russell Meriwether ("La Meri"). *Hindu Dance.* New York: Benjamin Blom, 1963.
  La Meri, one of the greatest of ethnic dancers and teachers has organized a book of more than 200 photographs of single and double hand combinations (mudras) with descriptions and explanations. There is also history and help for the potential ethnic dancer.

———. *Spanish Dancing.* 2d ed. Pittsfield, Mass.: Eagle Printing and Publishing Co., 1968.

Descriptions of four major styles of Spanish dance are given along with biographies of great performers. From the dance of the twenties, in Spain, to the present day, La Meri has provided an excellent contribution to the literature of ethnic dance.

———. *Dance as an Art Form.* New York: Barnes, 1933.

Here is another contribution to better understanding of ethnic dance, by a performer, teacher, choreographer, and historian.

Kurath, Gertrude Prokosch, and Marti, Samuel. *Dances of Anahuac.* Chicago: Aldine Publishing Co., 1964.

This is number 38 in a Viking Fund Series in anthropology and, edited by Sol Tax, is a magnificent record of the choreography and music of Maya and Aztec dances and rituals of the precortesian period. Related to the social structure, the dances are not only described verbally but are, in part, Labanotated.

Umemoto, Rikuhei, and Ishizawa, Yukata. *Introduction to the Classic Dances of Japan.* Tokyo: Sanseido Co., 1935.

With only thirty-two pages, this book provides an excellent orientation to these fascinating ancient dances of Japan.

FOLK DANCE

Alford, Violet, ed. *Handbooks of European National Dance.* New York: Chanticleer Press, 1948-1951. (Published under the auspices of The Royal Academy of Dancing and the Ling Physical Education Association.)

Here is a rich source of simple and well-described folk dances from Austria to Norway, Scotland to Spain, some twenty odd little books.

Ellfeldt, Lois. *Folk Dance.* Dubuque, Iowa: Wm. C. Brown Company Publishers, 1969.

This small book is concerned with basic identification of characteristics of the form, basic steps, means of translating dances from words to movement, aspects of style, and aids to dancers. No dances are presented.

Harris, Jane, Pittman, Anne, and Waller, Mattie. *Dance Awhile.* Minneapolis: Burgess Publishing Co., 3d printing, 1965.

This is one of the most useful and informative of all handbooks, and covers square and round dances as well as standard folk dances. Easy to read and translate into movement.

Lawson, Joan. *European Folk Dance, Its National and Musical Characteristics.* London: Sir Isaac Pitman and Sons, 1953.

This is a survey of all aspects of folk dancing, from the earliest to fairly recent times. Life, origin, character, costume, and tradition of a people are discussed. Similarities as well as differences between European people's dance is suggested.

Sharp, Cecil J. *An Introduction to English Country Dance.* London: Novello and Co., n.d. (In New York, H. W. Gray).

One of the great historians in folk dance, both in England and the eastern United States, also wrote *The Country Dance Book, The Morris Books,* and *The Sword Dances of Northern England.* Perhaps no one has been so influential in preserving and teaching these old country dance forms.

Shaw, Lloyd. *Cowboy Dances.* Caldwell, Idaho: Caxton Press, 1939.

This is certainly the classic among descriptions and stories of the western square dances of this country. Written by the beloved "Pappy" Shaw, this is a great book to read and even a better source for dances, calls, and inspiration. He also wrote *The Round Dance Book*, which describes over a hundred old-time American round dances and circle mixers. Details of the waltz, polka, schottische, two-step, and others are well worth reading.

SOCIAL DANCE

Blake, Dick. *Discotheque Dances.* New York: World Paperback, 1965.
  Included in this book are a number of short descriptions of some of the major rock dances.
Castle, Irene. *Castles in the Air.* Garden City, New York: Doubleday, 1958.
  Of particular historical interest with descriptions of early social dances, this is written as a biography.
Dannett, Sylvia, G. L., and Rachel, Frank R. *Down Memory Lane, Arthur Murray's Picture Story of Social Dancing.* New York: Greenberg, 1954.
  Here is a record of leading dances and dancers told in pictures, from primitive time to the time of publication. A nostalgic record; it will fascinate anyone who has ever heard of dancing.
Ellfeldt, Lois, and Morton, Virgil L. *This is Ballroom Dance.* Palo Alto, Calif.: National Press, 1974.
  A broad view of social-ballroom dance today with directions and discussion of both the traditional couple dance and the rock forms.
Pillich, William F. *Social Dance.* Dubuque, Iowa: Wm. C. Brown Company Publishers, 1967.
  Written by an experienced and able teacher, this is designed for beginners and presents cue charts and illustrations to aid the student.
Richardson, P. J. S. *The Social Dances of the 19th Century.* London: Herbert Jenkins, 1960.
  This book is the story of social dances in favor during the nineteenth century in England. Some aspects of their origins and development are explored, all of which are most relevant to the dance in this country. Photographs and directions are included.
Rust, Frances. *Dance in Society.* London: Routledge and Kegan Paul, 1969.
  This shows an approach to social dance in England from the Middle Ages to today and examines both the function of dance in this society and tests the hypothesis that variations are never random but closely related to: class relationships, ideology, social customs, attitude toward women, and level of industrialization and technology. Results of a questionnaire study are given.

CHILDREN'S DANCE

AAHPER Publication (243-25446) *Children's Dance.* Washington, D. C.: 1201-16 St. N. W., 1974.
  Based on a six-year study by a special committee of the Dance Division, this is a valuable 96-page booklet that includes materials on the theory and approach to recommended dance activity for children.

Andrews (Fleming), Gladys. *Creative Rhythmic Movement for Children.* Englewood Cliffs, N. J.: Prentice-Hall, 1954.

This is one of the great sources for both material and inspiration for working with children in creative movement. Excellent for both teachers and parents. It is being revised.

Joyce, Mary. *First Steps in Teaching Creative Dance.* Palo Alto, Calif.: National Press, 1973.

This is a teacher's handbook for grades K through 6; includes lessons and photographs.

Murray, Ruth Lovell. *Dance in Elementary Education.* 2d ed. New York: Harper & Row, 1963.

This has long been considered the classic in dance for children, especially as it is offered in the school.

Winters, Shirley. *Creative Rhythmic Movement for Children of Elementary School Age.* Dubuque, Iowa: Wm. C. Brown Company Publishers, 1974.

This is a charming book with a refreshing point of view. The emphasis is upon children rather than dance, and, while the materials are most useful for both teachers and parents, Winters has managed to capture something of the quality of magic that is so close to the surface among children, and is always present in her classes as she works with them.

SPECTACULAR DANCE (Theatrical Show)

Astaire, Fred. *Steps in Time.* New York: Harper and Brothers, 1959.

The story of one of the great tap dancers of the age; an autobiography.

Cayou, Dolores Kirton. *Modern Jazz Dance.* Palo Alto, Calif.: National Press, 1972.

The first technique book to present jazz dance as an art. It is illustrated with sequence drawings of some of the routines.

Hungerford, Mary Jane. *History of Tap Dancing.* New York: Prentice-Hall 1939.

This is a remarkable picture of the growth of tap dancing from its earliest beginnings to a major dance form.

Green, Stanley, and Goldblatt, Burt. *Starring Fred Astaire.* New York: Dodd, Mead, 1973.

This is the story of the one who elevated tap dancing to a peak of perfection. Called "the greatest tap dancer in the world," this text tells his story, views, and most important, shows a magnificent array of photographs from Astaire's childhood vaudeville acts through captivating movies and television shows.

Stearns, Marshall and Jean. *Jazz Dance.* New York: Macmillan, 1968.

This is a lengthy story of American vernacular dance, with its inevitable influences on social/recreational dances of the people. The extent to which popular music and dance are related, as well as how each have been influenced by jazz and the changing status of the American blacks are pointed out. Basic Afro-American action has been Labanotated.

PRE-CLASSIC DANCE

Arbeau, Thoinet. *Orchesographie.* London: Beaumont, 1925. Dance Horizon reprint available, 1965.

Translated from the original edition published in France in 1588, this is the valuable expose of the earliest of social dances so favored in the aristocratic courts and from which grew the ballet. The form, language, and style of the book are delightful.

Dolmetsch, Mabel. *Dances of England and France, 1450-1600.* London: Routledge and Paul, 1949.

A collection of authentic and well-documented dances which were hard to determine before this author's careful work. In 1954 she published *Dances of Spain and Italy 1400-1600,* an equally fine addition to the literature.

Horst, Louis. *Pre-Classic Dance Forms.* San Francisco: Impulse, 1961. Also available as Dance Horizons Reprint.

Class notes of the great Louis Horst, telling his favorite stories about the period, style, music, and authentic dance of the courts.

Wood, Melusine. *Some Historical Dances* (12-19c). London: Beaumont, 1952.

This is another careful collection of old dances, style and story. Wood followed the first with *More Historical Dances* in 1956 and *Advanced Historical Dances* in 1960.

NOTATION

Hutchinson, Ann. *Labanotation: The System for Recording Movement.* New York: New Directions 1961, (Oxford GB60).

Basic principles of Labanotation and practical suggestions for its use. This is a simplified, clear and sensible book. While no one is going to be proficient quickly, they will understand the process in one reading.

CREATIVITY

Ghiselin, Brewster. *The Creative Process.* New York: New American Library (Mentor MD132), 1952.

A compilation of the views of many outstanding artists on the nature of the creative process. Fascinating reading.

Koestler, Arthur. *The Act of Creation.* New York: Macmillan, 1964.

This is a large, long, and difficult book to read, but looking through it and reading the summaries is well worth the trouble.

ADVICE TO DANCERS

Como, William. ed. Raoul Gelabert's *Anatomy for the Dancer,* vol. 1 (1964), vol. 2 (1966). New York: Dance Magazine.

These two handbooks will be of great value to any dancer, for in dancer's language, here are warnings, exercises, and excellent advice regarding the dancer's joints, muscles, and movement skills.

De Mille, Agnes. *To A Young Dancer.* Boston: Atlantic-Little, Brown, 1962.

An immensely helpful book for anyone who longs to be a dancer, who wants to know what it is like to be a dancer, and who needs the advice of one who has had the experience.

Mara, Thalia. *So You Want to Be a Ballet Dancer.* New York: Pitman, 1959.

Advice to the aspiring dancer about the personal, physical, and intellectual qualities that are important.

Penrod, James, and Plastino, Janice Gudde. *The Dancer Prepares*. Palo Alto, Calif.: 1970.

A little booklet for those taking a first course in dance. It includes an overview of the dancer's craft and needs.

Notes

CHAPTER 1
1. Sheldon Cheney, *Expressions in Art* (New York: Liveright, 1962), pp. 409-12.

CHAPTER 2
1. Curt Sachs, *A World History of Dance* (New York: W. W. Norton, The Norton Library, 1963), p. 3.
2. Ibid., p. 6.
3. *Webster's New World Dictionary of the American Language,* College Edition (New York: World Publishing Co., 1960), p. 372.
4. W. D. Hambley, *Tribal Dancing and Social Development* (London: H. F. G. Witherby, 1926), p. 276.
5. Jane E. Harrison, *Ancient Art and Ritual* (New York: Holt, 1913), p. 236.
6. W. O. E. Oesterly, *The Sacred Dance: A Study in Comparative Folklore* (Brooklyn: Dance Horizons, 1968), p. 6.
7. Sachs, *A World History of Dance,* p. 4.
8. Ethel Urlin, *Dancing, Ancient and Modern* (London: Simkin, Marshall, Kent and Co., [ND]), p. xiii.
9. Yrjo Hirn, *Origins of Art* (New York: Macmillan, 1900), p. 87.
10. Wolfgang Kohler, *The Mentality of Apes* (New York: Humanities Press, 1927), p. 95.
11. Ananda K. Coomaraswamy, *The Dance of Shiva* (New York: Noonday Press, 1957), pp. 66-78.
12. Joseph Campbell, *The Masks of God: Primitive Mythology* (New York: Viking Press, 1959), pp. 435-36.
13. R. D. Simpson, "The Hopi Indians," Los Angeles: *Southwest Museum Leaflets,* No. 25, 1953, pp. 22-23.
14. George B. Grinnell, *Blackfoot Lodge Tales* (New York: Charles Scribner's Sons, 1892), pp. 104-107; 220-24.
15. A. E. Jensen, as cited in Joseph Campbell's *The Masks of God: Primitive Mythology,* pp. 173-76.
16. Bronislaw Malinowski, *Myth in Primitive Psychology* (New York: W. W. Norton, 1926), p. 30.
17. Pierre Grimal, ed., *Larousse World Mythology* (New York: Hamlyn, 1973), p. 9.
18. Campbell, *The Masks of God: Primitive Mythology,* p. 375.
19. Ibid., pp. 106-8.

CHAPTER 3
1. Curt Sachs, *A World History of Dance* (New York: W. W. Norton, The Norton Library, 1963), p. 207.
2. W. D. Hambley, Tribal Dancing and Social Development (London: H. F. G. Witherby, 1926), pp. 271-72.
3. Daniel Sutherland Davidson, "Aboriginal Australian and Tasmanian Rock Carvings and Paintings," *Memoirs of the American Philosophical Society* (Philadelphia: American Philosophic Society, 1936), vol. 5, p. 151.

4. Joseph Campbell, *The Masks of God: Primitive Mythology* (New York: Viking Press, 1959).
5. Franz Boas, *The Mind of Primitive Man*, rev. ed. (New York: Macmillan, 1938), pp. 240-41.
6. Lucien Levy-Bruhl, *Primitives and the Supernatural*, trans. Lillian A. Clare (New York: E. P. Dutton, 1935), p. 127.
7. Sachs, *A World History of Dance*, pp. 4-5.
8. Levy-Bruhl, *Primitives and the Supernatural*, p. 116.
9. Jane E. Harrison, *Ancient Art and Ritual* (New York: Holt, 1913), p. 171.
10. Sachs, *A World History of Dance*, pp. 17-40.
11. Carroll Russell and Louis Horst, *Modern Dance Forms* (San Francisco: Impulse Publications, 1961), pp. 52-65.
12. Sachs, *A World History of Dance*, pp. 144-45.
13. Susanne K. Langer, *Feeling and Form* (New York: Charles Scribner's Sons, 1953), p. 191.
14. Robert F. Thompson, *African Art in Motion* (Los Angeles: University of California Press, 1974), pp. 1-45.
15. Thurston Knudson, personal conversation, 1953.
16. Hambly, *Tribal Dancing and Social Development*, p. 80.
17. Geoffrey Gorer, *Africa Dances* (New York: Norton, 1962), p. 124.
18. W. O. E. Oesterly, *The Sacred Dance: A Study in Comparative Folklore* (Brooklyn: Dance Horizons, 1968), p. 22.
19. Ibid., pp. 204-14.
20. M. Vieyra, "Empires of the Ancient Near East: The Hymns of Creation," *Larousse World Mythology* (New York: Hamlyn, 1973), pp. 64, 68.
21. Sachs, *A World History of Dance*, p. 221.
22. Ibid., p. 105.
23. Ibid., p. 231.
24. Ibid., pp. 87-88.
25. Xenia Zarina, *Classic Dances of the Orient* (New York: Crown Publishers, 1967), p. 1.
26. Faubion Bowers, *Theatre in the East* (New York: Thomas Nelson and Sons, 1956), pp. 8-9.
27. Ananda K. Coomaraswamy, *The Dance of Shiva* (New York: Noonday Press, 1957), pp. 66-67.
28. Ibid., pp. 67-69.
29. Ibid., p. 77.
30. Pierre Grimal, ed., *Larousse World Mythology* (New York, Hamlyn, 1973), p. 13.

CHAPTER 4

1. Henri Frankfort, *The Birth of Civilization in the Near East* (Garden City, New York: Doubleday, Anchor Book 89, 1956), pp. 29-30.
2. Joseph Campbell, *The Masks of God: Primitive Mythology* (New York: Viking Press, 1959), p. 148.
3. Ibid., p. 404.
4. Ibid., p. 143.
5. Ibid., pp. 406-9.
6. Samuel Noah Kramer, *History Begins at Sumer* (Garden City, New York: Doubleday, Anchor Book A175, 1959), p. ix.
7. C. W. Ceram, *Gods, Graves, and Scholars* (New York: Alfred A. Knopf, 1964), pp. 194-202.

CHAPTER 5

1. George Schweinfurth, *The Heart of Africa* (New York: Harpers, 1874), p. 75.
2. Baldwin Spencer and J. F. Gillen, *The Native Tribes of Central Australia* (London: Macmillan and Co., 1889), pp. 497-511.
3. A. N. Tucker, *Tribal Music and Dancing in the Southern Sudan* (Africa), *At Social and Ceremonial Gatherings* (London: William Reeves, [N.D.] post 1931), @ to foreword, pp. 2-5.
4. C. M. Bowra, *Primitive Song* (New York: New American Library, a Mentor Book [MT499], 1962), p. 50.
5. Napoleon A. Chagnon, "Feast: With Biographical Sketch," *Natural History* 77 (April 1968):4, 34, 41.
6. Geoffrey Gorer, *Africa Dances* (New York: Norton, 1962), p. 224.
7. Bowra, *Primitive Song*, p. 168.
8. Robert F. Thompson, *African Art in Motion* (Los Angeles: University of California Press, 1974), p. 166.
9. Gorer, *Africa Dances*, p. 119.
10. Odette Blum, "Dance in Ghana," *Dance Perspectives* 56 (winter 1973):29-31.
11. Franz Boas, "Dance and Music in The Life of The Northwest Coast Indians of North America," *Function of Dance in Human Society*, a Seminar directed by Franziska Boas, The Boas School, 1944, p. 9.
12. Thompson, *African Art in Motion*, pp. 173-187.
13. Ibid., pp. 190-192.
14. Franziska Boas, "Kwakuitl Indians," *The Function of Dance in Human Society* (New York: The Boas School Seminar report, 1944), pp. 14-15.
15. Franz Boas, "Dance and Music in The Life of The Northwest Coast Indians of North America," *The Function of Dance in Human Society*, the Boas School, pp. 7-9. Seminar report, pp. 7-9.
16. Gorer, *Africa Dances*, p. 221.
17. Ibid., pp. 223-224.
18. A. R. Radcliffe-Brown, *The Andaman Islanders* (Cambridge: The University Press, 1922), p. 251.
19. Rafael Karsten, *The Civilization of the South American Indian* (London: Kegan, Paul, Trench, Trubnor, 1926), p. 18.
20. S. D. Porteus, *Primitive Intelligence and Environment* (New York: Macmillan Co., 1937), pp. 113-114.
21. Ruth Benedict, *Patterns of Culture* (New York: The New American Library, a Mentor Book, M89, 1953), pp. 84-85.
22. Pamela Johnson Meyer, "Foxes Foretell the Future in Mali's Dogon Country," *National Geographic* 135 (March, 1969):430-48.
23. Z. Estreicher, "Chants et rythmes de la danse d'hommes Bororo," (enregistrements Henry Brandt), Bulletin de la Societi Neuchateloise de geographie, Neuchatel, 1 (5) (1955):54-55.
24. Arthur L. Basham, "The Mahabharata and The Ramayana," *The Courier*, Dec. 1967. Paris: UNESCO, pp. 4-5; 8-10.
25. Lillian Lawler, *The Dance in Ancient Greece* (Middletown, Conn.: Wesleyan University Press, 1964), pp. 160.
26. Thoinot Arbeau, *Orchesography* (New York: Dover Publications [T1745], 1967), pp. 266 [original in 1589].
27. John Playford, *The English Dancing Master* (New York: Schott and Co., 1957).
28. E. Pemberton, "Dancing Master: An Essay for the Further Improvement of Dancing," *British Museum of Printed Books*, vol. 183, col. 200, London, 1711.

29. Allen Dodsworth, *Dancing and Its Relations to Education and Social Life* (London: Harper and Bros., 1895). [In Library of Royal Academy of Dancing].
30. Mrs. Lily Grove, "Dancing," *Badminton Library of Sports and Pastimes* (London: Longmans Green and Co., 1895).

CHAPTER 6

1. Jean Georges Noverre, *Letters on Dancing and Ballet* (London: C. W. Beaumont, 1930). [First published in 1760.] Dance Horizons reprint available.
2. Sheldon Cheney, Expression in Art (New York: Liveright, 1962), p. 386.
3. Dance Division, A.A.H.P.E.R., "Report: Task Force—Children's Dance," *Journal A.A.H.P.E.R.*, June 1971, p. 21.
4. La Meri, "The Ethnological Dance Arts," *The Dance Has Many Faces*, Walter Sorrell, ed. (New York: World Pub. Co., 1951), p. 4.
5. Faubion Bowers, *Theatre in the East* (New York: Thomas Nelson and Sons, 1956), pp. 30-52.
6. Marshall and Jean Stearns, *Jazz Dance The Story of American Vernacular Dance* (New York: Macmillan Co., 1968), p. 109.
7. Susanne K. Langer, *Feeling and Form* (New York: Charles Scribner's Sons, 1953), p. 203.
8. Reverend W. W. Gardner, *Modern Dancing: In The Light of Scripture and Facts*, (Louisville, Ky.: Baptist Book Concern, 1893), pp. 30-31.
9. Weston La Barre, "The Ghost Dance: The Origins of Religion," *Real Time I*, eds. John Brockman and Edward Rosenfeld. (Garden City, New York: Anchor Press/Doubleday, 1973), p. 76.

CHAPTER 7

1. Alwin Nikolais, "No Man From Mars," *The Modern Dance: Seven Statements of Belief*, ed. Selma Jeanne Cohen. (Middletown, Conn.: Wesleyan Press, 1956), p. 74.
2. Clive Bell, *Art* (New York: Capricorn Books, 1958), p. 15.
3. John Dewey, *Art As Experience* (New York: Minton, Balch and Co., 1934), p. 57.
4. George Santayana, *The Sense of Beauty* (New York: Collier Books, [BS34yv], 1961), pp. 24, 26.
5. Melvin Rader, *A Modern Book of Esthetics* (New York: Holt, Rinehart & Winston, 1962), p. 540.
6. W. E. Kerrick, *Art and Philosophy* (New York: St. Martins Press, 1964) p. 674.
7. Susanne K. Langer, *Reflections on Art* (New York: Oxford University Press, a Galaxy Book, [GB60], 1961), p. 364.
8. R. G. Collingwood, *Principles of Art* (New York: Oxford University Press, a Galaxy Book [GB11], 1958), pp. 68-69.
9. Susanne K. Langer, *Philosophy in a New Key* (New York: The New American Library, a Mentor Book [MD 101], 1961), p. 52.
10. Arthur Koestler, *The Act of Creation* (New York: Macmillan Co., 1964), p. 343.
11. John Dewey, *Art As Experience*, p. 271.
12. Collingwood, *Principles of Art*, p. 69.
13. Alexander Eliot, *Sight and Insight* (New York: E. P. Dutton & Co., Inc., 1960), p. 57.

CHAPTER 8

1. Allen Leepa, *The Challenge of Modern Art* (New York: A. S. Barnes, a Perpetua Book [P4023], 1961), p. xxiii.
2. John Dewey, "Having An Experience," in Melvin Rader, *A Modern Book of Esthetics*, pp. 181-182.
3. R. G. Collingwood, *The Principles of Art* (New York: Oxford University Press, a Galaxy Book, [GB11], 1958).
4. Irwin Edman, *Arts and The Man* (New York: W. W. Norton, The Norton Library, revised 1928), p. 17.
5. Herbert Read, *To Hell With Culture* (New York: Schocken Books, [SB81] Third Printing 1967), p. 7.
6. Susanne K. Langer, *Problems of Art* (New York: Charles Scribner's Sons, 1957), p. 26.
7. E. H. Gombrich, *Art and Illusion* (London: Phaidon Press, 1962).
8. Eugene F. Kaelin, *An Existentialist Aesthetic* (Madison: University of Wisconsin Press, 1966), pp. 273-274.
9. Oskar Kokoschka, "Statements and Documents," *Daedalus*, Journal of The Academy of Arts and Sciences, Special Issue, Winter 1960, p. 121.
10. John Dewey, "Having an Experience," pp. 182-183.
11. Paul Klee, as quoted in Will Grohmann, *Paul Klee*, (New York: Henry N. Abrams, N.D.), p. 365.
12. Wassily Kandinsky, *Concerning The Spiritual in Art* (New York: George Wittenborn offset reprint, 1970), p. 75 [Original 1947].
13. Arturo B. Fallico, *Art and Existentialism* (Englewood Cliffs, N. J.: Prentice-Hall, 1962), p. 109.
14. Alexander Eliot, *Sight and Insight* (New York: E. P. Dutton & Co., Inc., 1960), p. 28.
15. David Smith, "Toward a Sculptural Renaissance," *Readings in American Art Since 1900*, ed. Barbara Rose. (New York: Frederick A. Praeger, 1968), p. 192.
16. R. G. Collingwood, *Essays in the Philosophy of Art*, ed. Alan Donagan (Bloomington: Indiana University Press, 1964), p. 195.
17. Allen Leepa, *The Challenge of Modern Art*, p. 5.
18. Marcel Duchamp, "Statements and Documents," *Daedalus*, Journal of the Academy of Arts and Sciences, Special Issue, Winter 1960, p. 112.
19. Dewey, "Having an Experience," p. 182.
20. Joan Miro, "Two Statements," *Surrealists on Art*, ed. Lucy R. Lippard. (Englewood Cliffs, N. J.: Prentice-Hall, a Spectrum Book [S235], 1970), p. 172.
21. Joan Miro, "Statements and Documents," *Daedalus*, Journal of the Academy of Arts and Sciences, Special Issue, Winter, 1960, p. 93.
22. Duchamp, Marcel, "The Creative Act," *Surrealists on Art*, ed. Lucy R. Lippard. (Englewood Cliffs, N. J.: Prentice-Hall, a Spectrum Book [S235], 1970), p. 113.
23. Harold Rugg, *Imagination* (New York: Harper & Row, 1963), pp. 296, 298.
24. Vincent Thomas, "Creativity in Art," *Art and Philosophy, Readings in Esthetics*, ed. W. E. Kennick (New York: St. Martin's Press), p. 285.
25. Langer, *Problems of Art*, p. 28.
26. Gay Ellen Cheney, "From Authenticity to Art: A Search for Significance in Choreographic Process," University of Southern California Ph. D. dissertation, 1970, p. 183.
27. Langer, *Problems of Art*, p. 26.

28. Dewitt H. Parker, "The Problems of Esthetic Form," *A Modern Book of Esthetics,* ed. Melvin Rader (New York: Holt, Rinehart & Winston, 1962), pp. 323-331.

CHAPTER 9

1. Edwin Denby, *Looking at The Dance* (New York: Curtis Books [02028], 1968), p. 337.
2. Martha Graham, "Martha Graham Speaks. . . ," *Dance Observer,* 30-4 (April 1963):53.
3. George Santayana, *The Sense of Beauty* (New York: Collier Books [BS34yv], 1961), pp. 36-37.
4. Robert Frost, quoted in Alexander Eliot, *Sight and Insight* (New York: E. P. Dutton & Co., Inc., 1960), p. 29.
5. Walter Sorell, *The Dancer's Image* (New York: Columbia University Press, 1971), p. 16.
6. Marcel Duchamp, as cited in *Surrealists on Art,* ed. Lucy R. Lippard (Englewood Cliffs, N. J.: Prentice-Hall, a Spectrum Book [S235], 1970), p. 113.
7. Erick Hawkins, *The Modern Dance: Seven Statements of Belief,* ed. Selma Jeanne Cohen (Middletown, Conn.: Wesleyan Press, 1956), pp. 47-48.
8. Isadora Duncan, *The Art of The Dance,* Sheldon Cheney, ed. (New York: Theatre Arts, 1928), p. 51.
9. R. G. Collingwood, *The Principles of Art* (New York: Oxford University Press, a Galaxy Book [GB11], 1958).
10. Susanne K. Langer, *Problems of Art* (New York: Charles Scribner's Sons, 1957).

Index

Ailey, Alvin, 203
Allemande, 126
Altamira, 21
Ama-no-Uzeme, 16
Amaterasu, 16
Ameta, 18
Anderson, Jack, 193, 197
Arbeau, Thoinot, 104
Arnheim, Rudolf, 149, 194, 201
Arpino, Gerald, 205, 210
Art: consensus on, 158-59; content, 172-75; criticism, 159-61; form, 172-75; origins of, 143-44; style, 175-79
Ashton, Dore, 146, 174
Ashton, Frederick, 205
Astaire, Fred, 129

Bacon, Francis, 151
Baile de los Seises, El, 101, 103
Balanchine, George, 123, 202, 205, 211
Ballet: classical or traditional, 110-11; contemporary or modern, 111
Ballroom dance, 104-6
Barnes, Albert C., 154
Barnes, Clive, 195
Basse dance, 126
Baudelaire, Charles, 145
Baumgarten, A. G., 133, 176
Beiswanger, George, 198-99, 205
Bejart, Maurice, 202-3
Bell, Clive, 133, 149, 150, 155, 174, 177
Benedict, Ruth, 29, 94
Bergson, Henri, 149
Bettelheim, Bruno, 148
Bharata Natya Sastra, 117-18
Bharata Natyam, 99, 118
Black Crook, The, 123
Blackfoot Indians, 17
Blake, William, 190
Blum, Odette, 89
Boas, Franz, 29-30, 91
Boas, Franziska, 90-91
Book of the Dead, 81
Bouree, 126
Bournoville, August, 194
Bowers, Faubion, 58

Brahma, 58, 59, 77-78
Branle, 126
Bruhn, Erik, 200, 207
Bruner, Jerome, 152, 168
Buddha (Siddhartha, Guatama), 78-79
Buffalo Dance, 17-18

Cage, John, 211
Calas, Nicolas, 150, 152
Calder, Alexander, 157
Campbell, Joseph, 35, 37, 65, 71, 72
Camus, Albert, 146
Carole, 126
Cassirer, Ernst, 72, 156
Castle, Irene and Vernon, 127
Caudwell, Christopher, 146
Cecchetti, Enrico, 202
Ceram, C. W., 68-69
Ceremony, 28-32; African, 32; Dravidian, 77; Egyptian, 80-81; Eskimo, 31-32; Indian, 82; initiation, 32; Navajo, 30, 31; Near Eastern, 80
Cezanne, Paul, 155
Chaconne, 126
Chaplin, Charlie, 124
Cheney, Gay, 173
Cheney, Sheldon, 4
Children's dance, goals for, 112-13
Choreography, 204-6
Cohen, Selma Jeanne, 198
Cole, Jack, 123
Coleridge, Samuel Taylor, 151
Collingwood, R. G., 143, 157, 164, 166, 190
Coomaraswamy, Ananda K., 15, 59, 155
Corroboree Jump, 37
Courante, 126
Courtenay, Ted, 168
Creative people, characteristics of, 169-72
Creativity, 167-72
Croce, Benedetto, 147
Cubism, 178
Cunningham, Merce, 122, 123, 175, 198, 199, 203, 211

Dance: acrobatic, 109; aerobic, 109-10; African, 38, 44, 52, 84-85, 86-90, 91-93; artist, 199-201; artist-choreographer, 188-89; artist-performer, 189; Babylonian, 54; character, 111-12; children's, 112-13; creative, 116-17; definitions of, 10-12, 189-99; drama, 113; dramatic, 114-15; educational, 115-16; Egyptian, 55-58; esthetic, 116-17; esthetics of, 189-92, 194-99; ethnic, 98-103, 117-19; forms, 109-130; Indian, 59; interpretive, 116-17; jazz, 121; natural, 116-17; origins of, 12-19; preclassic, 124-27; spectacular, 129; Sumerian, 54-55; technique, 201-3; theater, 114-15; therapy, 113-14
Dancers, on dance, 206-11
Dances: communication, 49; ecstatic, 52; fertility, 92; food, 46, 94-97; funeral, 51; healing, 50-51, 86-87; initiation, 38-39, 45-46, 88; marriage, 46-47; pleasure, 52; political, 52; secret society, 47; totem, 47; war, 49; worship, 50
Davidson, Daniel Sutherland, 37
Decroux, Etienne, 124
De Kooning, William, 147
Demeter, 16
de Mille, Agnes, 123-24
Denby, Edwin, 182, 200-1
Denishawn, 121-22
Descartes, Rene, 213
Devidasi, 118
Dewey, John, 133, 144, 145, 154-55, 165, 166
Dobzhansky, Theodosius, 61
Dodsworth, Allen, 105
Dubuffet, Jean, 175
Ducasse, Curt John, 148
Duchamp, Marcel, 163, 166, 167, 187
Duncan, Isadora, 116-17, 122, 123, 189, 193, 198, 207-8
Dunn, Judith, 202
Dutsova, Hilda, 201

Echaurren, Matta, 146
Edman, Irwin, 164
Eliot, Alexander, 33, 144, 145, 147, 166
Erdman, Jean, 193
Esthetics, 132-60
Expressionism, 178

Fallico, Arturo B., 158, 166
Fancy Free, 124
Fetish, 25
Flannagan, John B., 174
Fokine, Michel, 202
Folk Dance, 103, 119-21
Fraleigh, Sondra Horton, 196
Frazer, Sir J. G., 24
Freud, Sigmund, 154
Fromm, Eric, 168
Frost, Robert, 185
Fry, Roger, 148-149-150
Fuente, Luis, 202

Gabo, Naum, 151
Galliard, 126
Gardner, Rev. W. W., 130
Gavotte, 126
Gide, Andre, 156-65
Gigue, 126
Gilgamesh, 73-75
Gilson, Etienne, 174
Gleizes, Albert, 177
Goethe, Wolfgang, 152
Gombrich, E. H., 151, 156, 165, 173, 175
Gorer, Geoffrey, 49, 88-89, 91-92
Gosslar, Lotte, 124
Gottlieb, Adolph, 148
Graham, John, 150
Graham, Martha, 121-22, 155, 183, 193-94, 196, 206, 207, 209, 210
Grimal, Pierre, 27
Grove, Mrs. Lily, 105
Guerard, Albert L., 146, 151
Guilford, J. P., 169

Hainuwele, 18-19
Halprin, Ann, 208, 211
Hambly, W. D., 13, 37
Hare, David, 147
Harkarvy, Benjamin, 200, 204, 208
Harrison, Jane, 13, 40
Harrison, Lou, 172
Hauser, Arnold, 150
Hawkins, Erick, 122, 197
H'Doubler, Margaret, 149, 152, 196-97, 198, 202
Hegel, George Wilhelm, 133
Helion, Jean, 145
Henri, Robert, 152, 156
Hirn, Yrjo, 14, 154

Hofmann, Hans, 174
Holm, Hanya, 207
Hopi, 16, 96-98
Horst, Louis, 42-43, 194
Hoving, Lucas, 210
Humphrey, Doris, 121-22, 123, 193, 197-98, 204, 206, 208

Indra, 59
Ishtar, 14, 74
Isis, 14, 75-76
Iwamatsu, Shizuko, 137, 168

Jenkins, Iredell, 145
Johns, Jasper, 148
Joyce, James, 175
Jung, Carl, 145

Kabuki, 101, 118-19
Kaelin, Eugene F., 165
Kandinsky, Wassily, 145, 156, 165, 166-67, 175
Kant, Immanuel, 133, 147
Karsten, Rafael, 93
Katchinas, 25
Kathak, 99, 118
Kathakali, 99, 118
Kaye, Nora, 201
Kealiinohomoku, Joann, 199
Kerrick, W. E., 141-42
Kidd, Michael, 123
Kirby, Michael, 157
Kirstein, Lincoln, 199
Klee, Paul, 151, 152, 155, 165
Kline, Franz, 150
Knudson, Thurston, 45
Koestler, Arthur, 144, 168
Kohler, Wolfgang, 14
Kokoschka, Oskar, 1, 165
Koner, Pauline, 203, 206, 208
Krishna, 15
Kubler, George, 83
Kuh, Katherine, 131, 175, 178-79

La Meri (Hughes, Russell Meriwether), 117-18
Lange, Konrad, 153
Langer, Susanne, 43, 127, 133, 142, 143, 148, 150, 153, 156, 165, 169-170, 174, 181, 194, 195
Lawler, Lillian, 101
Lawrence, D. H., 145

Le Corbusier, 156
Lee, Richard B., 86-87
Leepa, Allen, 148, 149, 152, 153, 164, 166, 169
Levy-Bruhl, Lucien, 39
Limon, Jose, 195, 205
Lipchitz, Jacques, 151, 152, 175
Lippincott, Gertrude, 204
Litz, Katherine, 122, 209
Louis, Murray, 199
Lowell, Amy, 168

McKayle, Donald, 195
MacLeish, Archibald, 158
McLuhan, Marshall, 134
Magic: contagious, 24; elements of, 22-25; Paleolithic, 20-22
Mahabharata, 82, 98-99, 117
Malinowski, Bronislaw, 27
Manipuri, 99, 118
Marceau, Marcel, 124
Marisicano, Merle, 122, 197
Maritain, Jacques, 147
Markova, Alicia, 203
Marks, Bruce, 209
Martin, John, 193, 196, 201
Masks, 26-27
Maslow, Abraham H., 170
Masson, Andre, 189-90
May, Rollo, 168
Metheny, Eleanor, 7
Milar, Chet, 100, 102
Minuet, 126
Miro, Joan, 166, 167, 173
Modern dance: classical, 121-22; contemporary, 122-23
Moore, Henry, 150, 174
Morris, Charles W., 147
Mudras, 118
Murray, Arthur, 127-28
Mythology, 27-28, 71-73; Babylonian, 73; Egyptian, 75-76; Indian, 76-79; Sumerian, 73-75

Nietzsche, Friedrich, 146, 154
Nikolais, Alwin, 123, 194, 196, 204
Noh, 99
Noverre, Jean Georges, 199, 200, 202
Nureyev, Rudolf, 207

Oesterly, W.O.E., 13-14, 50, 51
Oklahoma!, 123-24

On the Town, 124
Osiris, 14-15, 75-76, 81
Ozenfant, Amadie, 156

Page, Ruth, 197
Pantomime, 124
Parker, De Witt H., 174-75
Participation, dance, 41
Pavanne, 126
Pemberton, E., 105
Performance dance, 41
Persephone, 16, 71
Picasso, Pablo, 140, 153, 155, 175, 190, 206
Plato, 151
Playford, John, 104-5
Porteus, S. D., 93
Primitive, definitions of, 34-35
Primitive dance: categories of, 43, 45, 52; characteristics of, 40-45; functions of, 36, 53; hunters', 84-93; planters', 93-98; recurring, 84-98

Radar, Melvin, 141, 149, 172
Ramayana, 11, 82, 99, 117
Rauschenberg, Robert, 151
Read, Herbert, 149, 152, 153, 154, 164-65
Realism, 177-78
Reinhardt, Ad., 158
Rick, Cary, 210
Rickey, George, 146, 157
Rigaudon, 126
Rig-Veda, 77, 82
Riley, George, 173
Robbins, Jerome, 123-24, 201
Robinson, Bill, 129
Rogers, Carl, 169
Rosenberg, Harold, 145
Rothko, Mark, 148
Rugg, Harold, 169

Sachs, Curt, 11, 14, 39, 42-43
Santayana, George, 133, 147, 184
Sarabande, 126
Schoenberg, Arnold, 175
Schweinfurth, George, 85
Shahn, Ben, 134, 147, 173, 174
Shaman, 24, 37, 39
Shearer, Sybil, 122
Shiva (Siva), 15, 58, 59, 76
Siddhartha (Buddha, Guatama), 78-79
Siegel, Marcia B., 196

Slavenska, Mia, 203
Sloan, John, 153
Smith, David, 166
Social dance, 104-6, 127-28
Sokolow, Anna, 201-2
Sorell, Walter, 107, 151, 187
Spencer, Baldwin, and J. F. Gillen, 85
Stern, Paul, 174
Stodelle, Ernestine, 195-96
Superrealism, 178

Taboos, 22-23
Tamiris, Helen, 121-22, 123, 195
Tap dance, 129-30
Taylor, Paul, 207, 209, 210
Terry, Walter, 194
Tharp, Twyla, 208
Thomas, Vincent, 169
Thompson, Robert F., 44, 88
Tolstoy, Leo, 146, 150
Tomasson, Helgi, 209
Totem, 25; Bandicoot (Australian), 28; dance (South African), 37; witchetty grub (Australian), 31
Trois Freres, 21
Tuc d'Audobert, 29
Tucker, A. N., 85-86
Tudor, Antony, 200
Tune, Tommy, 205

Urlin, Ethel, 14

Varése, Edgard, 173
Veron, Eugene, 149
Villella, Edward, 209
Vishnu, 59, 76, 77, 78

Weidman, Charles, 121-22, 155, 207, 210
Weitz, Morris, 150, 153-54, 157-58
Whitehouse, Mary, 206-7
Whitman, Walt, 157
Whyte, Lancelot Law, 146, 172-73
Wigman, Mary, 152, 155, 193
Wilenski, R. H., 153
Wooley, Sir Leonard, 66-67
Wright, Frank Lloyd, 146

Youskevitch, Igor, 199, 208

Ziggurat, 64
Zola, Emile, 151